StoneBridge Art Guide

STONEBRIDGE ART GUIDE

A CHRISTIAN HISTORY CURRICULUM GUIDE FOR TEACHING AND LEARNING ART IN THE AMERICAN CHRISTIAN PRINCIPLE APPROACH

KINDERGARTEN THROUGH EIGHTH GRADE

DEVELOPED BY WENDY GIANCOLI

EDITED BY ELIZABETH YOUMANS

Preface BY CAROLE G. ADAMS

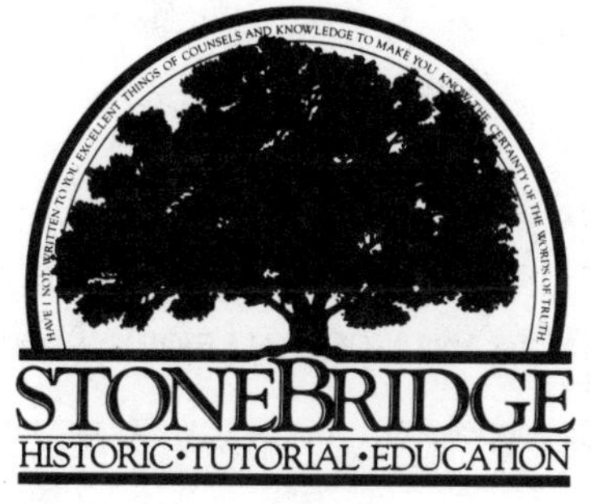

STONEBRIDGE EDUCATIONAL FOUNDATION
1992

STONEBRIDGE ART GUIDE

A CHRISTIAN HISTORY CURRICULUM GUIDE FOR TEACHING AND LEARNING ART IN THE AMERICAN CHRISTIAN PRINCIPLE APPROACH

KINDERGARTEN THROUGH EIGHTH GRADE

DEVELOPED BY WENDY GIANCOLI

EDITED BY ELIZABETH YOUMANS

PREFACE BY CAROLE G. ADAMS

PUBLISHED FOR

STONEBRIDGE EDUCATIONAL FOUNDATION

P.O. BOX 9247, CHESAPEAKE, VIRGINIA 23321 • (804) 465-2598

PUBLISHED BY

FOUNDATION FOR AMERICAN CHRISTIAN EDUCATION

P.O. BOX 27035, SAN FRANCISCO, CALIFORNIA 94127 • (415) 661-1775

TYPOGRAPHY BY DESTA GARRETT

ISBN 0-912498-12-9

ACKNOWLEDGEMENTS

Thanks be to God – Creator, Designer, Sculptor, Architect.

My husband Tom and my cherished daughters, Jeni and Ami, gave me abundant love and support in a multitude of ways.

This Guide was accomplished through the combined efforts of: Verna Hall – the discoverer of America's Christian history and government, founder of the Foundation for American Christian Education, and restorer of the vision to American Christians; Rosalie Slater – the architect of the Principle Approach, America's traditional Biblical philosophy of education, for the teaching and learning of America's Christian history and unification of all subjects in the curriculum, whose loving acceptance and whose wealth of knowledge and wisdom inspired my thought and brought clarity of mind; Carole Adams – beloved founder of StoneBridge Schools, from whose vision the seeds of this art program were planted and nurtured. Her love of beauty and her elevated artistic appreciation both infused and framed this work; Elizabeth Youmans – a dear friend and respected colleague, whose gifts of writing, editing, and creativity were invaluable to the practical use of this Guide; Sheree Beale – my kindred spirit, whose editing and encouragement were essential; Donna Buck – art instructor, who shared her God-given gift of creativity in the instruction of students; StoneBridge Students – whose work has delighted my heart and brought life to this program; and other friends and colleagues – who have enriched this program in a variety of ways.

To God be the glory.

– Wendy Giancoli

TABLE OF CONTENTS

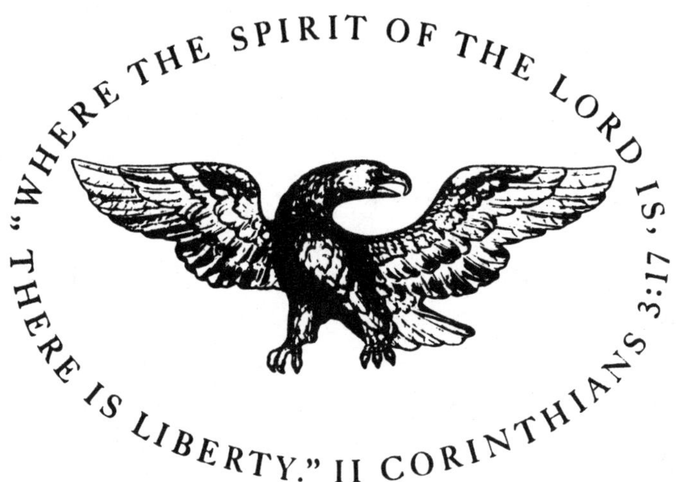
"WHERE THE SPIRIT OF THE LORD IS, THERE IS LIBERTY." II CORINTHIANS 3:17

BEHOLDING THE BEAUTY OF THE LORD

THE FINE ARTS IN EDUCATION *

by Carole G. Adams

The central idea of Providential history is the impact of Christ, the Word of God, through time on a man or a nation. This idea is the essential orientation for every Christian in identifying the purpose of all things. Because the fine arts serve to nourish the spirit of man and to reflect his relationship to God, they serve both as agents of the Gospel and as records of its work. By nature and integrity, therefore, the arts have an essential role in the propagation of the Gospel.

Art considered in its whole purpose and providential meaning is more than mere aesthetics. Art for enjoyment and appreciation is the gift of our Creator God who put into man the senses and soul to embrace it. However, a Biblical view of art proceeds from a commitment to the unfolding revelation of truth in the scriptures and results in an identification of the interdependence of truth and beauty and faith as the principle of art.

The single man in scripture bearing the distinction of being sought of the Lord as a "man after his own heart" revealed what the desires of that heart were in his Psalm 27:

> *One thing have I desired of the Lord, that will I seek after; that I may dwell in the house of the Lord all the days of my life,* ***to behold the beauty of the Lord,*** *and to inquire in his temple.*

David's one desire – to behold the beauty of the Lord – is a statement of the Christian aesthetic making the pursuit of beauty an obligation not an option. The Bible depicts beauty as an attribute or perfection of God; He is the source of beauty, just as He is the source of truth. Our God made provision for the quality of human life, not simply its survival, suggesting that "artistic beauty needs not justification for its existence, any more than a happy marriage does, or a bird, or a flower, or a mountain, or a sunset."[1]

How much, then, is the God-shaped inner vacuum that can only be sufficiently filled by the Savior, fed in the tender ages of childhood by the hunger for beauty? Parents and educators must account for this avenue of bringing children to the full stature of Christ, reclaim it and place it in its proper realm. *We must ask what habits of the heart, mind, and soul, what qualities of character, are encouraged or discouraged by the aesthetic dynamics that influence our children.*[2]

> We are so accustomed to thinking of beauty as merely decorative and ornamental that we forget that beauty is a moral necessity. God wrought beauty in the structure of the universe. Beauty is the highest form of righteousness. Beauty and truth are not separated in God's world, and they ought not to be in human thought. God, who gave as much care to painting a lily as to forming the eternal hills, joined truth and beauty in holy union; and what God has joined together, man ought not attempt to put asunder, *because beauty has a moral value for truth.*
>
> This universal love of beauty is one of the resources of human life that Christianity ought to pervade with its spirit and claim as its own. It is to this instinctive love of the beautiful that the artist makes his appeal, and gets, therefore, *a wider hearing for the truth* he presents in this universally loved form.

---

* Reprinted from *The Journal of the Foundation for American Christian Education,* VOL. III, F.A.C.E., San Francisco, CA (1991), pp. 63–68.

> Art is the interpretation of the great eternal realities of life, and as soon as the artist tries to embody the greatest feelings and aspirations of the human soul, he gets on Biblical ground, for there is no great interest or aspiration of man which the Bible has not treated. It is for this reason that great artists have dealt so largely with Biblical themes. Painting and the Bible could not be kept separate. They are congenial companions, because they have one common characteristic: both deal, not with the immediate and material, but with the eternal and spiritual. The function of art is to embody the universal and the eternal. The function of religion is to help man to discover that his selfhood (soul) is eternal, that he is building it day by day; and that "as a man soweth, so shall he also reap."[3]

Aesthetic education, therefore, is essentially educating tastes and sensibilities, and is mandatory to the education of the whole child. To neglect the fine arts in education is to admit ignorance and vulgarity. "For every one pupil who needs to be guarded from a weak excess of sensibility there are three who need to be awakened from the slumber of cold vulgarity. The task of the modern educator is not to cut down jungles but to irrigate deserts. The right defence against false sentiments is to inculcate just sentiments. By starving the sensibility of our pupils we only make them easier prey to the propagandist when he comes. For famished nature will be avenged and a hard heart is no infallible protection against a soft head."[4]

The tendency towards anti-intellectualism that has sometimes appeared in evangelicalism has a less obvious counterpart in anti-aestheticism. Dorothy Sayers speaks of it as "the snobbery of the banal" which snares Christians into depriving our children of the riches of God's grace. This describes those who "look down upon good music as high-brow, who confuse worship with entertainment, who deplore serious drama as worldly yet are contentedly devoted to third-rate television shows, whose tastes in reading run to the piously sentimental, and who cannot distinguish a kind of religious calendar art from honest art."[5] The Bible teaches us that Christianity is an incarnational religion. It is truth embodied in a physical world containing the elements of design – form, shape, line, color, etc. – and truth embodied in real people to whom God gave the ability to respond to art by his grace. We do respond to art, to good art and to bad art. It imprints itself upon us and our children and becomes a reference point for our most subtle and profound needs. "Culture has very much to do with the human spirit. What we find beautiful or entertaining or moving is rooted in our spiritual life.... T. S. Eliot has noted that aesthetic sensibility and spiritual perception are very closely related."[6] The fine arts in high culture have transcendent properties, taking us beyond ourselves, and teaching through perception of spiritual truth.

This brings us to a realization of the Christian obligation for the stewardship of the fine arts. How do we "irrigate the deserts" to nourish the sensibilities of our children for Christ? Removing or diminishing the swamp of popular culture through television and the nearly-inescapable multi-media that inundate us every day is not the answer. It is a step that creates a vacuum which must be filled with the beauty of the Lord. The birth of a child extracts the most tender and noble sentiments of human nature. The business of Christian parents and educators is to nurture the smallest child in the living Word of God as it appears in the Person of Jesus and in the written language of the Bible, as it is reflected in creation, and as it is recorded in the annals of the fine arts.

The smallest child is naturally alert to color and tone, to all the elements of the arts. Children are delightfully and uninhibitedly creative by the gift of God. They are highly perceptive and receptive visually. They love pictures and respond to them enthusiastically. As children begin to express themselves, drawing and painting, singing and impromptu "instruments" appear. Art education begins here with the home environment, feeding the child through the aesthetic standards of home life.

As a child enters school too often his curriculum centers on "basics" literacy and a "craft experience" approach to art that excludes the true nurture of sensibilities and tastes which are left to popular culture for influence. What is needed is a propagation of the Gospel through art and music – genuine instruction in the elements of design, in art history and appreciation. The "basics" of design and music theory should be built into the education of children along with phonics and arithmetic. Masterpieces of art and music should become the intimate acquaintances of our children establishing the values and high standards early.

The practice of art and music is essential to a child's whole education. Drawing instruction in the early grades was seen as an aid to learning other subjects in pre-progressive American education, and there was evidence that good instruction counted at least as much as "talent."[7] Because the arts are channels to the soul, they are healing instruments to many children. The child who struggles with "classroom learning" often finds comfort in the art class where his stronger abilities have expression and affirmation.

The curriculum that combines these aspects of art in primary and elementary grades is a rich feast that cultivates talent, imparts a Christian world view, develops skills, and influences tastes for what is excellent. A recent first grade class art lesson consisted of studying Michelangelo (his individuality, his character, his contribution, and his work), making notes in their notebooks, and examining many examples. The children admired especially the Sistine Chapel ceiling which was completely understandable to them as it illustrated their own Bible lessons. The practice of line drawings was reviewed and each child created his own interpretation using the new skills taught in the lesson. The teacher then taped a mural-sized paper to the underside of their reading table, put a mat under it to cover the floor, and then allowed each child to transfer his line drawing to the "ceiling" just as Michelangelo must have done. The finished product then was attached to the first grade room ceiling for the rest of the year for further appreciation. This lesson is a memorial to high culture and to a great master in the minds and hearts of that class of first graders. It staked a claim on their hearts for the transcending effect of an experience in the fine arts.

The fine arts must have a more adequate place in Christian education and not be treated carelessly in the curriculum. In addressing the aesthetic problem, Frank Gaebelein says,

> Yet in actuality they are not marginal, peripheral subjects; they are close to the heart of Christian life and witness. At present evangelical education is strongest aesthetically in music, although even here it has far to go. When it comes to the visual arts such as painting and architecture, and to the other performing arts, including drama, much of evangelical education is like a fallow field that needs both planting and cultivation. Christian schools and colleges must practice the unity of truth they preach by giving the arts a greater place in the curriculum.
>
> The compelling motive for Christian action in the field of aesthetics lies in the nature of God. Christians are obligated to excellence because God himself is supremely excellent. In the Hall of Fame at New York University, these words are inscribed in the place given Jonathan Edwards, the greatest of American Christian philosophers: "God is the head of the universal system of existence from whom all is perfectly derived and on whom all is most absolutely dependent, whose Being and Beauty is the sum and comprehension of all existence and excellence." It is because of who and what God is, it is because of the beauty and truth manifest in his Son, it is because of the perfection of his redeeming work, that evangelicals can never be content with the mediocre in aesthetics. Here, as in all else, the call is to the unremitting pursuit of excellence to the glory of the God of all truth.[8]

NOTES

[1] Ryken, Leland, *Triumphs of the Imagination: Literature in Christian Perspective.* InterVarsity Press: Downers Grove, Illinois (1979).

[2] Myers, Kenneth A., *All God's Children and Blue Suede Shoes: Christians & Popular Culture.* Crossway Books: Westchester, Illinois (1989).

[3] Maus, Cynthia Pearl, *Christ and the Fine Arts.* Harper & Brothers Publishers: New York (1938), p. 8.

[4] Lewis, C. S., *The Abolition of Man: How Education Develops Man's Sense of Morality.* MacMillan Publishing Co., Inc.: New York (1947).

[5] Gaebelein, Frank E., *The Christian, The Arts, and The Truth: Regaining the Vision of Greatness.* Multnomah Press: Portland, Oregon (1985).

[6] Myers, *All God's Children,* p. 27.

[7] Edwards, Betty, *Drawing on the Artist Within.* Simon and Schuster: New York (1986).

[8] Gaebelein, *The Christian, The Arts, and The Truth,* p. 59.

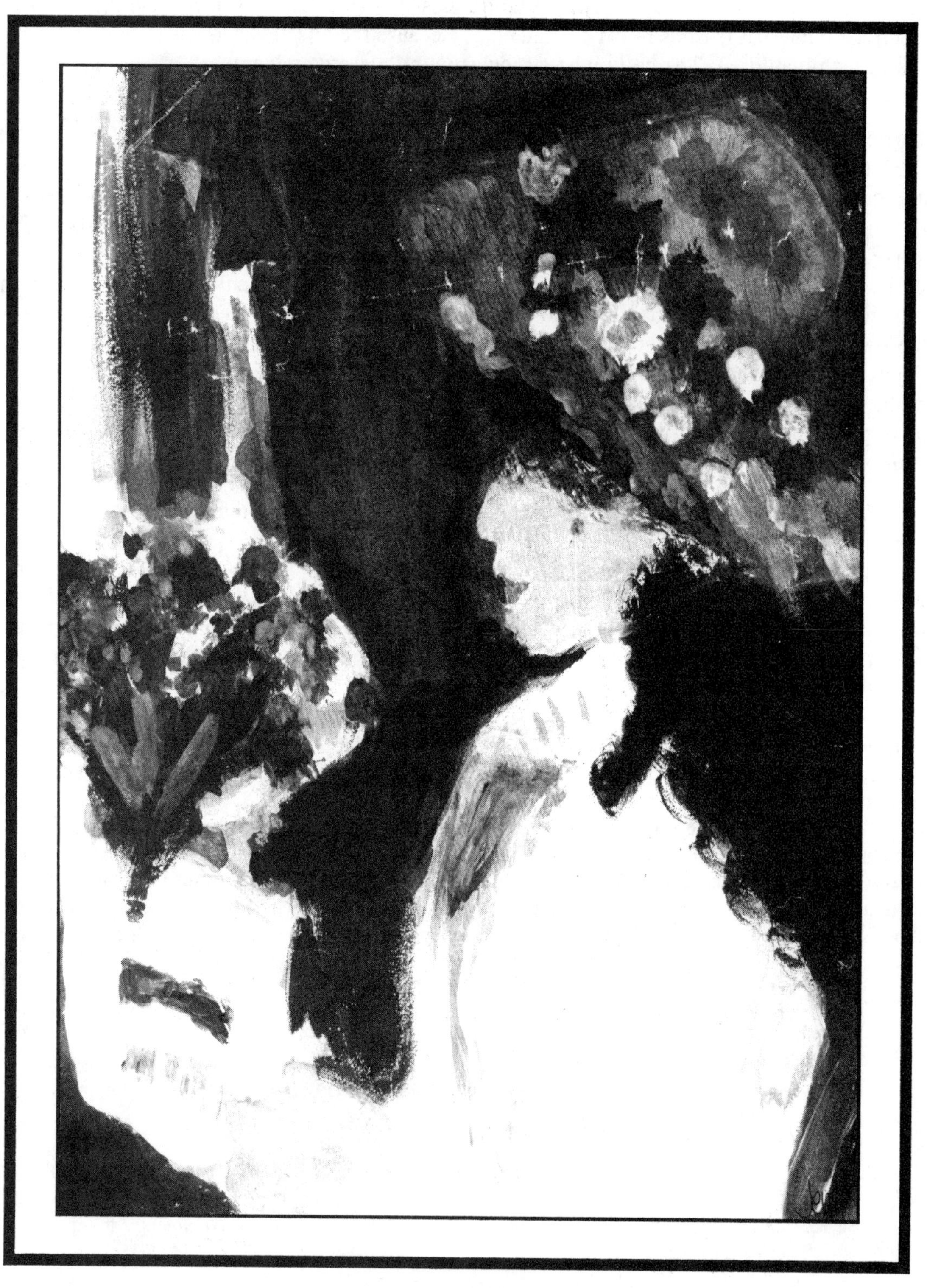

IMPRESSIONIST STUDY, COPY OF *TWO GIRLS READING IN A GARDEN* BY RENOIR
WATERCOLOR DETAIL, 8TH GRADE STUDENT

FOREWORD

The art program at StoneBridge has ministered to me since I first walked the hallways as a prospective parent. Even then I felt the excitement and electricity of learning as I viewed bulletin boards filled with student art work. These hallway exhibits proclaimed the individuality of each student while at the same time educated me about the master artist who had inspired the work. This experience was an affirmation to me that I had indeed found an approach to learning that would best serve my two precious daughters and would respect their unique learning styles.

As a parent, I am thrilled to report that today one of my daughters related in detail the story of Benjamin West, an early American painter whom she had studied four years ago. She loved telling me about how he plucked the hairs from his cat, Grimalkin, to make paintbrushes. She told me also about having made a brush just like his in art class, and she knew exactly where to find it in her art notebook. In literature that same year, her class had studied the biography of Benjamin West. It was obvious by her enthusiasm, love, and knowledge that the interweaving of art and literature had been extremely effective. True learning had taken place because the whole had been taught.

As I developed from parent to classroom teacher, the art curriculum continued to minister to me. As part of our fourth grade program we studied the Frances Hodgson Burnett classic, *The Secret Garden.* Mrs. Giancoli researched the Impressionist artist, Monet, and shared with us how he had been influenced by his garden and God's wondrous creations in it. She told us that Monet had said, "I perhaps owe having become a painter to flowers."

As I have been teaching, I have seen that all students have benefitted immensely from the art program. For some it has been the key that unlocked their entire educational future. One student was David, a dyslexic for whom reading, math and spelling seemed almost impossible. His progress in these areas was labored and measured in small steps. The art program, however, recognized his great artistic strengths, and allowed him the successes necessary to give the confidence he needed to continue working diligently in difficult areas. While some students memorized parts for a play, David designed the program cover. When some students received ribbons for Math Olympics, David received awards for the Art Festival. David's story is one of success, due largely to the confidence he developed through his art experiences. He made great gains in all areas because his uniqueness as an artist was recognized.

I obviously have a great love for art and a sincere belief that it is vital in educating the whole child. I invite you to be inspired by this Art Guide and challenge you to become an artist of the most significant kind: **one who paints on the hearts and minds of the children.**

– Liz Vansickle
StoneBridge Elementary Teacher

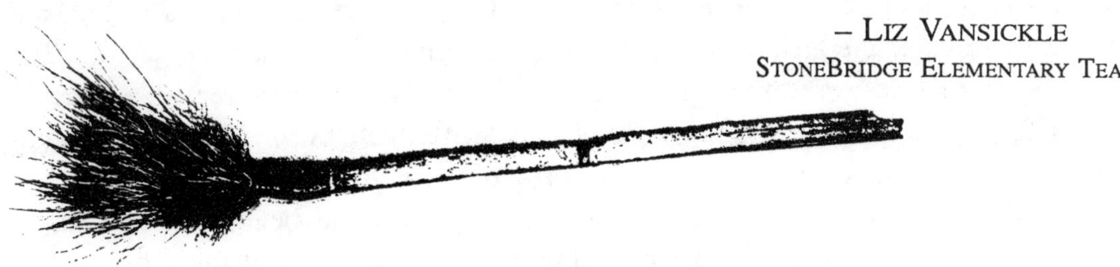

[STUDENT PAINT BRUSH CONSTRUCTED OF FOX TAIL HAIRS AND A MARSH REED; INSPIRED BY *Benjamin West and His Cat Grimalkin*]

INTRODUCTION

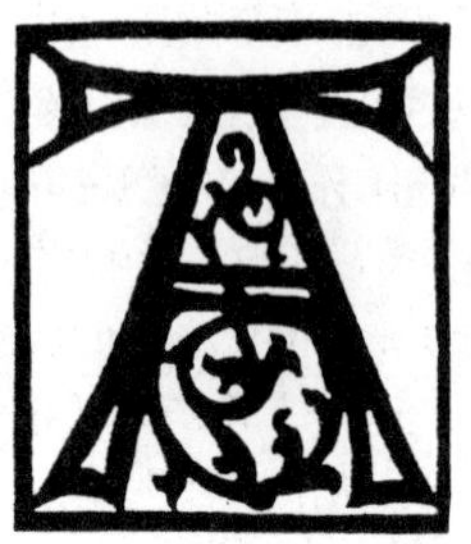

s when a painter, gazing on a face,
Divinely thro' all hindrance, finds the man
Behind it, and so paints him that his face,
The shape, and color of a mind and life,
Lives for his children ever at its best.

– Alfred Lord Tennyson, *Idylls of the King*

In the education of the **whole child**, the inclusion of the study and practice of art in the elementary curriculum is vital. For the very young child, who learns and expresses himself in concrete ways, the visual image plays a key role in his learning experience. We live in an age where "the predominant form of communication is visual rather than verbal, the image rather than the word, is the basic unit of communication. Unless we intentionally educate the aesthetic sensibilities of our children, we accept for them the standards and values of current popular culture. T. S. Eliot has noted that 'aesthetic sensibility and spiritual perception are very closely related. Great music, literature, painting, or architecture imprints itself in our lives and becomes a reference point for our most subtle and profound experiences.'"[1] The heritage of Christian art throughout the centuries has given us the greatest pictures of the world. Religious pictures from Bible narratives, as well as those masterpieces that teach great moral lessons, have a strong spiritual appeal to young children and should be displayed in the classroom and studied in the art curriculum.

"Art instruction in Christian schools today has a weightier accountability than it had just a few years ago. The art teacher must take responsibility for cultivating Godly tastes and sensitivities, as well as imparting knowledge and developing skills in her students. Children are bombarded daily with the crass, impersonal stimulus of electronic images to the point of visual fatigue and boredom. Through art education that is Biblically principled, that portrays Christ as the 'great masterpiece,' we can lead them into the appreciation of the beauty, order, and grandeur that will elevate their lives and poise their spiritual sensibilities towards God."[2]

Art has been defined as "the interpretation of the great eternal realities of life, and as soon as the artist tries to embody the greatest feelings and aspiration of the human, he gets on Biblical ground, for there is no great interest or aspiration of man which the Bible has not treated. Art deals with the eternal and the spiritual.... Because the principle of **art is the incarnation of God's eternal beauty,** beauty becomes a moral necessity,...the highest form of righteousness. God who gave as much care to painting a lily as to forming the eternal hills, joined truth and beauty in holy union. **Beauty has a moral value for truth.** It is the instinctive love of the beautiful that the artist makes his appeal, and gets, therefore, a wider hearing for the truth he presents in this universally loved form."[3] Therefore, art becomes a moral teacher!

The study of the great masterpieces and the practice of art skills aid in the formation and cultivation of students' use of imagination, creativity, and their God-endowed talents or abilities. In Jesus' "Parable of the Talents" in Matthew 25, the word *talent* is synonymous with the word *ability.* Doubtless, the primary application of the parable is to spiritual gifts, but may certainly be applied to artistic gifts. The phrase "each according to his talent" or "each according to his ability" requires accountability and wise stewardship of our God-endowed artistic gifts. It is imperative that the art teacher develop excellence in aesthetic tastes and critical judgments through artwork that reveals Godly beauty and truth. Excellence in the arts is fundamental simply because of God's surpassing excellence in creation and beauty! As Jonathan Edwards said, "God is the head of the universal system of existence from whom all is perfectly derived and on whom all is most absolutely dependent, whose Being and Beauty is the sum and comprehension of all existence and excellence." Such a God demands our best in the use of our talents and their products for **His praise and glory!**

In his book, *The Christian, the Arts and the Truth: Regaining the Vision of Greatness,* Frank Gaebelein challenges the contemporary Christian educator to seek evangelical answers to the issue of aesthetics and points clearly to the need for immediate action. He suggests three proposals: (1) the formulation of a Christian theory of aesthetics based first of all upon the insights of the Bible rather than upon extrabiblical sources; (2) the cultivation of good taste and the development of the critical faculty; and (3) the revision of educational programs to give a more adequate place to the arts.[4]

This *StoneBridge Art Guide* presents the many contributions that art in the elementary curriculum has made in the lives of its students and teachers and of the value in **educating the whole child.** At StoneBridge Schools art instruction is available for **every** child, teaching the knowledge of the character of God, the Ultimate Master Artist, and the appreciation of His masterpiece, Creation. This Guide also highlights the experiences and Christian character of the Art Director, who has been inspired by God in the writing of her curriculum, in the methods she has employed in teaching the lessons, and in the rapport she has developed with every child, calling forth each child's fullest measure of creative expression. This Art Guide is not intended to be a series of "how to" lesson plans, but to assist the aspiring art teacher in developing a Principle Approach art curriculum through his or her own research and creativity. The Guide acknowledges the diversity of gifts of each individual art teacher and encourages the expression of those gifts as God inspires and directs.

The real joy for the art teacher is the inspiration that flows from his or her personal research. As the elements of design are searched out in the scriptures and observed in nature, the hand of God as Creator, Designer, and Architect is clearly imprinted in one's heart and mind. The teacher becomes acutely aware of God's love of beauty, infinite detail, variety, harmony, balance, and order. As individual master artists, often chosen for their love of God as expressed in their artistic gifts, are researched through reading biographies and studying their masterpieces, many project ideas for use in the classroom begin to develop. The artist becomes an intimate friend of the teacher, who is then able to relate "friendship" and love for the artist to the classroom students. Art "His" Story becomes the source for the practice of art within the lesson, as the artist's work – either through subject matter, media, or style

– inspires a project. Personal childhood anecdotes about the artist are also a rich source for project ideas for elementary children.

A successful art program should have well defined purposes and goals of learning art established within the curriculum. The art teacher's methods should expect and direct the participation of every student. Discipline problems often arise in classes where there are no specific goals articulated to the students. At StoneBridge an overview is written by the art teacher for each grade level, reviewed with the students the first class period, and filed in their notebook. Well defined goals enable each student to evaluate his own performance which is not based on whether the student is "gifted and talented." Through the philosophy and methodology used at StoneBridge, every student experiences success in the art program.

Art should be integrated throughout the entire curriculum providing enrichment in many subject areas. Teachers can display masterpieces to adorn their classroom, to inspire creative writing, to highlight an historical event, or to teach a principle. Students should be encouraged by every teacher to illustrate and color their notebook work, an aspect of the Notebook Method which the children enjoy. Art is a vital part of the literature program and is frequently used on Special Day Celebrations at StoneBridge Schools.

Teaching art to the faculty has been another facet of the StoneBridge art program that bestows value to the role of art in the life of the school. At the Annual Teachers' Retreat, the Art Director presents a lesson introduced through Art "His" Story. The teachers become students and learn the joys and frustrations that their classroom children experience in art class. Some teachers who were discouraged in their own art education as children, now come to realize that **art is a skill that can be learned** and delightfully achieve immediate success in these art lessons.

Student art work is always tastefully displayed on bulletin boards throughout the school hallways. The beauty of the students' work radiates a special message for all who behold it. A permanent collection of framed student masterpieces also hangs in the hallways. The art curriculum is a vital part of our total elementary school program.

The StoneBridge Schools art program testifies to the value of elevating students' and teachers' aesthetic tastes in the visual arts through the philosophy of the Principle Approach. It is also a witness to the joy experienced by the students in participating in an art project that draws upon their God-given creativity in the use of their gifts and abilities to the glory of God. It meets the challenge for guiding our next generation of Christians for leadership in the visual arts.

– Elizabeth Youmans
StoneBridge Educational Foundation

---

[1] Kenneth A. Myers, *All God's Children and Blue Suede Shoes: Christians and Popular Culture*. Crossway Books: Westchester, IL (1989). As quoted in "The Principle Approach Classroom: Art Education Today," *The American Christian Prompter* Newsletter, Vol. 2, No. 2 (February 1991), F.A.C.E., S.F., CA, p. 4.

[2] "The Principle Approach Classroom: Art Education Today," by Carole Adams, Editor, *The American Christian Prompter* Newsletter, Vol. 2, No. 2 (February 1991), F.A.C.E., S.F., CA, p. 4.

[3] Maus, Cynthia Pearl, *Christ and the Fine Arts*. Harper & Row Publishers: New York (1938, 1959), p. 8.

[4] Gaebelein, Frank E. *The Christian, The Arts, and Truth: Regaining the Vision of Greatness*. Multnomah Press: Portland, Oregon (1985), p. 55.

CHAPTER 1

THE PRINCIPLE APPROACH TO ART EDUCATION

Great are the works of the Lord: They are studied by all who delight in them.
[PSALM 111:2]

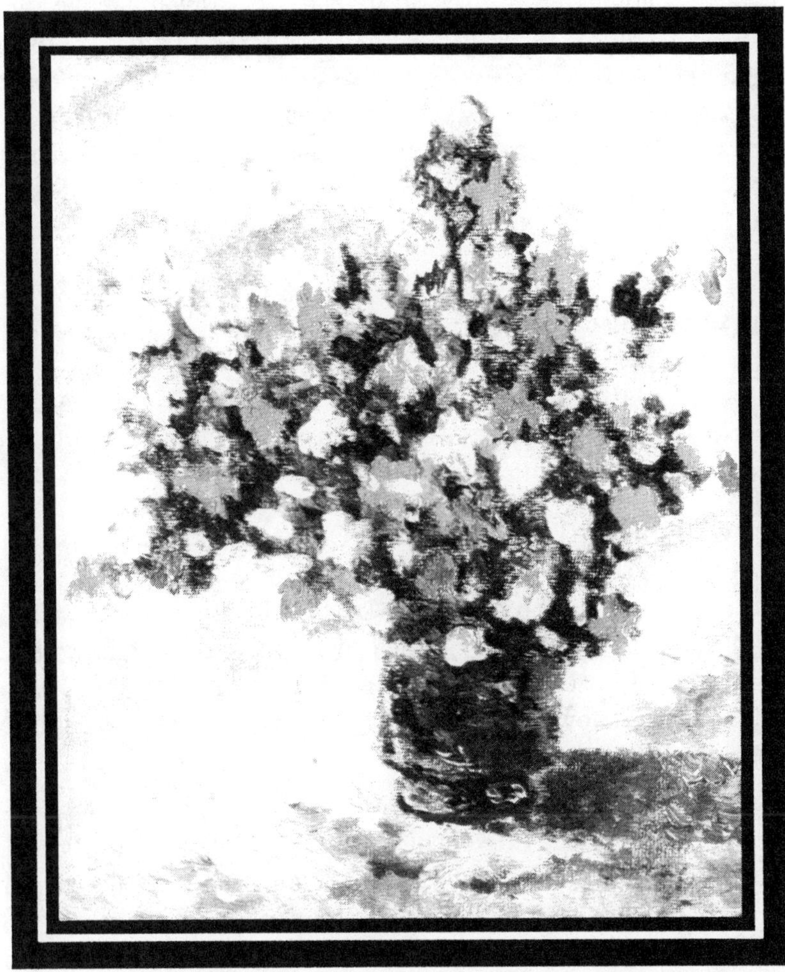

IMPRESSIONIST STUDY, COPY OF *VASE OF FLOWERS* BY MONET
ACRYLIC, 8TH GRADE STUDENT

This *StoneBridge Art Guide* is predicated upon the philosophy, scholarship, and methodology of The Principle Approach to American Christian education and government. Defined by its architect and restorer, Rosalie J. Slater, "The Principle Approach is America's historic Christian method of Biblical reasoning which makes the Truths of God's Word the basis of every subject in the school curriculum."[1] The application of this method to the subject of art has restored the 4 R's and the doctrine of Providence to its teaching and learning; has identified the Biblical principles of art and God's individuality as Creator and Master Artist; has defined God's purposes for art in the lives of individuals and of nations; has restored art to its rightful place in the education of the whole child; and is preparing young American Christians for future leadership in reclaiming the visual arts for the glory of God and their Gospel purpose in our Republic and around the world.

THIS ART GUIDE IS A PRIMER WITH THREE EMPHASES:

1. **Art "His" Story**
   The art curriculum contains the history of art and its westward move on the Chain of Christianity. As a "handmaid of the Bible," art has served both as a **teacher** of God's Word and the Gospel and as a **visual record** of Christ, His Story. The character and contributions of individual master artists and of nations are studied as they relate to God's purposes for the visual arts and liberty for the individual. When the Christian idea of man and liberty for each individual providentially achieved its fullest expression and protection in America's Christian Constitutional Republic, art flowered into full bloom for the individual.

2. **God's Elements of Design**
   Biblically researched and identified, God's elements of design reveal His majesty and glory as Creator and Master Artist. God's elements of design are the rudiments of art taught as the seedbed in the kindergarten program and systematically developed through the scope and sequence of an eight-year program.

3. **Development of Individual Talent and Character Through Art Practice**
   The discipline of art is a skill like composition that can be learned, exercised, and refined. The students receive instruction in the basic skills of art practice and their application in the liberal and useful arts. The Christian idea of man bestows value to each individual, his creative abilities, and his expressed application of them. Therefore, each child, made in the image of God, is acknowledged as having creative expression and is encouraged to participate in the art program.

The inclusion of a comprehensive art course of study, beginning in the kindergarten program of instruction, contributes to educating the **whole** child and actually nurtures the learning of other subjects. "In an obscure 1916 book, two insightful teachers recommended intensive drawing instruction in the early grades as an aid to learning other subjects. The book offers evidence that good instruction counts at least as much as 'talent'."[2]

The first step in establishing curriculum in any subject is to define the word using Noah Webster's 1828 Dictionary. The whole subject is revealed and its principles are illuminated as the *vocabulary of the subject* is identified from this definition and the *key words* are then defined. Using a Bible concordance, the key words or their synonyms are researched to *identify* God's purpose and the governing Biblical principles. For further instruction in researching and developing curriculum, see "4 R-ing Curriculum," Appendix III.

---

[1] Rosalie Slater, *Teaching and Learning America's Christian History: The Principle Approach.* F.A.C.E.: San Francisco, CA (1965), p. 88.

[2] Betty Edwards, *Drawing On the Artist Within.* Simon and Schuster: New York (1986), p. 6.

THE DEFINITIONS OF ART VOCABULARY

NOAH WEBSTER'S 1828 DEFINITIONS: (Key Words in bold print added for identification.)

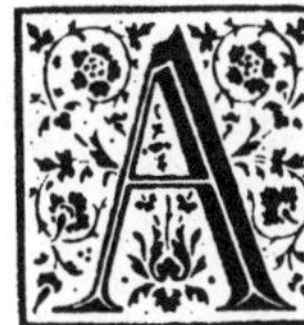

rt, n. [L. *ars, artis;* probably contracted from the root of W. *cerz,* Ir. *ceard.* The radical sense is *strength,* from *stretching, straining,* the primary sense of strength and power, and hence of skill. See an analogy in *can.*]

1. The disposition or modification of things by human **skill**, to answer the **purpose** intended. In this sense *art* stands opposed to *nature. Bacon. Encyc.*

2. A system of rules, serving to facilitate the performance of certain actions; opposed to *science,* or to speculative principles; as the *art* of building or engraving. Arts are divided into *useful* or *mechanic,* and *liberal* or *polite*. The mechanic arts are those in which hands and body are more concerned than the mind; as in making clothes, and utensils. These arts are called *trades*. The liberal or polite arts are those in which the **mind** or **imagination** is chiefly concerned; as poetry, music and painting. "In America, literature and the elegant *arts* must grow up side by side with the coarser plants of daily necessity." *Irving.*

3. Skill, **dexterity,** or the performing of certain actions, acquired by **experience**, **study**, or **observation**; as, a man has the *art* of managing his business to advantage.

KEY WORDS IDENTIFIED FROM THE DEFINITION AND DEFINED:

Skill, *n.* 1. The familiar knowledge of any art or science, united with readiness and dexterity in execution or performance, or in the application of the art or science to practical purposes. Thus we speak of the *skill* of a mathematician, of a surveyor, of a physician or surgeon, of a mechanic or seaman. 2. Any particular art.

Purpose, *n.* 1. That which a person sets before himself as an object to be reached or accomplished; the end or aim to which the view is directed in any plan, measure or exertion. We believe the Supreme Being created intelligent beings for some benevolent and glorious *purpose,* and if so, how glorious and benevolent must be his *purpose* in the plan of redemption! 2. Intention; design. Every *purpose* is established by counsel. *Prov. xx.*

Mind, *n.* 1. Intention; purpose; design. 2. Inclination; will; desire. 3. Opinion. 4. Memory; remembrance. 5. The intellectual or intelligent power in man; the understanding; the power that conceives, judges, or reasons. 6. The heart or seat of affection. 7. The will and affection; as readiness of *mind. Acts xvii.* 8. The implanted principle of grace. *Rom. vii.*

Imagination, *n.* 1. The power or faculty of the mind by which it conceives and forms ideas of things communicated to it by the organs of sense. *Ency. "Imagination* I understand to be the representation of an individual thought." *Bacon.* "The business of conception is to present us with an exact transcript of what we have felt or perceived. But we have also a power of modifying our conceptions, by combining the parts of different ones so as to form new wholes of our own creation. I shall employ the word *imagination* to express this power. I apprehend this to be the proper sense of the word, if imagination be the power which gives birth to the productions of the poet and the painter." *Stewart.* "We would define *imagination* to be the will working on the materials of memory; not satisfied with following the order prescribed by nature, or suggested by accident, it selects the parts of different conceptions, or objects of memory, to form a whole more pleasing, more terrible, or more awful, than has ever been presented in the ordinary course of nature." *Ed. Ency.* 2. Conception; image in the mind; idea. 3. Contrivance; scheme formed in the mind; device. 4. Conceit; an unsolid or fanciful opinion. "We are apt to think that space, in itself, is actually boundless; to which *imagination,* the idea of space itself leads us." *Locke.* 5. First motion or purpose of the mind. *Gen. vi.*

Dexterity, *n.* 1. Readiness of limbs; adroitness; activity; expertness; skill; that readiness in performing an action, which proceeds from experience or practice, united with activity or quick motion. We say, a man handles an instrument, or eludes a thrust, with *dexterity.* 2. Readiness of mind or mental faculties, as in contrivance, or inventing means to accomplish a purpose; promptness in devising expedients; quickness and skill in managing or conducting a scheme of operations.

Experience, *n.* 1. Trials, or a series of trials or experiments; active effort or attempt to do or to prove something, or repeated efforts. A single trial is usually denominated an *experiment; experience* may be a series of trials, or the result of such trials. 2. Observation of a fact or of the same facts or events happening under like circumstances. 3. Trials from suffering or enjoyment. 4. Knowledge derived from trials, use, practice, or from a series of observations.

Study, *n.* 1. Literally, a setting of the mind or thoughts upon a subject; hence, application of mind to books, to arts or science, or to any subject, for the purpose of learning what is not before known. "*Study* gives strength to the mind; conversation, grace." *Temple.* 2. Attention; 3. Any particular branch of learning that is studied. Let your *studies* be directed by some learned and judicious friend. 4. Subject of attention. "The Holy Scriptures, especially the New Testament, are her daily *study.*" *Law.*

Observation, *n.* 1. The act of observing or taking notice; the act of seeing or of fixing the mind on any thing. We apply the word to simple vision, as when one says, a spot on the sun's disk did not fall under his *observation.* 2. Notion gained by observing; the effect or result of seeing or taking cognizance in the mind, and either retained in the mind or expressed in words. 3. Observance; adherence to in practice; performance of what is prescribed.

Beauty, *n.* [Fr. *beautè*, from *beau.*] 1. An assemblage of graces, or an assemblage of properties in the form of the person or any other object, which pleases the eye. In *the person,* due proportion or symmetry of parts constitutes the most essential property to which we annex the term *beauty.* In *the face,* the regularity and symmetry of the features, the color of the skin, the expression of the eye, are among the principal properties which constitute *beauty.* But as it is hardly possible to define all the properties which constitute beauty, we may observe in general, that beauty consists in whatever pleases the eye of the beholder, whether in the human body, in a tree, in a landscape, or in any other object. Beauty is *intrinsic,* and perceived by the eye at first view, or *relative,* to perceive which the aid of the understanding and reflection is requisite. Thus, the beauty of a machine is not perceived, till we understand its uses, and adaptation to its purpose. This is called the beauty of utility. By an easy transition, the word beauty is used to express what is pleasing to the other senses, or to the understanding. Thus we say, the beauty of a thought, of a remark, of sound, "So *beauty,* armed with virtue, bows the soul with a commanding, but a sweet control." *Percival.* 2. A particular grace, feature or ornament; any particular thing which is beautiful and pleasing; as the *beauties* of nature. 3. A particular excellence, or a part which surpasses in excellence that with which it is united; as the *beauties* of an author. 5. In the *arts,* symmetry of parts; harmony; justness of composition. *Encyc.* 6. Joy and gladness. *Is. lxi.* Order, prosperity, peace, holiness. *Ezek. xvi.*

OTHER DEFINITIONS:

"Art is the incarnation of God's eternal beauty,... the interpretation of the great eternal realities of life...."
[Cynthia Maus, *Christ and the Fine Arts.* Harper & Brothers Publishers: New York (1938)]

"As in all cultures and at all times, art is not a luxury but a necessity without which we would be vastly impoverished.... Western art is exceptional and distinct from the other great arts.... Our art is part of us; in it flows the spiritual and intellectual lifeblood which still nourishes and sustains our ancient civilization. It is also a living, redemptive force in an age that has witnessed the madness and destruction which is also, unfortunately, our Western heritage. Art can embody and transcend both its creators and its times to reveal enduring truths about the human condition; the more we understand art, the more we understand ourselves and the complexities of our world." [Cole and Gealt, *Art of the Western World.* Summit Books: New York (1989)]

"By viewing Nature, Nature's handmaid Art, Makes mighty things from small beginnings grow."
[John Dryden, *Annus Mirabilis* (1667), stanza 155]

"May not a work of art speak to people of all times as long as it survives? The key to the question is the word 'speak.' Indeed, it may speak, but what is its language?"
[Gardner, *Art Through the Ages.* Harcourt Brace Jovanovich Publishers, New York (1980)]

"'Christian art?' Art is art; painting is painting; music is music; a story is a story. If it's bad art, it's bad religion, no matter how pious the subject. If it's good art – and there the questions start coming, questions which it would be simpler to evade."
[Madeleine L'Engle, *Walking on Water: Reflections on Faith and Art.* Harold Shaw Pub.: Wheaton, Illinois (1980), p. 14]

"Basically, there can be no categories such as 'religious' art and 'secular' art, because all true art is incarnational, and therefore, 'religious'." [L'Engle, *Walking on Water,* p. 25]

"For since the creation of the world His invisible attributes, His eternal power and divine nature, have been clearly seen, being understood through what has been made...."
[Romans 1:20]

"Now the material in which God worked to fashion the first man was a lump of clay. And this was not without reasons for the Divine Architect of time and of nature, being wholly perfect, wanted to show how to create by a process of removing from and adding to material that was imperfect in the same way that good sculptors and painters do when, by adding and taking away, they bring their rough models and sketches to the final perfection for which they are striving. He gave His model vivid colouring; and later on the same colours, derived from quarries in the earth, were to be used to create all the things that are depicted in paintings."
[Giorgio Vasari]

WRITE YOUR OWN DEFINITION HERE:

THE BIBLICAL PRINCIPLES OF ART

(*Principle* is defined by Noah Webster in his 1828 Dictionary as: "the cause, source, or origin of anything; a constituent part, ground, foundation, and general truth of something.")

1. **Creation is the masterpiece of all time. Our Divine Creator spoke into existence all things. He formed man and in him breathed the breath of life.**

   "And God said . . . ." [Genesis 1:3-26]
   "For everything God created is good. . . ." [I Timothy 4:4]
   "And the Lord God formed man from the dust of the ground and breathed into his nostrils and the breath of life and man became a living being." [Genesis 2:7]

2. **Our Lord's creative nature is revealed to us throughout Scripture and in creation. We need only gaze about us, observing creation, to see His divine qualities of beauty, balance, variety, detail, unity, and order. Likewise, an artist's creative expression reflects the Lord in the artist and should glorify Him.**

   "For since the creation of the world His invisible attributes, His eternal powers and the divine nature have been clearly seen being understood through what has been made. . . ." [Romans 1:20]
   "A good man out of the good treasure of his heart bringeth forth good things. . . ." [Matthew 12:35]

3. **The elements of design originated with God in creation and are the building blocks with which the artist creates.**

   The elements of design He created are:

   Color and **Value** (the degree of lightness or darkness of an object)

   "In the beginning God created the heavens and the earth. And the earth was formless and void and darkness was over the surface of the deep; and the Spirit of God was moving over the surface of the waters. Then God said 'Let there be light,' and there was light. And God saw that the light was good, and God separated the light from the darkness." [Genesis 1:1-5]

   Space (the distance between things)

   "In the beginning God created the heavens and the earth." [Genesis 1:1]
   "Then God said, 'Let there be a firmament in the midst of the waters, and let it divide the waters from the waters.' " [Genesis 1:6-8]

   "Then God said, 'Let the waters under the heavens be gathered together into one place, and let the dry land appear'; and it was so. And God called the dry land Earth, and the gathering together of the waters He called seas. And God saw that it was good." [Genesis 1:9,10]

   Shape (The Hebrew word for "formed" means to shape or to mold as a potter molds clay.)

   "And the Lord formed man of the dust of the ground. So God created man in His own image." [Genesis 1:26]

   Line and **Texture** (the toughness or smoothness of a surface) Artists show texture by repetition of a line.

   "Then God said, 'Let the earth bring forth grass, the herb that yields seed and the fruit tree that yields fruit according to its kind . . . ,' and it was so." [Genesis 1:11]

4. **God, whose image man bears, has endowed each individual with His inherent creative ability.**

   "And God created man in His own image, in the image of God He created him." [Genesis 1:27]

5. **It is man's responsibility to acknowledge, develop, and steward the gifts God has so graciously given him.**

   "To one He gave five talents of money, to another two talents, and to another one talent, each according to his ability. . . ." [Matthew 25:15-29]

6. **In order for an artist to fully develop his creative ability he must become a keen observer.**

   ". . . Lift up your eye and see." [Zechariah 4:2]

7. **With our study of the individual lives of master artists throughout history, the student learns not only of varied art techniques, but more importantly, of how others have used their God-given talents. He learns how God has moved through individual lives as the chain of Christianity moves westward. He learns that art is a visual record of HIS STORY.**

   "For God has allowed us to know His secret plan and it is this: He purposed long ago in His sovereign will that all human history should be consummated in Christ Jesus." [Ephesians 1:9,10]

8. **Our American Christian heritage affirms and protects the individual's God-given right to develop to his fullest potential.**

   ". . . where the spirit of the Lord is, there is liberty." [II Corinthians 3:17]

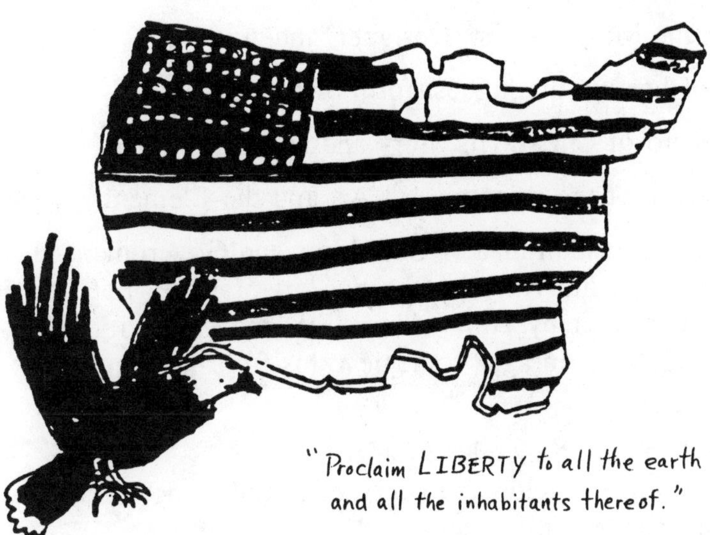

"Proclaim LIBERTY to all the earth and all the inhabitants thereof."

THE GOVERNING PRINCIPLES OF ART EDUCATION

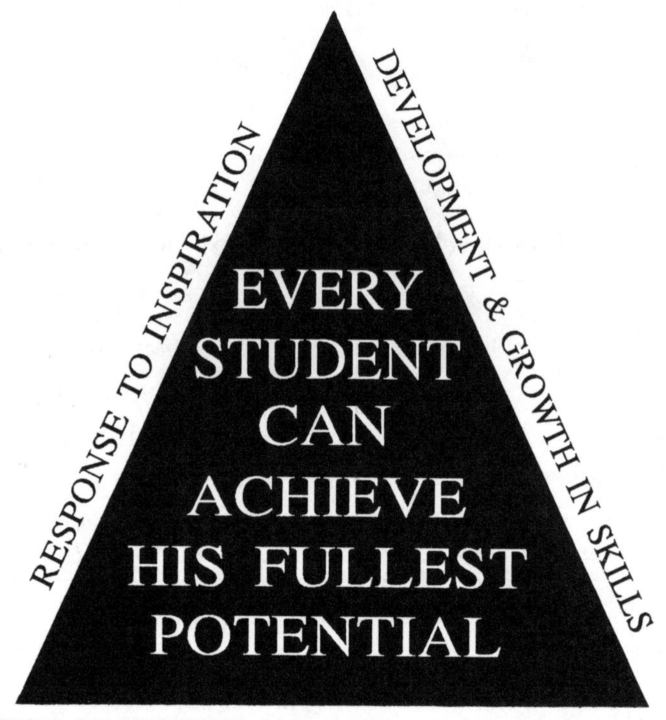

1. God, as Creator, is the Master Artist, Designer, and Architect.
2. God is the source of beauty, the highest form of righteousness.
3. Art is the visual record of Christ, His Story and His Gospel.
4. The Bible is the source of the Principles of Art and the Elements of Design.
5. The philosophy of the Christian Idea of God, Man, and Government liberates each student to express his God-given individuality through art practice. Each student, made in the image of God and endowed by Him with ability and creativity, is inspired to steward these artistic gifts and is encouraged to achieve his fullest potential.
6. The role of the art teacher is:
   a. To teach the fundamental principles of art practice.
   b. To inspire each child to develop and achieve his fullest potential of artistic expression.
   c. To create a lifelong love of the fine arts.
   d. To develop a Biblical view of the fine arts, thereby elevating aesthetic tastes and critical faculties and redeeming the standard of excellence in their expression.

CHAPTER 2

4 R-ING ART

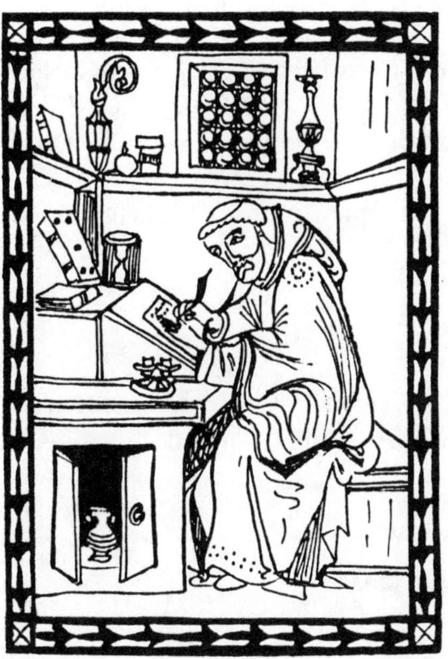

When introduced to the Principle Approach to American Christian Education and its tool, the Notebook Method, each of us is challenged to personally take the responsibility for our own **re-education.** As teachers we must become learners. As we begin the process of 4 R-ing a subject, "real learning" takes place! Through the structure of sound discipline and study skills, mastery of that subject grows and a wonderful thing happens – the subject comes alive and becomes our property. The value of the Notebook Method is its ability to liberate the teacher to be the **living textbook** with the opportunity to inspire and produce true learning in individual students.

Biblically ***researching, reasoning, relating,*** and ***recording*** art will enable each art teacher to take possession of the Biblical truths that govern art in His Story. 4 R-ing gives the direction necessary for the teacher to develop curriculum and art projects and identifies the personal character demanded by art to master and teach it Biblically and creatively. Please see "**4 R-ing Curriculum**" in Appendix III for further assistance. Several basic research tools and readings, listed on p. 10, are foundational for study and mastery and a good public library should provide additional resources for research. 4 R-ing is an ongoing process in the life of a teacher and one that requires time. If you are new to 4 R-ing, take caution lest the method become too tedious and time consuming, and you lose sight of the vital principles to be discovered and taught. Be careful to balance the ***letter*** of the method with its ***spirit***. The spirit of the Notebook Method gives the teacher access to flexibility, creativity, spontaneity, inspiration, an elevated curriculum, and most importantly, to individuals! It is the excellent method of real education, time-tested, and enduring when practiced in spirit as well as in letter.

Summers are an ideal time for teachers to bask in the joy and inspiration derived from personal study and to develop curriculum and projects. Attempt to study several master artists each summer as you build a Biblically-based Christian history art curriculum. As art project ideas formulate, summers also provide the necessary time to refine them for classroom use and to determine the best method, tools, and art supplies that will be needed in the classroom setting. As you study and document your research, always permit your love of art and the inspiration of the Holy Spirit to teach, illumine, and guide your curriculum development and lesson plans!

TEACHER RESEARCH AND PREPARATION

I. Research and study the philosophy of the Principle Approach and its tool, the Notebook Method. Suggested research tools and readings are:

The Christian History of the Constitution of the United States of America: Christian Self-Government, compiled by Verna M. Hall. Foundation for American Christian Education (F.A.C.E.), San Francisco, CA (1960).

Teaching and Learning America's Christian History: The Principle Approach by Rosalie J. Slater. F.A.C.E., San Francisco, CA (1967), pp. 90–110.

A Guide to American Christian Education for Home and School: The Principle Approach by James B. Rose. American Christian History Institute (A.C.H.I.): Palo Cedro, CA (1987), pp. 113–158.

The Bible

The Exhaustive Concordance of the Bible by James Strong.

Commentary on the Whole Bible by Matthew Henry.

American Dictionary of the English Language (Facsimile 1828 Ed.) by Noah Webster. F.A.C.E., San Francisco, CA.

The Book of Life (eight volumes, arranged and edited by Hall and Wood). John Rudin and Company, Inc., Chicago (1923–1952 editions).

II. Compile and document your research and study of art as follows:

A. Set up three notebooks for recording your research and filing ideas:

1. **ART "HIS" STORY** Notebook.

a. Label divider for each period of art or artist studied.

b. For each artist studied, entitle a notebook page with the following for recording research:

- Character qualities
- Childhood influences
- Education
- Masterpieces
- Contributions to Christian history
- Vocabulary
- Ideas for practical lessons – let the artist's work inspire a project either through his subject matter, media, or style.

2. **ELEMENTS OF DESIGN** Notebook – Label a divider for each element of design:

- Value
- Color
- Space
- Shape
- Line
- Texture

3. **ART FORMS** Notebook – Label dividers with the following:

- Drawing
- Painting
- Architecture
- Sculpture
- Crafts

B. As your research and understanding of the Principle Approach to art grow and develop, write your definition of art and your philosophy of American Christian history art education in your own words.

III. Collect and compile visuals for classroom use such as:

A. Visuals for Art "His" Story: reproductions of masterpieces – prints, postcards, posters, greeting cards, duplicated copies from textbooks, and museum catalogues (see Reference List on p. 18).

B. Visuals for practical lessons: photographs, magazine clippings, greeting cards, postcards, and calendars.

IV. Visit local museums. Gather and record information about their collections.

V. Select an artist to research.

  A. Read biographies and autobiographies. Find materials written by the artist's contemporaries. Record anecdotes about his childhood to share with your students. Identify his childhood influences, education, Christian experience, and character qualities. Study the historical setting(s) of his life. Identify his place on the Chain of Christianity and complete a time line. Study the artist's style, subject, and medium used most often. Record his major masterpieces and search for visuals of them.

  B. Rembrandt is an excellent first choice because he is considered the first Biblical artist. Unlike his 17th century contemporaries, he was not commissioned to paint Biblical themes. His art work reflects his love and understanding of the Scriptures and he illustrated nearly every book of the Bible. (See following page for an example of inspiring material for use in teacher research and study.)

VI. Develop student art projects inspired from Creation or from your study of a master artist using one of God's elements of design. See p. 15 for Rembrandt-inspired student art.

VII. Prepare your lesson plan. See pp. 43–52 for further ideas and detailed methods.

VIII. Write student hand-out for use in teaching a master artist to be filed in the students' notebooks.

  A. This is a modification of the Notebook Method as it is used in the teaching and learning of other subjects. The elementary students at StoneBridge Schools have only one 35–40 minute art period a week. In that time the art teacher must teach the lesson, work with each student, and clean up the classroom. In order to incorporate an enriched art appreciation program, an elevated art practice program, and to ensure that the students have a record of the master artists studied on the Chain of Christianity, the StoneBridge Art Director prepares hand-outs for the artists that are taught.

  B. Illustrations and pictures are included, as well as a brief biographical sketch appropriate for the grade level being taught. Often, the hand-out is used for two or three art periods. See pp. 16–17 for a sample hand-out prepared for a study of Rembrandt with eighth grade students. Also, see pp. 41–42 for other methods used with the students in recording art notes.

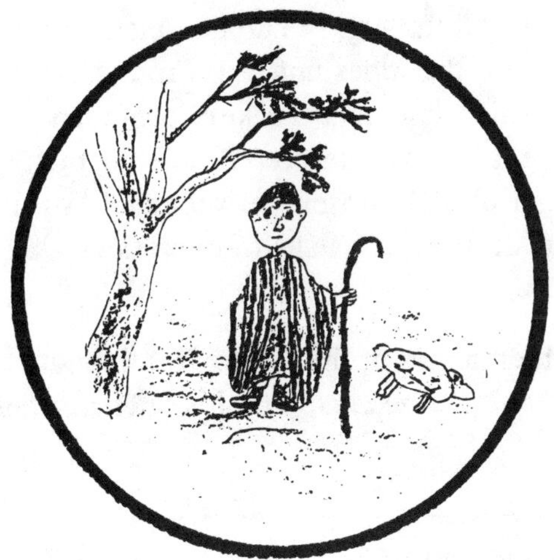

STUDENT WORK INSPIRED BY THE STUDY OF GIOTTO, THE 14TH C. SHEPHERD BOY WHO BECAME THE PATHFINDER IN THE ART OF PAINTING

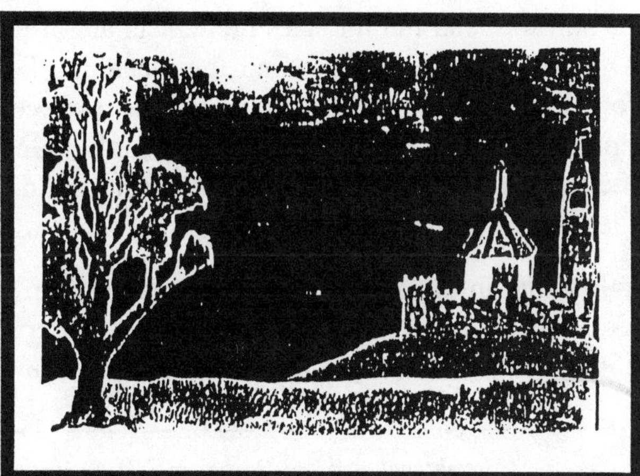

STUDENT'S THREE-DIMENSIONAL LANDSCAPE ALSO INSPIRED BY A STUDY OF GIOTTO WHO DEVELOPED A DEPTH OF SPACE IN PAINTING

REMBRANDT AND THE GOSPEL*

The Painter of the Bible

A contemporary painter and pupil of Rembrandt's remarks bitterly that since the churches are closed to Dutch painters 'their best careers' are spoilt for most of them, and they content themselves with 'lowly things' or 'futilities' for their subjects. This judgment may be exaggerated or superficial, since portraits, landscapes and still life may also have their deeper meaning, and do not deserve such contempt. But it is true all the same that in Rembrandt's time great religious themes play an inferior part and that apart from his own school Dutch painters of the seventeenth century rarely take them for their subjects. Not that the Dutch Protestants went so far as to condemn religious painting as a whole; on the contrary, we know that it had a ready market. But the Church did not provide any commissions, and private people mainly ordered portraits. So a painter had no reason to choose religious subjects unless he did so of his own inclination. 'The choice of the theme was left to the decision of the artist; he shaped it after his own judgment; no criticism of the patron influenced the execution. The advantages arising out of such freedom amply compensated for everything the Calvinist spirit suppressed by abandoning the tradition of Madonnas and Legends of Saints.'

In his choice of a subject for his work Rembrandt always surprises us by his love of the Bible. This man who in 145 paintings (out of about 650), 70 etchings (out of about 300), and 575 drawings (out of 1,250 to 1,500), took biblical themes and treated all of them in an individual manner, did indeed live with the Bible. In this regard the drawings are particularly enlightening because they are mostly not destined for the public. They are like the pages of a diary where all through his life Rembrandt noted down the discoveries he made in the Bible.

In what way does the artist translate the Scriptures? We have seen – and shall see it confirmed again and again – that the Rembrandt of the forties, fifties, and sixties had a different relation to the Bible from the young Rembrandt. His work reflects his development, not only leading him to choose different subjects, but also shaping old themes in a new way.

As a young man, Rembrandt looked for the dramatic. The Scriptures were an excellent source of stories full of tension and movement. It was in that period that he conceived the highly baroque pictures of Balaam and Samson, and the miracles he depicts are in reality sorcery. But that does not last. From 1643 onwards, in his loneliness, he discovered the meaning of the message which contains the key to human existence. From that time he no longer sought to exploit the Bible; he tried to interpret it. In his mature years Rembrandt became the servant of the Word of God. He no longer placed himself between that Word and the spectator, nor directed attention to his technical devices and the skill of his means of expression. He wanted to let the gospel speak for itself.

Nothing in this regard is more revealing than to compare the manner of the young Rembrandt, when he paints themes like *The Raising of Lazarus* or *Ecce Homo* or *Christ at Emmaus,* with his later manner, about 1650, when he takes up the same themes once more.

**Rembrandt and the Gospel* by W. A. Visser 'T Hooft. Excerpted from Chapter Two: "The Painter of the Bible," pp. 24–32. A Living Age Book, published by Meridian Books, Inc.: New York (1960). Used by permission from Viking-Penguin Press.

Neumann is right when he says that no other religious pictures are so little influenced by ecclesiastical considerations, and so wholly biblical as those of Rembrandt. The mature artist wants no commentary for the Bible other than the Bible itself. He remains independent of any tradition. But independence does not mean indifference or hostility. He knows his predecessors and often borrows from them an idea, an attitude, or an illuminating thought. But his conception of the biblical message is always personal, he never feels bound by any precedent. He never grants the right to anyone to force a particular interpretation upon him.

In his *History of Religious Art since the Council of Trent* Emile Mâle stresses the fact that painters of Catholic countries were not allowed to choose themes from the Bible themselves. Their theme was prescribed. 'So the artist did not need to invent anything. The subjects demanded of him corresponded to the religious sentiment of his time: everywhere the Church was present in them.'

Thus practically all official religious painting was restricted to the traditional iconography and certain selected scenes from the Bible. In Rembrandt's time there was in existence a kind of canon which provided a painter with a list of themes. Certain themes belonged to the official treasure of Christian art; others were omitted. Besides this the point of view from which the subject was to be treated was clearly laid down. Recent studies have shown with what loyalty, even a sense of routine, painters have often followed those laws. But Rembrandt is quite the opposite. When he represents a biblical story, it has come alive, and real, for him; the mature Rembrandt has himself seen and heard something in the story.

Thus we see in his work a far-reaching reduction. Innumerable religious themes which had been added in the tradition of the Church to the biblical themes proper find no more room in his work. But at the same time there is a liberation. In their liturgical selections the Middle Ages left little room for the Bible story itself: only four parables, very few scenes from the life of Jesus, even fewer from the Old Testament and principally those events which are regarded as prefigurations of the New Testament. The Counter-Reformation was dominated by polemical and didactic aims, and had put all the stress on subjects connected with the Church, without being concerned with the Bible as a whole. For Rembrandt, on the other hand, the Bible alone determines the subject. For that reason his painting is the first example in the history of art of work inspired by the biblical message in all its richness.

Rembrandt read the *whole* Bible. None of the important series of biblical pictures of other painters comprises the whole Bible in this way. From what other painter's work can we publish the Bible in pictures? Fra Angelico confined himself to the New Testament. Dürer represents only four scenes from the Old Testament, so does Rubens; and what is known as Raphael's Bible is only illustrations from the Old Testament painted by Raphael and his pupils to which four or five pictures from the life of Jesus are added. The other painters of the sixteenth and seventeenth centuries are content to follow the tradition. Thus Rembrandt is the only great painter not only of the Netherlands but also of the whole world to deserve the name of a biblical painter, for he roams through the Bible from beginning to end, and gives us what he discovers.

But we may go even further. Rembrandt not only looks for themes for his pictures in the Bible, he also interprets the texts of Scripture. He by no means restricts himself to general illustration of one story or another, but he presents a special moment, he interprets a certain verse. Hence the names given to the various paintings cannot express their full meaning. We must always go back to the text on which they are based.

For instance, when Rembrandt tells the story of Hagar, he portrays six different scenes: Sarah leading Hagar to Abraham, Sarah complaining about Hagar, Hagar at the well on the way to Sur, the expulsion of Hagar, Hagar in the desert, the angel appearing to Hagar. In his account of Joseph, too, we can take part in all the main events of that tempestuous existence. We see all the scenes of David's drama. Nor is the temptation of Jesus a static subject, but the unrolling of a dramatic action. Gethsemane is seen from very different sides, whether the stress lies on the 'sorrow unto death,' on the prayer 'not as I will, but as thou wilt,' or on the reproaches to the sleeping disciples.

But all this has not petrified into a system. Rembrandt did not work in series. He only showed what he had heard in the message of the Bible, he only painted what he had 'seen.'

Does this mean that Rembrandt treated *all* the great biblical themes? Certainly not. The 'Rembrandt Bibles' published in Holland and Germany show that there are few books of the Bible with which he has not been concerned, and that he has dealt with many subjects which have been deliberately left out by the iconographic tradition. We note, however, that certain themes frequently recur, while others are missing. We do not intend to enumerate them, but it may serve as an example to note that he treated the story of Abraham thirty-one times, the parable of the Good Samaritan fifteen times, Emmaus eighteen times, whereas he did not handle at all such famous themes of mediaeval painting as the *Last Judgment,* the *Parable of the Ten Virgins, The Rich Man and Lazarus,* or themes popular in baroque painting such as the *Transfiguration,* the *Power of the Keys,* and the *Wedding of Cana.*

The inventory of Rembrandt's collections shows that he possessed engravings of the entire works of Titian, Lucas of Leyden, and Raphael. Thus he was very probably able to study three of the most famous representations of Mary Magdalen every day. He certainly knew the *Transfigurations* of Raphael and Rubens. He owned a *Rich Man and Lazarus* by Palma Vecchio. Those works never inspired him to make his own version of the themes. Why not? The mature Rembrandt represented only 'what he had seen and heard,' what he had understood in such a way that he could hand it on.

So the question arises whether we may not elicit Rembrandt's beliefs from his choice of subjects. This question has received detailed attention from Hans Martin Rotermund. He names as the chief omissions from Rembrandt's work the story of Whitsun, Old Testament prefigurations, the Revelation of St. John, and the life of St. Paul. There is no doubt that the first three of these themes play no part in Rembrandt's work. But it is not true that St. Paul is of little or no interest to Rembrandt. From his earlier period there are four paintings, one etching, and three drawings representing themes from the life of St. Paul, from his later life three paintings. What is even more important, Rembrandt identified himself with St. Paul in such a way that he actually depicted himself as St. Paul. This painting of 1661 (Collection de Bruyn) shows most clearly of all the self-portraits of the later years how Rembrandt had detached himself from the world and turned towards the things that are eternal. He who has seen the look on this face will not easily forget it. He is St. Paul; but he is also Rembrandt. Both have heard the word, 'My grace is sufficient for thee.'

Rotermund names other themes which play a special part in Rembrandt's work. He rightly emphasizes how Rembrandt in dealing with the Old Testament chooses themes connected not with the struggles of the people of the covenant but with the individual human being meeting God. In his representations of the New Testament we notice his special interest in the teaching and healing Christ, his preference for the humanity of the Mother of Jesus, and his presentation of Jesus' temptation and tribulation in its extreme form of mortal dereliction.

Student Art Inspired by the Teacher's Study of Rembrandt

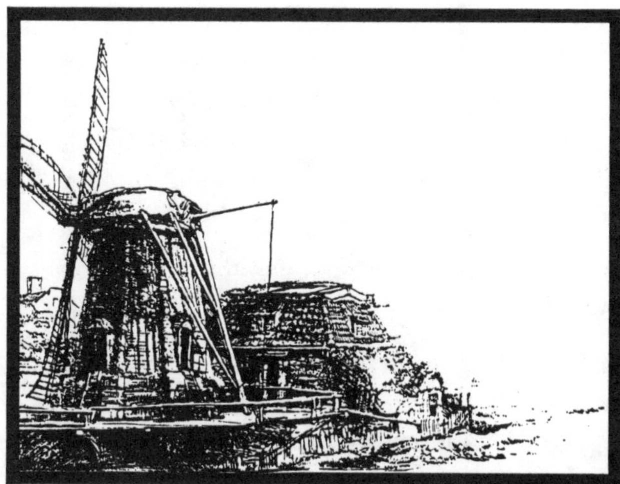

Mill by Rembrandt

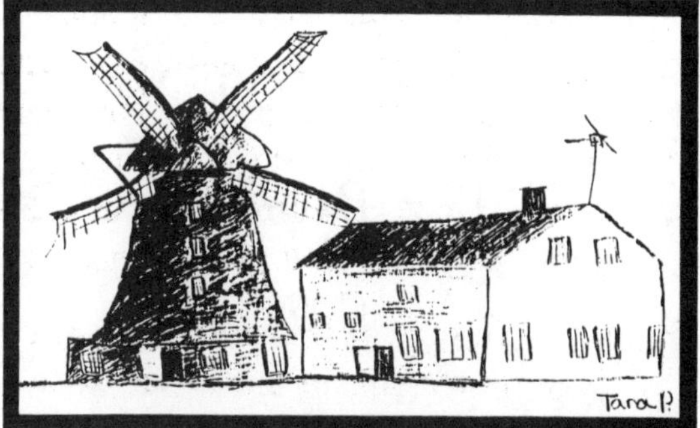

Mill by Tara Peppos
[value study – fifth grade]

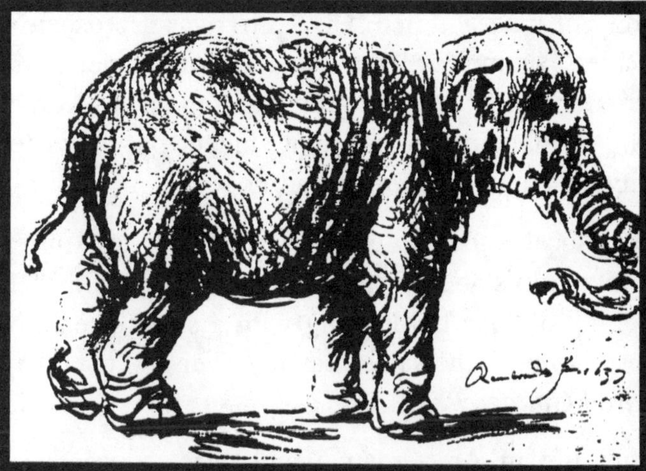

Elephant by Rembrandt

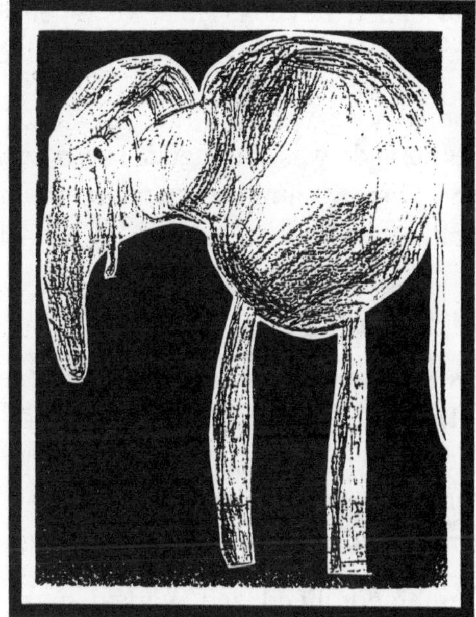

Elephant by Devin Whalen
[Rembrandt study – kindergarten]

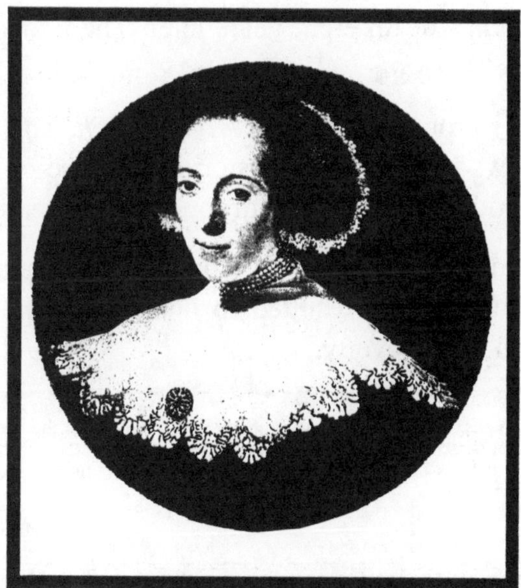

Dutch Woman by Rembrandt

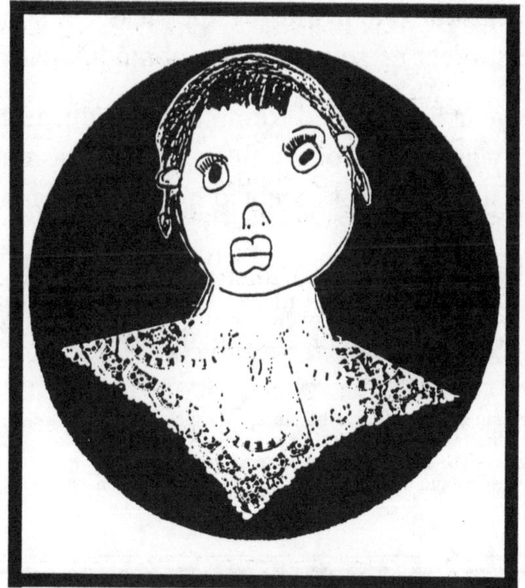

Dutch Woman by Natalie Thompson
[Rembrandt study – kindergarten]

SAMPLE HAND-OUT PREPARED BY TEACHER
FOR 8TH GRADE STUDENT NOTEBOOK RECORD*

REMBRANDT VAN RIJN

"The Biblical Artist"

(1606 – 1669)

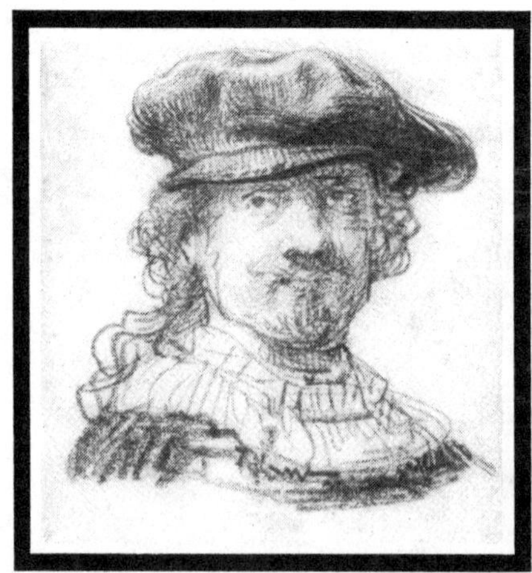

Rembrandt.

Rembrandt lived in a tiny country in Europe called The Netherlands. He was born in a western section of the country called Leyden, Holland. When Rembrandt was a young school boy, the Pilgrims also lived in Leyden before coming to America in 1620.

Rembrandt was the eighth son born into a family of nine children. His father was a prosperous miller whose windmill was located on the Rhine River. His mother, who was a devout reader of the Scriptures, introduced her son to the Bible. When Rembrandt was in grammar school he learned about the Bible and other classics every day. Young Rembrandt was a bright student but his vision for himself was to become an artist, not a university scholar as his father had hoped.

As a young man Rembrandt apprenticed under a local artist in Leyden and another in Amsterdam. It was under these masters that he learned to mix colors and prepare canvases. And it was here that he learned to draw and to do etchings. An etching is done by drawing with a silver needle on copper plates and inking them. The plates can be used to print the same drawing over and over. One of Rembrandt's most famous etchings is *The Hundred Guilder Print.*

Rembrandt lived and worked most of his adult life in Amsterdam which was the center of intellectual life in Holland. He became a very successful artist and was much sought after as a portrait painter. His portraits were realistic and showed depth of character. In 1634 he married his beloved Saskia. Their life together was cut short by Saskia's death eight years later. Their son Titus was the subject of several of Rembrandt's paintings.

The year Saskia died Rembrandt produced his famous group portrait, the *Night Watch.* This huge painting was revolutionary in its composition and it shows Rembrandt's mastery in the use of light. His new style was not accepted by his contemporaries and his commissions dropped off dramatically.

Rembrandt was an avid collector of paintings, etchings, and other art objects. He acquired a remarkable collection, but he managed his finances poorly which resulted in bankruptcy in 1656. This great master spent the remaining years of his life in near poverty.

*When studying the life of an artist, students in the art class are not required to take notes. In order to have as much time as possible for the students to interact with the project, this art teacher types up a brief summary of the biographical sketch and has the students file these notes in the art section of their notebooks. The average length of an art period is 35–40 minutes. In that time Art "His" Story is highlighted, an art project is taught, and the art teacher must distribute and clean up all the tools and materials needed for the project.

While Italian artists were ornately decorating their churches and composing religious paintings, the Dutch masters in the seventeenth century were painting mainly portraits and landscapes. Rembrandt painted about ninety self-portraits. He enjoyed painting rich fabrics and would often do his portraits in costumes. One of his mature portraits is entitled *Self-Portrait as St. Paul.* It is possible that he saw himself as an apostle of Christ. Rembrandt was the first to use the self-portrait as a major means of artistic expression.

Rembrandt has also left us with many Biblical pictures. He had a loving, forgiving concept of Christ. He was the first to portray Christ with Jewish features. It is interesting that the picture he was doing when he died was of Simeon.

Inventory of Rembrandt's meager belongings at the time of his death show that he had only one book, an old Bible. Rembrandt had obviously lived with his Bible. He illustrated almost every book in the Old and New Testaments. Visser 'T Hooft states that "His drawings, most not meant for public view, are like pages of a diary where all through his life Rembrandt noted down the discoveries he made in the Bible."

Earlier artists had painted religious works in a prescribed manner. Rembrandt's paintings, however, are unique because in them he interpreted the Scripture. This is why he is known as a Biblical artist, not a religious artist. Rembrandt is a focal point in the history of Christian art.

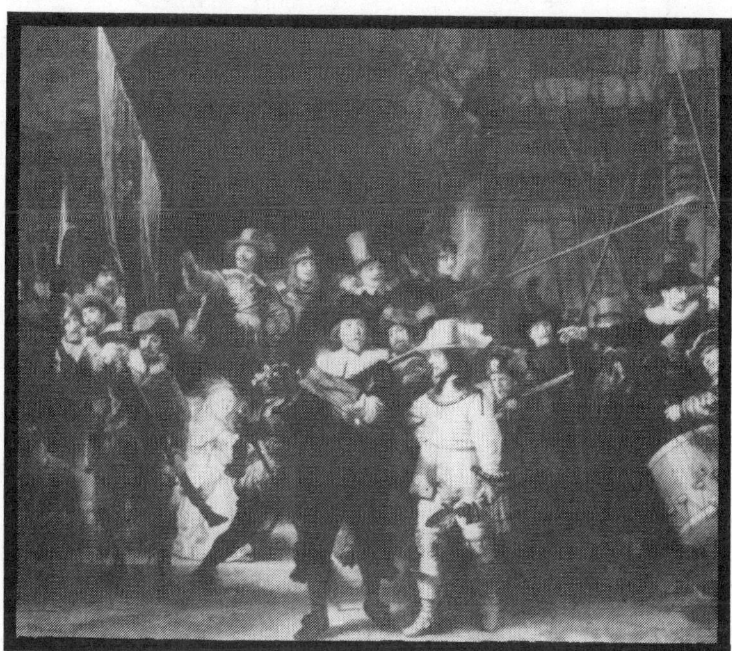

Night Watch BY REMBRANDT

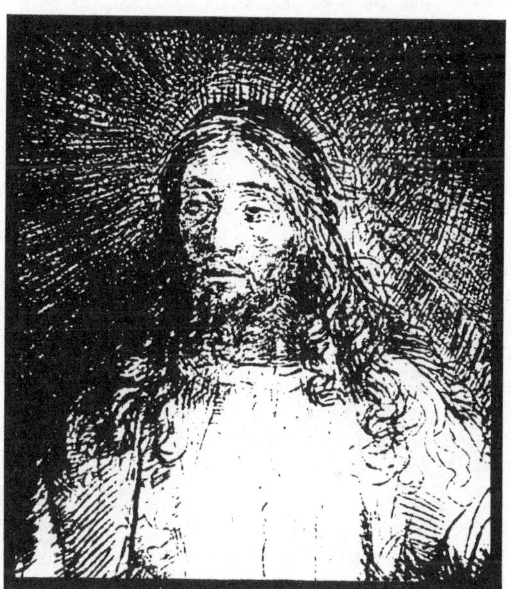

FROM *The Hundred Guilder Print* BY REMBRANDT

The National Gallery of Art in Washington, D.C. houses 23 of Rembrandt's paintings.

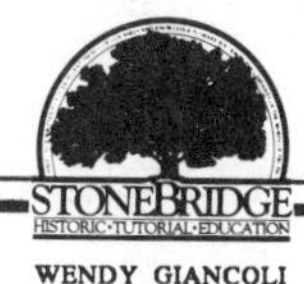

READING AND REFERENCE LIST BY BOOK TITLES

Addicted to Mediocrity by Franky Schaeffer. Crossway Books: Westchester, Illinois (1981)

All God's Children and Blue Suede Shoes: Christians and Popular Culture by Kenneth A. Myers. Crossway Books: Westchester, Illinois (1989)

American Art by Milton W. Brown, Sam Hunter, John Jacobus, Naomi Rosenblom, David M. Sokol. Harry N. Abrams, Inc.: New York (1987)

Art and Man (various magazine issues), pub. by Scholastic, Inc. under the direction of the National Gallery of Art. [Order back issues: 730 Broadway, New York, New York, 10003-9538. Ask for Teacher's Edition which includes a poster.]

Art Smart by Susan Rodriguez. Prentice Hall: New Jersey (1988)

Atlas of the Bible: An Illustrated Guide to the Holy Land. The Reader's Digest Association, Inc.: Pleasantville, New York (1981)

Benjamin West and His Cat Grimalkin by Marguerite Henry, illustrated by Wesley Dennis. Macmillan: New York (1947); Order from F.A.C.E. with study Syllabus: *William Penn and the Colony of Religious Toleration* by Rosalie J. Slater. F.A.C.E.: San Francisco, California

Bequest of Wings by Annis Duff. The Viking Press: New York (1954)

The Bible and Its Painters, by Bruce Bernard. Orbis Pub., London (1983)

The Book of Life, eight-volume set arranged and edited by Hall and Wood. John Rudin & Co., Inc., Chicago; (1923–1952 editions).

A Child's History of Art, by V. M. Hillyer & E. G. Huey. Appleton S.Q.: New York, (1934)

Christ and the Fine Arts by Cynthia Maus. Harper: New York (Revised edition, 1959)

The Christian Teaching of Art. Bob Jones University Press: Greenville, South Carolina (1986)

The Christian, the Arts, and Truth: Regaining the Vision of Greatness, by Frank Gaebelein. Multnomah Press, Portland (1985)

The Creation, by Ernest Haas. Penguin Books: Canada (photography/nature)

Dictionary of Art and Artists by Peter and Linda Murray. Penguin Books Ltd.: New York (1968)

Doing Art Together by Muriel Silberstein-Storfer and Mableu Jones. Simon and Schuster: New York (1982)

Drawing on the Artist Within by Betty Edwards. Simon and Schuster: New York (1986)

Drawing on the Right Side of the Brain by Betty Edwards. St. Martin's Press: New York (1989)

Five Hundred Years of Art and Illustration from Dürer to Kent by Howard Simon. The World Pub. Co., Cleveland (1942)

The Great Masters, by Giorgio Vasari. Park Lane: New York (1986)

Great Painters, by Piero Ventura. G. P. Putnam's Sons, New York, (1984)

History of Art by H. W. Janson. Prentice Hall, Inc.: Englewood Cliffs, New Jersey; Harry N. Abrams, Inc.: New York (1986)

History of Art for Young People by H. W. Janson. Harry N. Abrams, Inc., New York (1987)

How Should We Then Live? by Francis Schaeffer. Fleming H. Revell Co.: New Jersey (1976)

An Illustrated Life of Jesus, by Richard I. Abrams and Warner A. Hurchinson. Abingdon: Nashville, Tennessee (1982)

Jesus Revealed (originally published as *His Face*) by Marion Wheeler. Portland House: New York (1988)

The Lives of Great Artists, by Giorgio Vasari. Penguin Books: New York, (1984)

The Living Gospels of Jesus Christ, by J. B. Phillips. Exeter Books: New York, (1984)

Men of Art by Thomas Craven. Simon and Schuster, New York, (1936)

Mommie It's a Renoir by Aline D. Wolf. Parent Child Press: Altoona, Pennsylvania (1984)

Rembrandt and the Gospel by W. A. Visser 'T Hooft. Meridian Books, Inc., New York, (1960)

Signs and Symbols in Christian Art by George Ferguson. Oxford University Press: Oxford, New York, (1961)

Time-Life Library of Art. Time., Inc., New York.

A Treasury of the Great Children's Book Illustrators, by Susan E. Meyer. Abrodale Press, New York (1987)

Walking on Water by Madeleine L'Engle. Harold Shaw Publishers: Wheaton, Illinois (1980)

Young Readers' Book of Christian Symbolism by Michael Daves; illustrated by Gordon Laite. Abingdon Press, Nashville (1967)

RESOURCES FOR LOCATING BOOKS, COLOR REPRODUCTIONS, POSTERS, AND SLIDES

CORCORAN GALLERY OF ART
17th Street & N.Y. Avenue, N.W.
Washington, D.C. 20006
(202) 638-3211
Attn: Corcoran Shop or Registrar's Office

CHRYSLER MUSEUM
Olney Road and Mowbray Arch
Norfolk, VA 23510; (804) 622-1211

METROPOLITAN MUSEUM OF ART
Fifth Ave. at 82nd St., NY, NY 10028
(212) 879-5500
Attn: Institutional Sales
Many Audio tape tours of the museum's permanent collection are available for rent if you choose to take an independent tour. They also have a large collection of prints, postcards, and slides.

MUSEUM OF FINE ARTS, BOSTON
465 Huntington Ave., Boston, MA 02115
(617) 267-9300, x 317
Attn: Photographic Services Dept./Slide Library

NATIONAL GALLERY OF ART
Constitution Avenue at 4th Street, N.W.
Washington, D.C. 20565
(202) 842-6462 or 6465
Attn: Publications Service
National Gallery has a slide and video extension program for which you pay only return postage. They also have a large collection of prints and postcards.

NATIONAL MUSEUM OF AMERICAN ART
Smithsonian Institution
Eighth & G Streets, N.W.
Washington, D.C. 20560
(202) 357-1626
Attn: Office of Research Support

NATIONAL PORTRAIT GALLERY
Smithsonian Institution
F Street at Eighth, N.W.
Washington, D.C. 20560
(202) 381-5380
Attn: Office of the Curator

PHILADELPHIA MUSEUM OF ART
Benjamin Franklin Parkway
Post Office Box 7646
Philadelphia, PA 19101-7646
(215) 763-8100
Philadelphia Museum of Art has a large print, postcard, and slide collection for sale.

PHILLIPS COLLECTION
Washington, D.C.; (202) 387-2151
Slides available

PRINT FINDERS
15 Roosevelt Place
Scarsdale, New York 10583
(914) 725-2332
Print Finders is a mail order company that will locate reproductions and mail them to you.

VIRGINIA MUSEUM OF FINE ARTS
Richmond, Virginia; (804) 367-0800
Virginia Museum of Fine Arts has a large slide and postcard collection for sale.

CHAPTER 3

GOD'S ELEMENTS OF DESIGN AS SEEN IN CREATION

"In the beginning GOD created...."

Our Heavenly Father's creative character is revealed throughout Scripture. In observing nature, His love for beauty, balance, variety, detail, order, and unity is seen. From the very beginning of time God gave the essential elements needed for the artist to create – the elements of design:

- **VALUE**
- **COLOR**
- **SPACE**
- **SHAPE**
- **TEXTURE**
- **LINE**

"In the beginning God created the heavens and the earth. And the earth was formless and void, and darkness was over the surface of the deep; and the Spirit of God was moving over the surface of the waters. Then God said, 'Let there be light,' and there was light. And God saw that the light was good; and God separated the light from the darkness." [Genesis 1:1-5]

"Then God made two great lights; the greater light to rule the day and the lesser light to rule the night." [Genesis 1:16]

These verses indicate that our Almighty Heavenly Father created the elements of design.

VALUE – (the degree of lightness or darkness of an object)

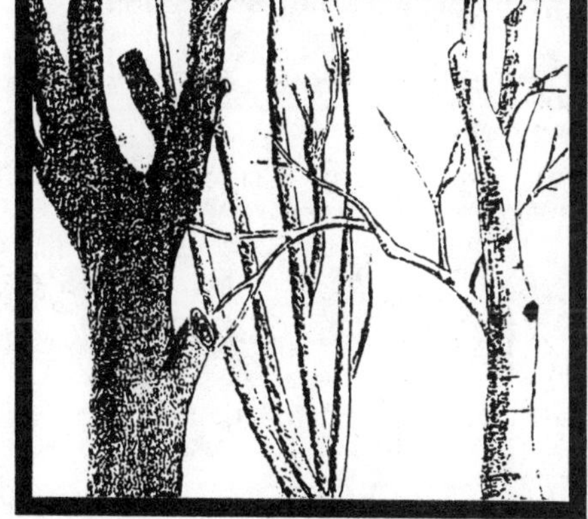

A baby when first opening his eyes does not see color for the first days of life. He sees only light and dark, the value of objects. An artist when working will frequently squint (or half shut) his eyes to clearly distinguish values.

Light n. – That ethereal agent or matter which makes objects perceptible to the sense of seeing, but the particles of which are separately invisible. Light when decomposed is found to consist of rays differently colored; as red, orange, yellow, green, blue, indigo, and violet. The sun is the principal source of light in the solar system; but light is also emitted from bodies ignited, or in combustion, and is reflected from enlightened bodies, as the moon.

Dark a. – Destitute of light; obscure

COLOR n. – In physics, a property inherent in light, which by a difference in the rays and the laws of refraction, or some other cause, gives to bodies particular appearances to the eye. The principal colors are red, orange, yellow, green, blue, indigo, and violet. 'White' is not properly a color; as a white body reflects the rays of light without separating them. 'Black' bodies, on the contrary, absorb all the rays, or nearly all, and therefore, 'black' is no distinct color. But in common discourse 'white' and 'black' are denominated 'colors.'

[Definitions are from Noah Webster's 1828 Dictionary]

Light makes all things visible, or affords illumination: a color depends on light. It's interesting that the Hebrew word for light includes "beauty" in its definition.

The sun is our most important natural light source.

Colors are not normally seen in light because light usually travels in a straight line when moving in the same kind of substance. A prism is a wedge of glass that is used to bend or refract light. Water will also bend light rays. A beam of light passes through a glass prism and a rainbow-like band of colors or a spectrum occurs. The shortest ray of light bends the most producing violet. The longest ray bends the least producing red. The others fall in between and tend to blend into each other. When mixed together, all the colors found in the spectrum give white light.

Red, yellow, and blue are called the primary colors. All other colors are made from different combinations of the primary colors.

Green, violet, and orange are called secondary colors.

> *"In the beginning God created the heavens and the earth."* [Genesis 1:1]
> *"Then God said, 'Let there be a firmament in the midst of the waters, and let it divide the waters from the waters.' "* [Genesis 1:6-8]

The Hebrew translation for the word "created" is *para*. It means to make something that did not exist before, such as matter, time, and space.

The Hebrew word for "firmament" means *expanse of atmosphere*. The water above was a canopy over the earth. The water under the heaven gathered together and dry land appeared.

> *"Then God said, 'Let the waters under the heavens be gathered together into one place, and let the dry land appear'; and it was so."*
> *"And God called the dry land Earth, and the gathering together of the waters He called the seas. And God saw that it was good."* [Genesis 1:10]

God created the earth and the seas. He created **SPACE** or the distance between things.

In order to create an interesting composition, an artist must think and plan the use of his background space, as well as the space of the object that is being drawn. In perspective drawing the background space is made to appear smaller and the color and details are blurred or drawn less distinctly.

> *"And the Lord formed man of the dust of the ground. So God created man in His own image; in the image of God He created: male and female He created them."* [Genesis 1:26,27]

The spoken word of God brought all that He had made into existence with the exception of man. When He was ready to create man, He did not say "Let there be man" as He said "Let there be light." Instead, God FORMED man's body.

The Hebrew word for formed means to **SHAPE** or to mold as a potter molds his clay.

> *"But now, O Lord, thou art our Father; we are the clay, and thou art our potter; and we all are the work of Thy hand."* [Isaiah 64:8]

Shape v. – To form or create; to mold or make into a particular form.

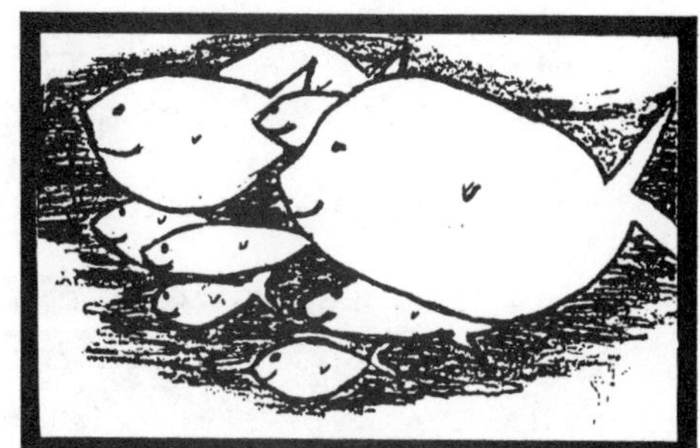

Shape n. – Form or figure as constituted by lines and angles; as the shape of a horse or a tree; the shape of the head, hand, or foot.

[Definitions are from Noah Webster's 1828 Dictionary]

The shape of an object is the outline or contour that describes it. Two-dimensional shapes have only length and width. Paintings and drawings are two-dimensional.

Three-dimensional shapes have length, width, and depth. Sculptures are three-dimensional. You could be considered a "living" sculpture.

Lines describe shapes. There are three basic shapes.

square  triangle 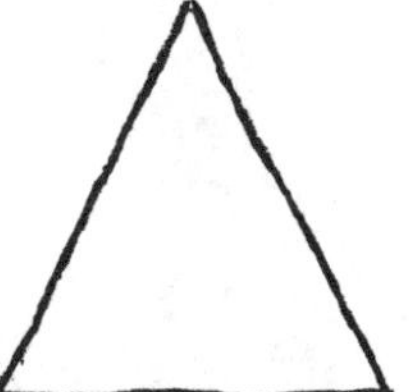 circle 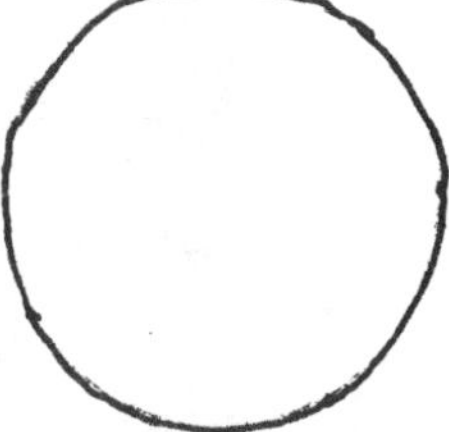

If these shapes are three-dimensional, they become

cube 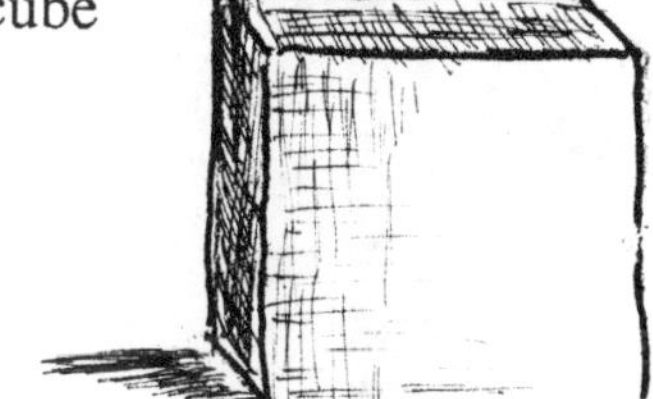 cone 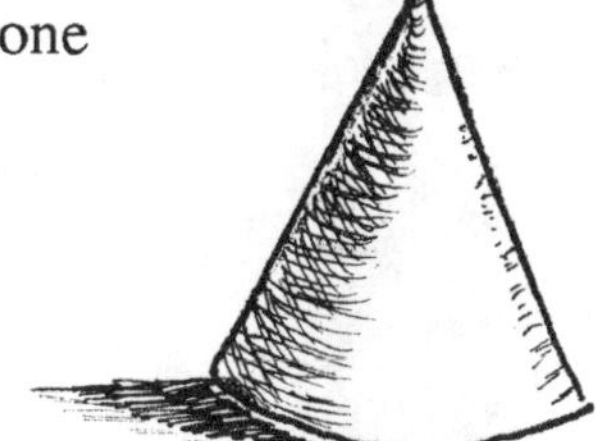 sphere 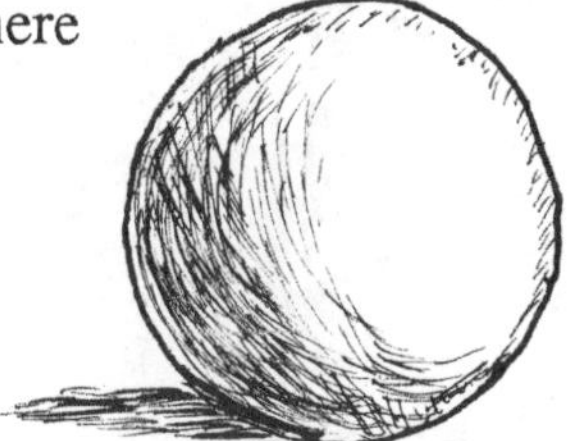

On a flat surface an object can be made to look three-dimensional by shading the part of it that is furthest away. This gives weight or volume to the object.

> *"Then God said, 'Let the earth bring forth grass, the herb that yields seed and the fruit tree that yields fruit according to its kind,...' and it was so."* [Genesis 1:11]

Through these verses we see that God also created the element of design **TEXTURE**. Texture is the roughness or smoothness of a surface.

An artist shows texture on a flat surface by repetition of **LINE**. Texture may also be made by repeating shapes to make a pattern. It is the only element that includes the sense of touch as well as the sense of sight.

"In the beginning God created...."

the elements of design: value, color, space, shape, line, and texture.

"For by Him all things were created that are in heaven and on earth." [Colossians 1:16]

CHAPTER 4

ART ON THE CHAIN OF CHRISTIANITY

– ART "HIS" STORY –

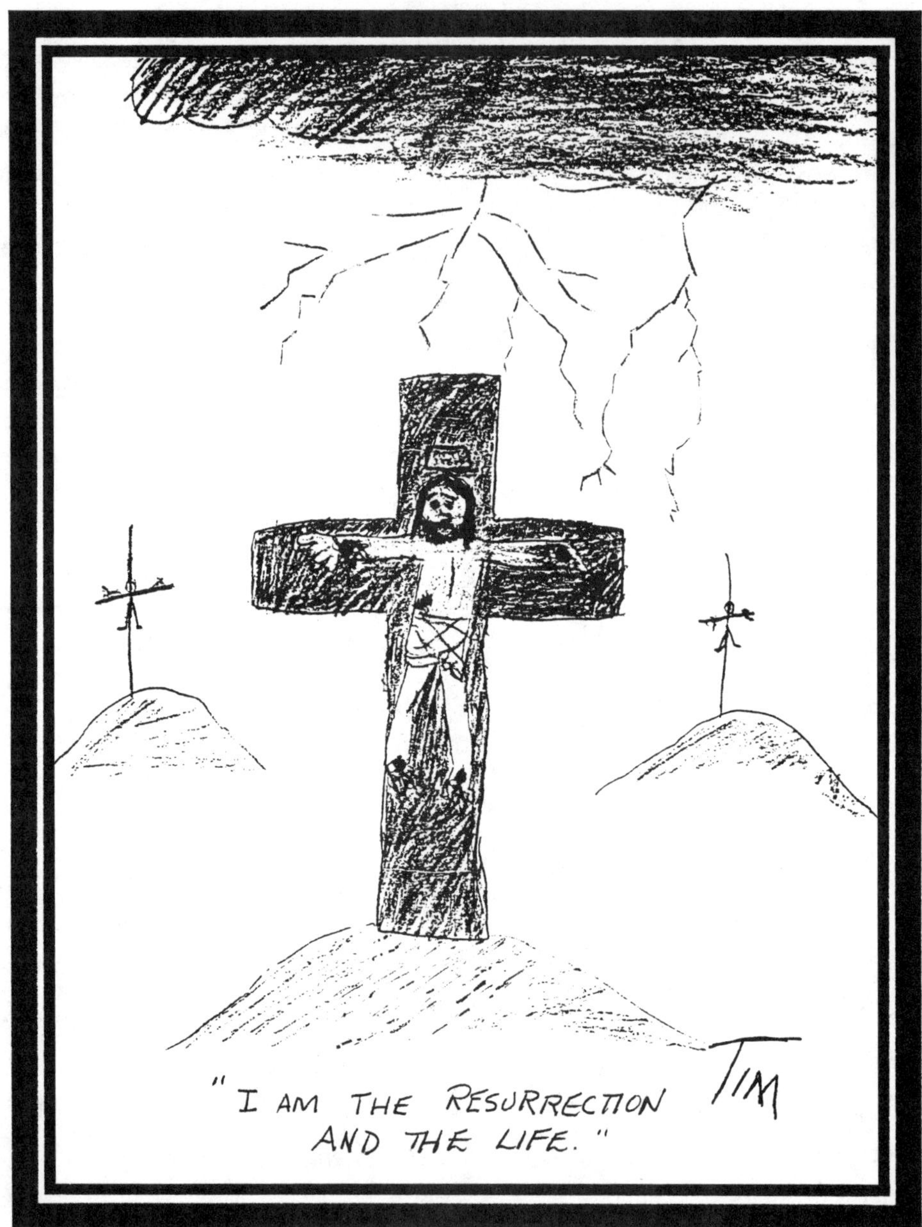

Art "His" Story is a revelation of Jesus Christ! *"For God has allowed us to know the secret of His plan, and it is this: He purposed long ago in His sovereign will that all human history should be consummated in Christ."* [EPHESIANS 1:9–10 PHILLIPS TRANSLATION] Throughout the ages, God purposed that the visual arts should serve as a **TEACHER** of the Bible and its Gospel message. Works of art have always been the people's Bible as artists throughout the centuries have portrayed the Bible in every media. Beginning with the first century Christian symbols and martyrs' paintings on the catacomb walls through the Middle Ages, the vast majority of the people were unable to read or write, so that the constant depiction of the Bible even upon familiar household objects made the stories almost universally known. When early Christian churches were first built, the glorious Byzantine mosaics pictured the Bible upon their walls in brilliant colored glass. During the time when barbarians overran Europe, the monks saved Christian art and had the Bible stories painted on church walls and sculpted in stone. Some of the most spiritual paintings of Christ are those frescoes painted by Italians, Giotto and Fra Angelico, during this time. When the great Gothic cathedrals were built by the people themselves, they were illustrated inside and out with Bible stories in stone sculptures, on friezes, in stained glass, on bronze doors, woven in tapestries, and crafted in gold, ivory, and wood! "The artist's brush taught the story of Christianity more convincingly than the pen of the theologian." [Cynthia Maus, *Christ and the Fine Arts*. Harper & Brothers Publishers: New York (1938)]

The past is our heritage and glory. God also purposed that the visual arts should serve as a RECORD of Christ, His Story and His relationship with man leaving a visual testimony of God's wondrous workings and mighty Hand! *We will not hide them from their children, shewing to the generation to come the praises of the Lord, and his strength, and his wonderful works that he hath done. For he established a testimony in Jacob, and appointed a law in Israel, which he commanded our fathers, that they should make them known to their children: That the generation to come might know them, even the children which should be born; who should arise and declare them to their children: That they might set their hope in God, and not forget the works of God, but keep his commandments.* [PSALM 78:4–7] **Christian art is the heritage of all the world!**

The study of great masterpieces is a source of immense pleasure even to the very youngest child who is deeply affected by the spirit of the masterpiece and who often delights in even the minutest details. Its inclusion in the study of art is central to the StoneBridge art curriculum, because the great masterpieces are used to teach the basic art principles, the elements of design, and frequently inspire the children's art projects. Children are highly impacted by visual images and it is the responsibility of the Christian educator to elevate aesthetic tastes and values through a carefully developed art appreciation curriculum and through the display of great artwork throughout the school or home.

CREATE A FINE ARTS GALLERY IN YOUR SCHOOL

- Make a list of the masterpieces that are studied in the art curriculum.
- Determine where reprints can be purchased and the cost to attractively frame them.
- Offer parents and grandparents an opportunity to donate the cost of a framed masterpiece.
- Hang the masterpieces with a nameplate attached citing the title and its artist and acknowledging the donor.

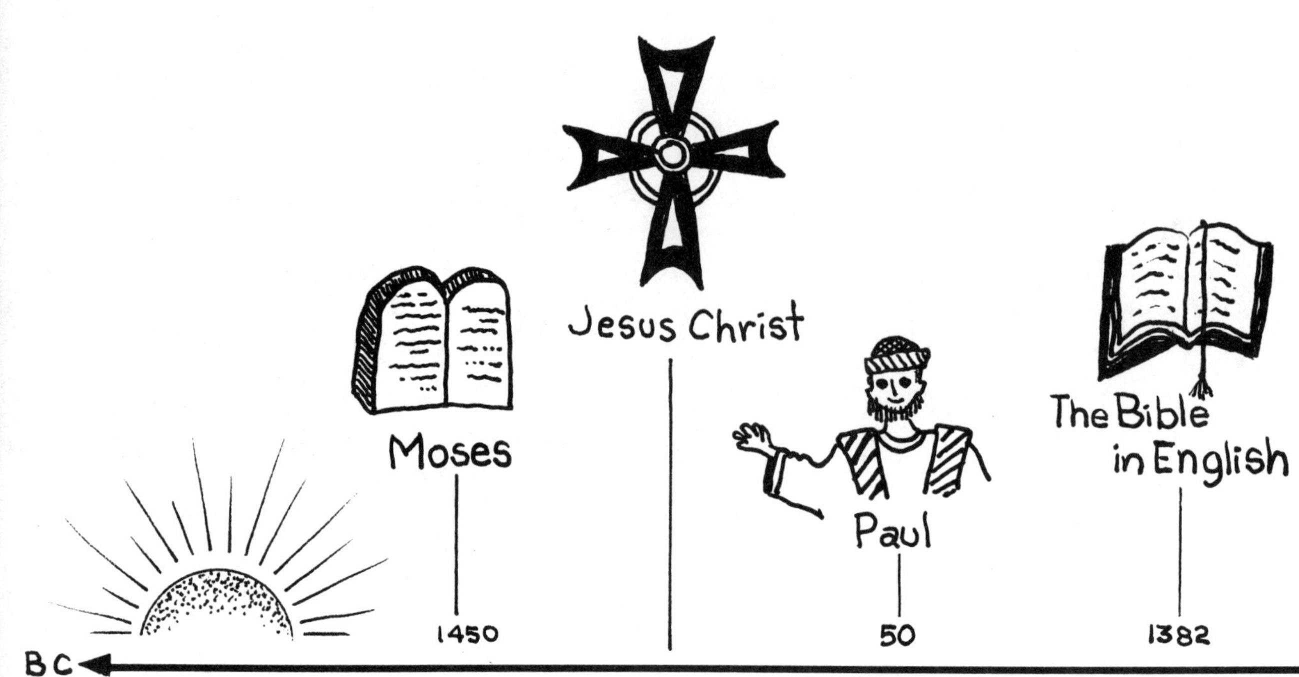

IN THE BEGINNING
GOD
CREATED

EARLY CHRISTIAN

GIOTTO
‹1266 · 1337›

ROME

JAN VAN EYCK
‹1380 · 1441›

GREECE

FRA ANGELICO
‹1400 · 1458›

EGYPT

CHRISTIAN CATHEDRALS

MESOPOTAMIA

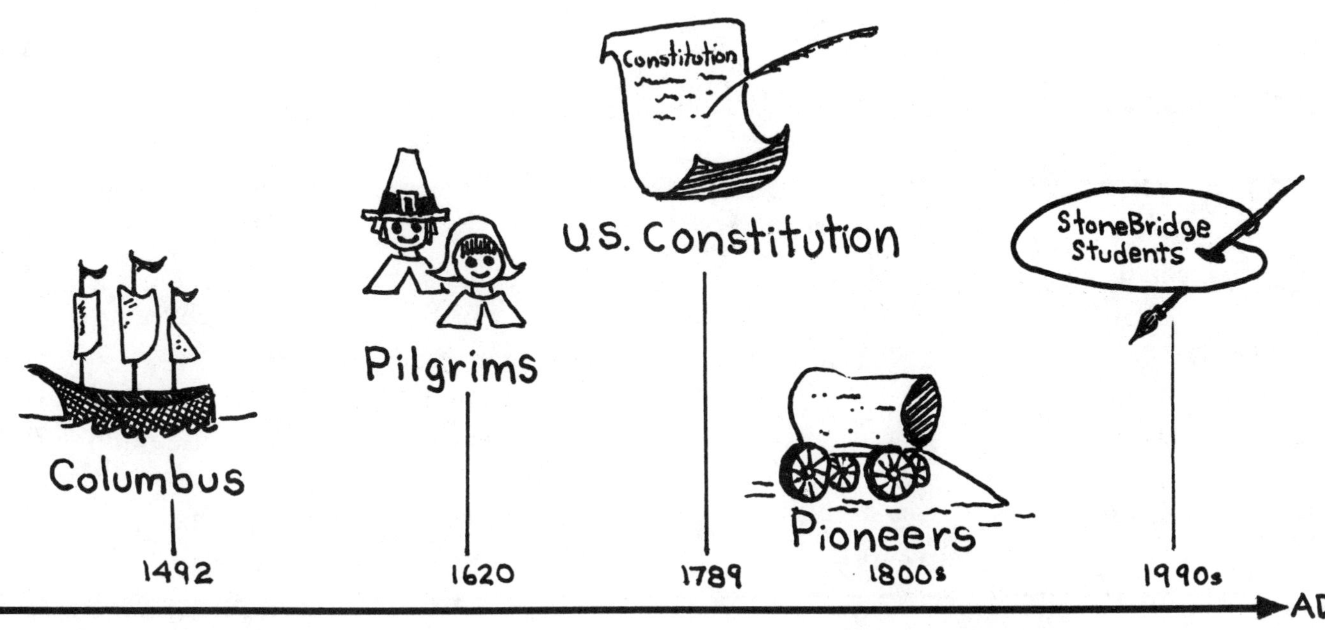

LEONARDO DA VINCI
<1452-1519>

ALBRECHT DÜRER
<1471-1528>

MICHELANGELO BUONARROTI
<1475-1564>

RAPHAEL SANTI
<1483-1520>

LORENZO BERNINI
<1598-1680>

REMBRANDT VAN RIJN
<1606-1669>

JAN VERMEER
<1632-1675>

JOSHUA JOHNSON
<1700s>

SIR JOSHUA REYNOLDS
<1723-1792>

BENJAMIN WEST
<1738-1820>

CHARLES W. PEALE
<1741-1827>

THOMAS JEFFERSON
<1743-1826>

JOHN J. AUDUBON
<1785-1851>

FREDERIC E. CHURCH
<1826-1900>

WINSLOW HOMER
<1836-1910>

CLAUDE MONET
<1840-1926>

PIERRE A. RENOIR
<1841-1919>

MARY CASSATT
<1845-1926>

HOWARD PYLE
<1853-1911>

JESSIE W. SMITH
<1863-1935>

NORMAN ROCKWELL
<1894-1978>

WALT DISNEY
<1901-1966>

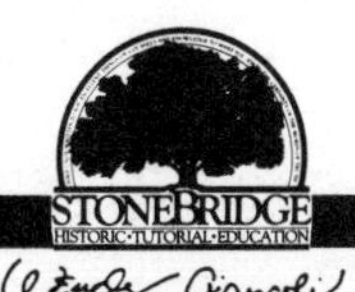

SELECTED ARTISTS ON THE CHAIN

ART OF ANTIQUITY

Mesopotamian	contemporary to Old Testament history
Egyptian	contemporary to Old Testament history
Greek	roots of Western Art
Roman	roots of Western Art

MIDDLE AGES

The Gospel Preserved and Taught

Christian Cathedrals	the Bible in stone, spiritual significance in architecture
Giotto (1266–1337)	Christian character; religious frescoes; use of space; three-dimensional effect
Jan Van Eyck (1380–1441)	Christian character; perfected the use of oil paint and brought it into popularity
Fra Angelico (1400–1458)	devotional spirit; Christian character; religious frescoes

ITALIAN RENAISSANCE AND BAROQUE

Expression of Individual Artists Liberated

Leonardo da Vinci (1452–1519)	creative and inventive genius; creator of the most famous religious painting and non-religious painting; his relationship with the church
Michelangelo (1475–1564)	contribution to the history of art; his love of God
Raphael (1483–1520)	religious frescoes; his relationship with the church
Bernini (1598–1680)	his faith, relationship to the church; his *Bust of a Savior* is in the Chrysler Museum, Norfolk, Va.

REFORMATION

The Individual Spirit Liberated

Dürer (1471–1528)	devout Christian character; understanding of God's diversity as seen in nature
L. Cranach (1472–1553)	his respect for and portraits of Martin Luther
Rembrandt (1608–1669)	first Biblical artist; he illustrated or painted almost every book in the Bible in a country and at a time when religious pictures were not being commissioned
Vermeer (1632–1675)	Dutch painter of domestic scenes

OF CHRISTIANITY: WHO AND WHY

ENGLISH

Sir Joshua Reynolds (1723–1792) .... influence on Benjamin West

AMERICAN

The Chain of Christianity Moving Westward

Benjamin West (1738–1820) .... Christian character; father of American painting

Charles W. Peale (1741–1827) .... Colonial craftsman and artist – reflection of the Republic; taught many others

Joshua Johnson (1700s) .... a slave who became free; a craftsman and an artist

Thomas Jefferson (1743–1826) .... introduced Neoclassicism to American architecture (Capitol in Richmond)

J. J. Audubon (1785–1851) .... pioneer who recorded America's natural wild life and spread knowledge of America

Frederic Edwin Church (1826–1900) .... Christian character; his appreciation for the detail and diversity of God; Hudson River School

Howard Pyle (1853–1911) .... Quaker heritage; illustrator of children's books; father of American illustrators; taught many others such as Jessie Willcox Smith and N. C. Wyeth

IMPRESSIONISM

W. Homer (1836–1910) .... watercolor paintings recorded the Civil War

Monet (1840–1926)
Renoir (1841–1919) .... founders of French Impressionist School of Art; appreciation of light and color

Mary Cassatt (1845–1926) .... representative of women's role in art; only American in the French Impressionist School

MODERNISM

Norman Rockwell (1894–1978) .... visual portrait of American life

Walt Disney (1901–1966) .... American cartoonist of exceptional creative talent

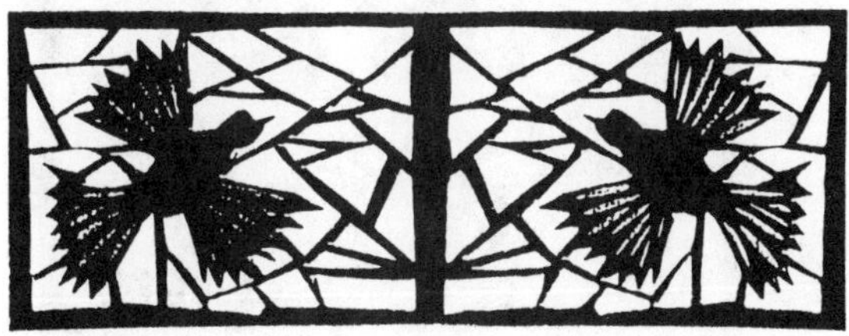

Art is a reflection of its creator

PORTRAITS OF

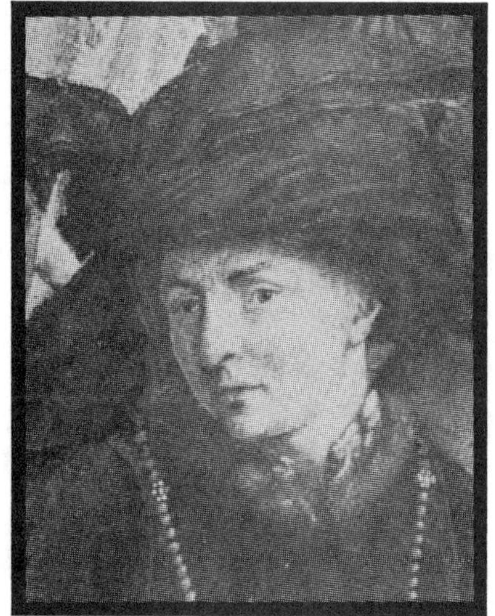
JAN VAN EYCK

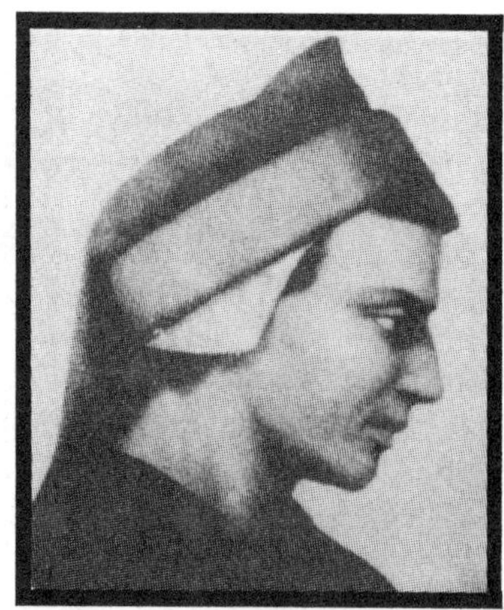
GIOTTO

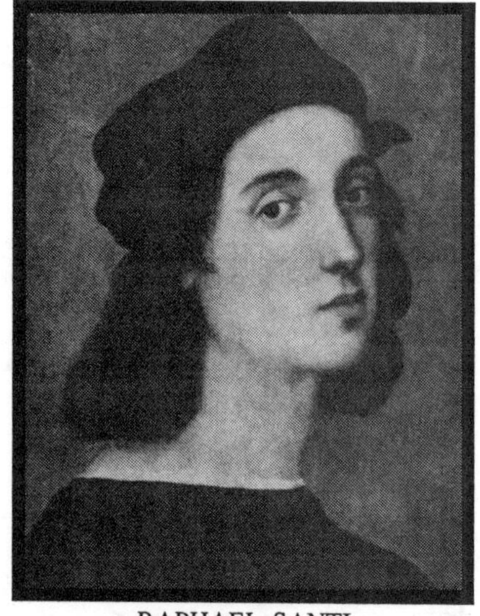
RAPHAEL SANTI

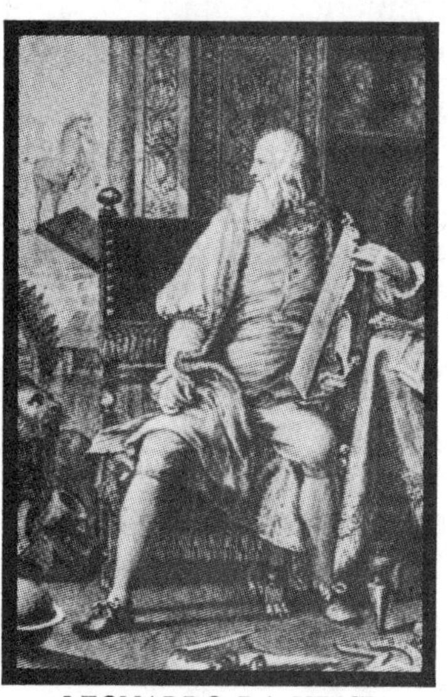
LEONARDO DA VINCI

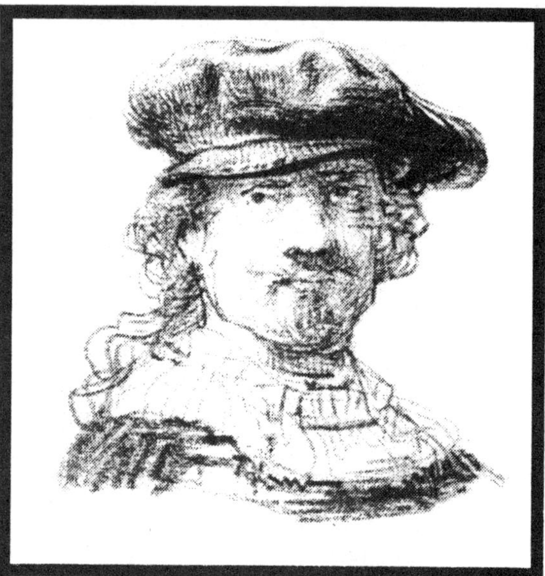
REMBRANDT VAN RIJN

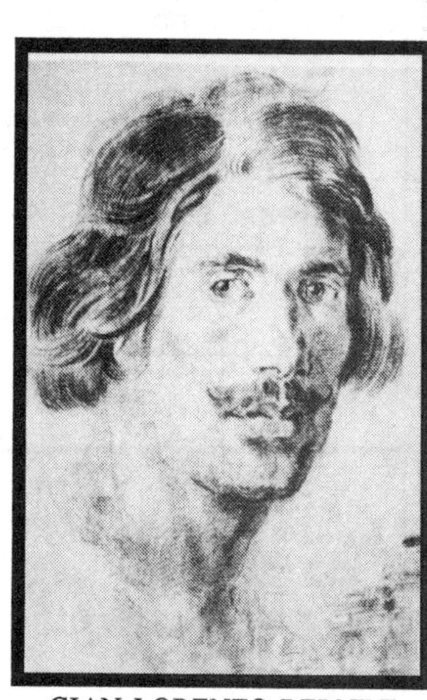
GIAN LORENZO BERNINI

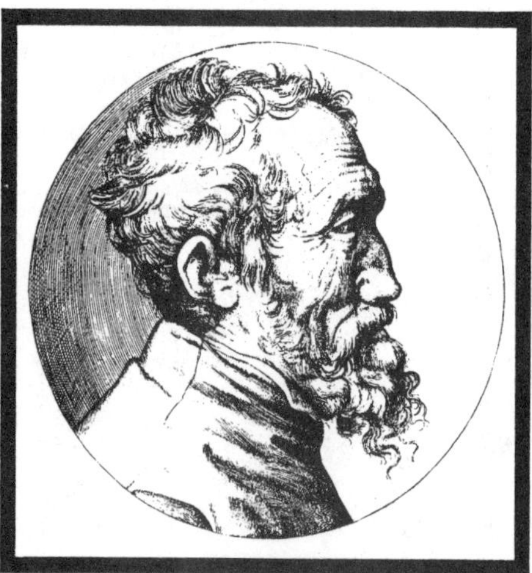
MICHELANGELO BUONARROTI

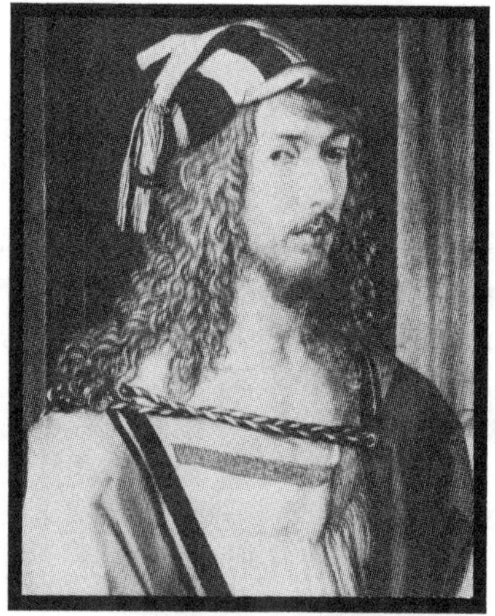
ALBRECT DÜRER

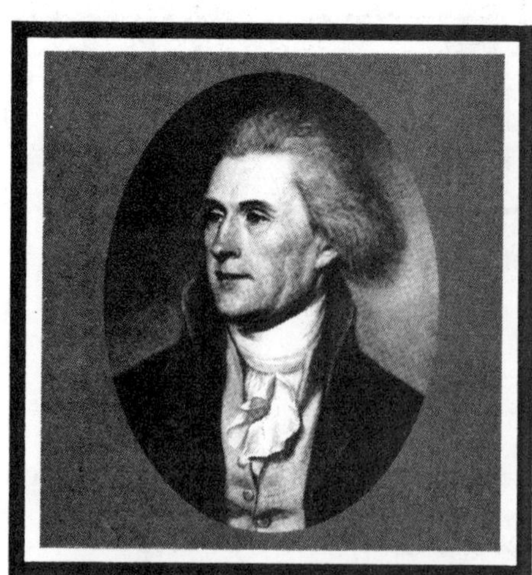
THOMAS JEFFERSON

Ennobled Artists

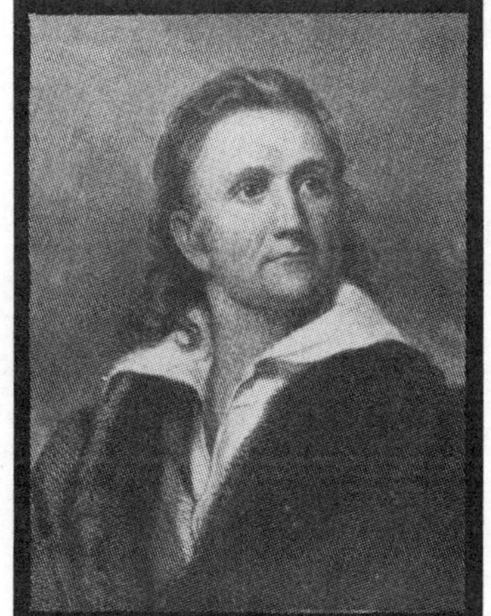

JOHN JAMES AUDUBON

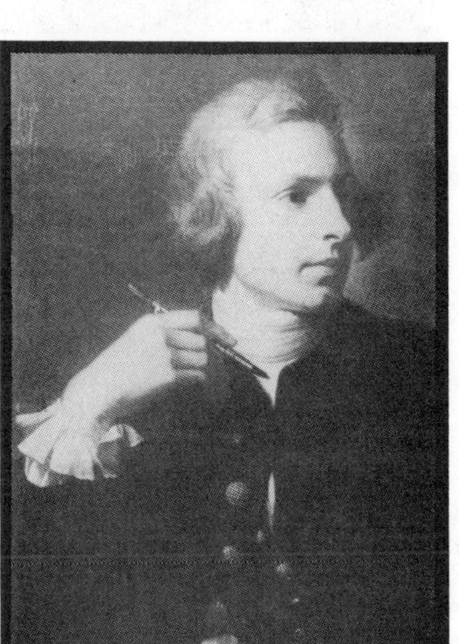

CHARLES WILLSON PEALE

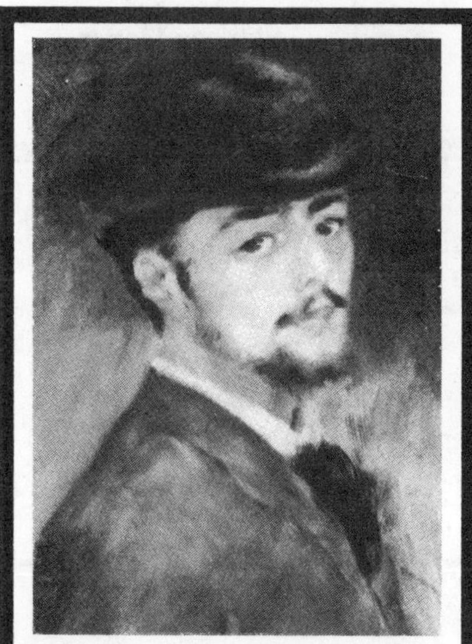

PIERRE AUGUST RENOIR

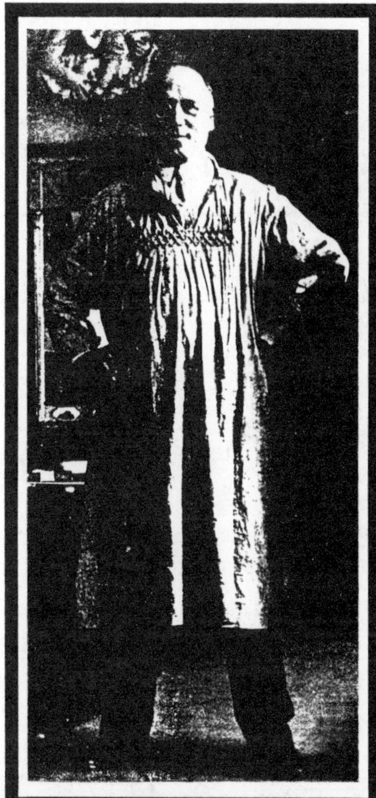

HOWARD PYLE

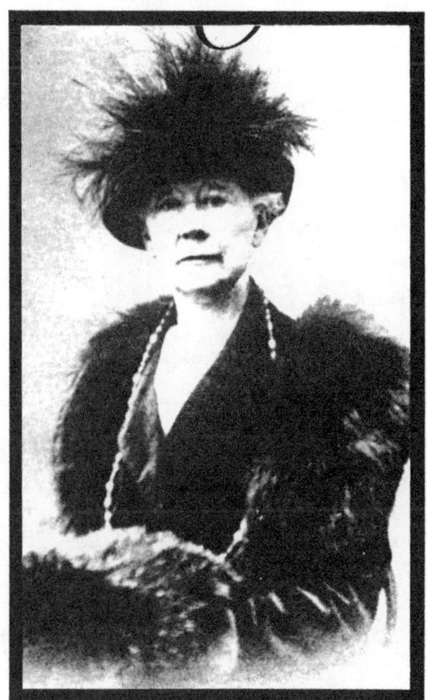

MARY CASSATT

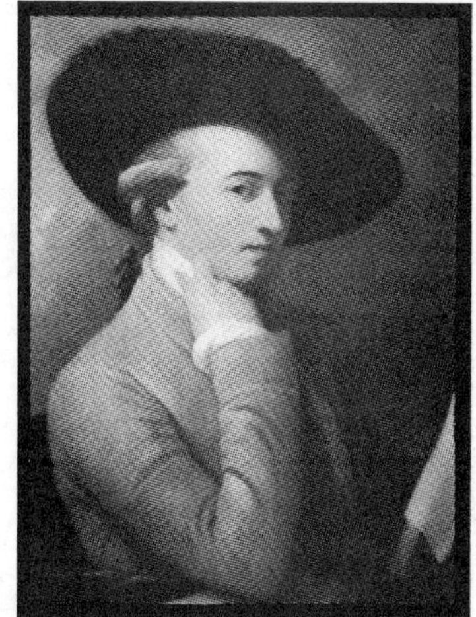

BENJAMIN WEST

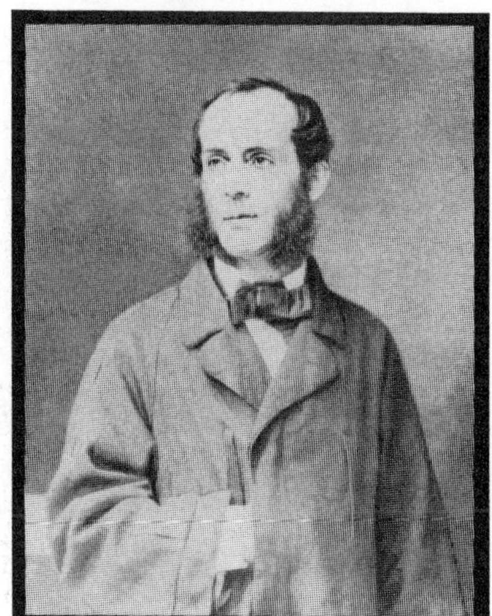

FREDRIC EDWIN CHURCH

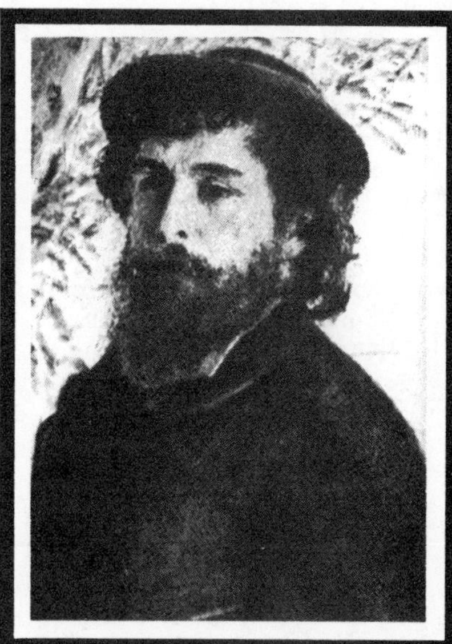

CLAUDE MONET

Four-Year Schedule

	CREATION	ART OF ANTIQUITY	MIDDLE AGES Gospel Preserved Through Artists & Monks	RENAISSANCE & ITALIAN BAROQUE
YEAR ONE	The Heavens and all that is therein –	**Mesopotamian** (2000–1700 B.C.) Subject Matter	**Giotto** (1266–1357) Space	**Gian Lorenzo Bernini** (1598–1680) Shape
YEAR TWO	The Seas and all that is therein –	**Egyptian** (1700–1450 B.C.) Shape	**Christian Cathedrals** Texture	**Leonardo da Vinci** (1452–1519) Space; Subject Matter
YEAR THREE	The Land and its inhabitants –	**Greek** and **Roman** Shape & Space	**Jan Van Eyck** (1380–1441) Texture	**Raphael** (1483–1520) Color; Subject Matter
YEAR FOUR	Shapes repeated in nature –	**Early Christian** Line	**Fra Angelico** (1400–1458) Color; Subject Matter	**Michelangelo** (1475–1564) Shape

OF THE ART CURRICULUM

REFORMATION	AMERICA The Flowering Period	IMPRESSIONISM	MODERNISM
Rembrandt (1608–1669) Value; Subject Matter	**Charles W. Peale** (1741–1827) – and/or – **Joshua Johnson** (1700s) Line	**Winslow Homer** (1836–1910) Color; Line; Style; Medium	Select a local Artist
Jan Vermeer (1632–1675) Color	**Benjamin West** (1738–1827) – and/or his teacher – **Sir Joshua Reynolds** (1723–1792) English Subject Matter	**Renoir** (1841–1919) Color; Style	**Norman Rockwell** (1894–1978) Subject Matter
Lucas Cranach (1472–1553) Line; Subject Matter	**Thomas Jefferson** (1741–1827) Space – and/or – **Howard Pyle** (1853–1911) Line	**Mary Cassatt** (1845–1926) Color; Style	Select a local Artist
Albrecht Dürer (1471–1528) Texture; Value; Subject Matter	**John J. Audubon** (1785–1851) Shape; Subject Matter – or – **Fredric E. Church** (1826–1900) Space	**Claude Monet** (1840–1926) Color; Style; Subject Matter	**Walt Disney** (1901–1966) Cartooning

SUGGESTED ART PROJECTS FOR YEAR FOUR

CREATION	*Shape*	Shapes repeated in nature – the spiral: Construction paper 3-D snails (K5–2nd) Torn paper seahorses (3rd & 4th) Crayon etchings of the shell (5th & 6th) Drawing of ram's horn (7th & 8th)
EARLY CHRISTIAN	*Line* *Texture*	Pencil drawings of early Christian symbols Mosaics (all grades) Ink drawings of early churches (6th-8th)
FRA ANGELICO	*Subject* *Line*	Construction paper angels (K5) Drawing angels (all grades) Illuminated letters (3rd–5th) Calligraphy using Scripture
MICHELANGELO	*Form* *Subject*	Clay (all grades) Clay nativity figures (6th–8th); see p. 50 Salt dough nativity figures (3rd–5th) Ceiling drawings (1st–3rd); see pp. 43–46 Drawing hands (all grades); see p. 51
ALBRECHT DÜRER	*Value* *Line*	Drawing from nature – plants Logos Printing: Thumbprints (K5) Styrofoam prints, string prints (1st-5th) Linoleum block prints (6th–7th) Silk screen printing (8th)
JOHN J. AUDUBON	*Subject* *Composition*	Bird mobiles (K5) Birds – paint, ink, or colored pencil Each grade does a different American bird and studies the habits and peculiarities of that bird. The bird is pictured in its natural surroundings as those done by Audubon. (1st–8th)
CLAUDE MONET	*Color, Space* *Style*	Copy masterpiece – landscapes Painting "impressionistically"
WALT DISNEY	*Line*	Flip books Drawing cartoons

CHAPTER 5

METHODOLOGY

The Principle Approach Art Curriculum uses a simple, basic method:

1. Identify an element of design in a masterpiece.
2. The study of this element instructs and inspires students to apply their knowledge in their practice of art skills.
3. The master artist's subject matter, medium, or style frequently sparks the development of classroom art projects.

The aspiring art teacher does not need to be a Michelangelo or a Rembrandt in artistic ability. The teacher should develop methods in the classroom that teach to the whole child and draw from every child the fullest potential of his God-given creativity and imagination. After the teacher's personal study and research is completed, he or she needs only to teach the art skills, inspire the heart of the student through his or her love of the subject matter, and provide a nurturing and elevated fine arts environment.

It is the supreme art of the teacher
to awaken ***joy*** *in creative expression and knowledge.*

– Albert Einstein –

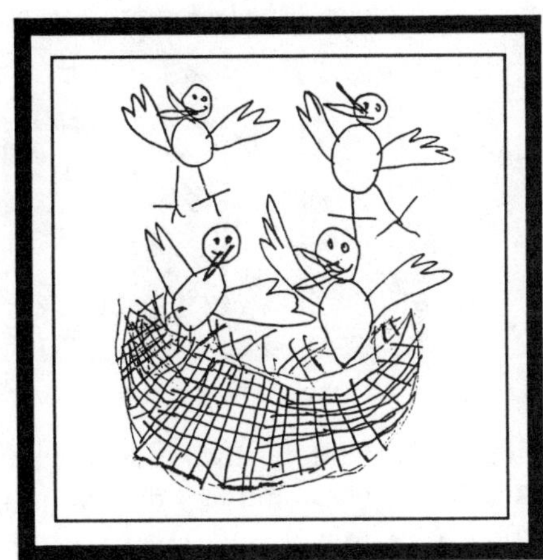

METHODS

HOW TO MAKE ART LIVE IN THE LIFE OF THE STUDENT

Teaching and learning begin by establishing a positive relationship with each student. Maximum learning takes place when the teacher touches the heart of every student and the student responds with his or her consent to learn. Interacting with each student in every class period is very important because the art teacher normally spends only one class period a week with each elementary class. The art teacher should move through the classroom during each lesson relating with each child through eye contact and words of encouragement, thereby inspiring and nurturing the "artist" within every child.

The methods of teaching art in this program were inspired from studying biographies and masterpieces of individual artists.

I. OBSERVATION

A. Each school year begins with the greatest masterpiece of all time, *Creation*. Students observe firsthand the interweaving of lines into spider webs and bird nests. They observe and create the contour lines of animals, trees, and the values as seen in mountains as they majestically overlap one another in a landscape. They discover that the change in value and the overlapping of objects indicate spatial relationships. They learn to create a three-dimensional surface with object placement and with varied values. They observe the beauty of color in a flower garden and a rainbow. These observations generally occur in the art studio. An object is placed where each student can easily see it. For best results, have one object or photograph for every two students so that details are easily observed. Often the subject matter to be created cannot be brought to the classroom. This is where a developed picture file is invaluable. To strengthen observation skills, the teacher should make comments or ask questions that can only be answered from close observation. [See "A Pencil Drawing from Nature Inspired by Albrecht Dürer" on p. 80.]

B. Another method of observation is the use of a view finder with students in the fifth to eighth grades. The cardboard frame of a slide is a ready-made, convenient view finder, which can be purchased at a photography supply store, or students can make their own from construction paper. View finders help in planning pictorial composition. Always hold the view finder at arm's length and close one eye to see various composition possibilities.

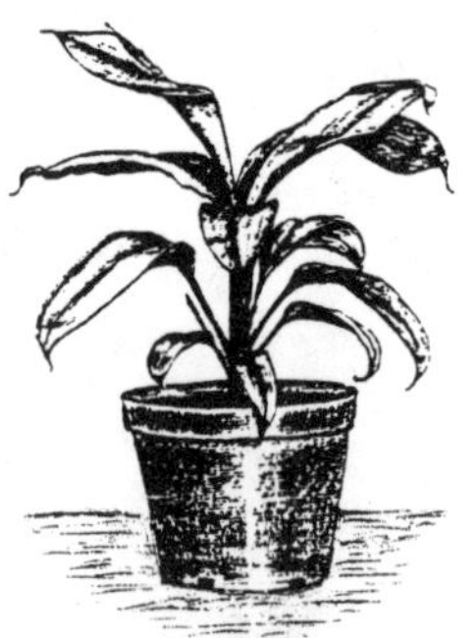
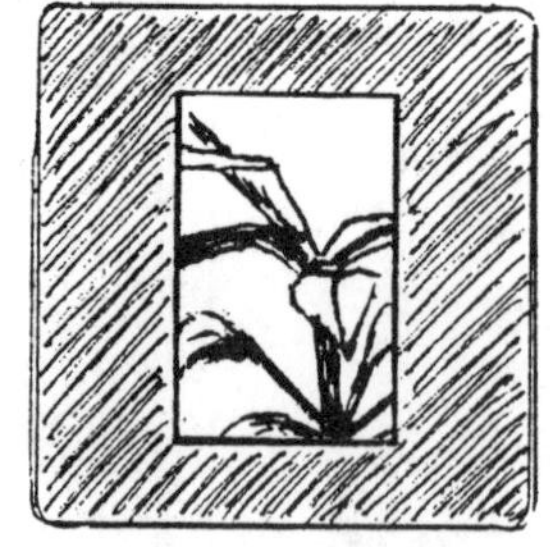
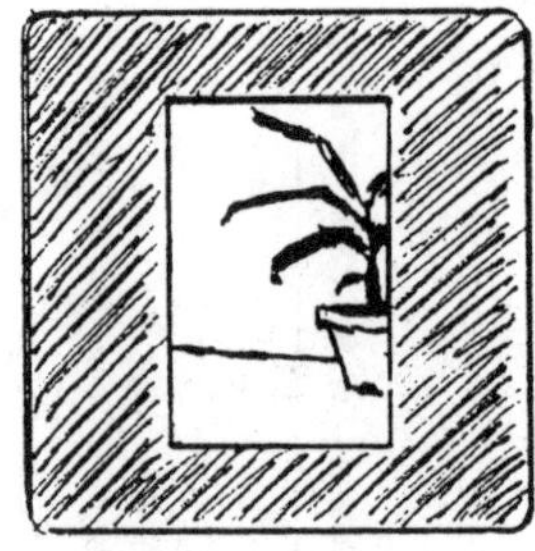
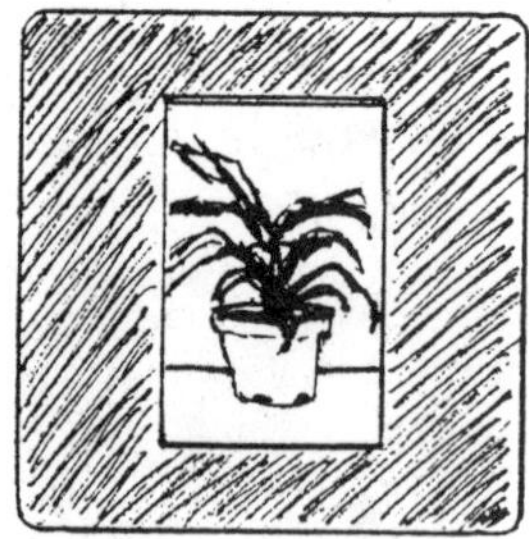

[EXAMPLES OF THE USE OF A SLIDE FRAME TO PLAN PICTORIAL COMPOSITION.]

C. Students are taught to "see with an artist's eye." So often we look at the detail and diversity in nature but so seldom do we actually see them. The mind and the eye must be trained to see. Teach students to be keen observers by asking questions that can be answered only after thoughtful looking. Students need to look beyond the obvious.

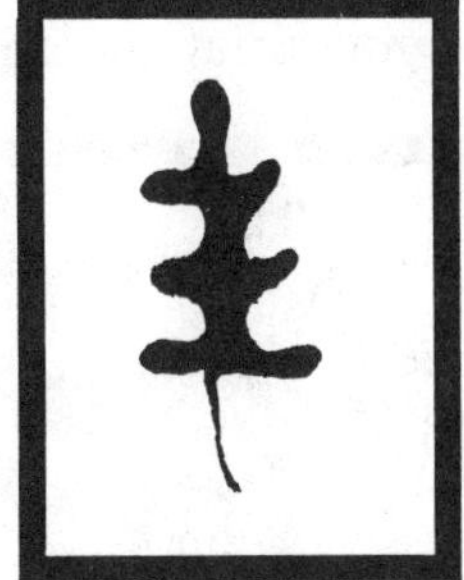

LEAF STENCIL

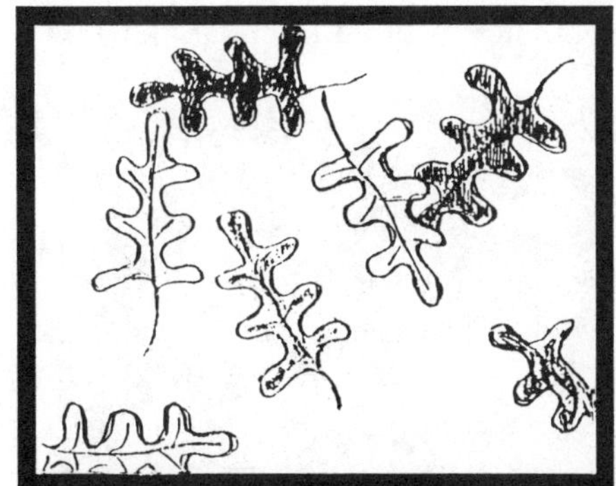

KINDERGARTEN COMPOSITION LESSON

II. STUDY

A. Students are taught that art begins *internally* in the heart and the mind before the eye and hand can create it. To encourage thinking ahead, projects are often begun with a visual plan of action or a thumbnail sketch.

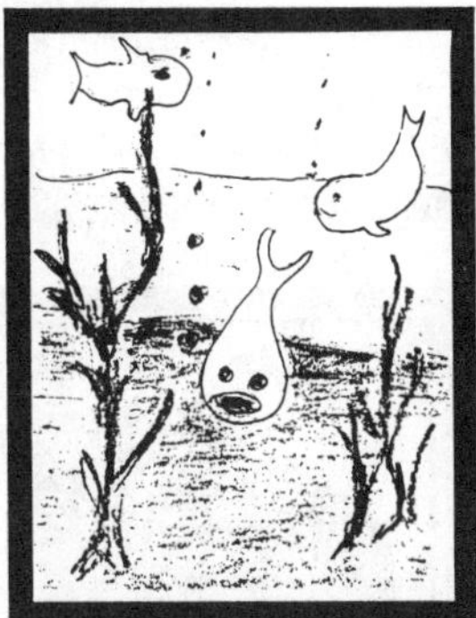

THUMBNAIL SKETCH

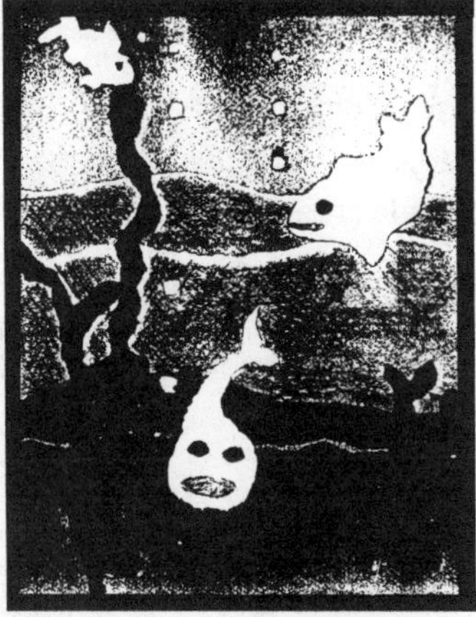

COMPLETED PROJECT

B. Masterpieces are used to instruct and inspire.

"If a man is to become a really great painter, he must be trained for it from his very earliest years. He must copy much of good artists until he has acquired the ability to draw easily." [Albrecht Dürer]

1) Students study images from great masterpieces, then reproduce their own.

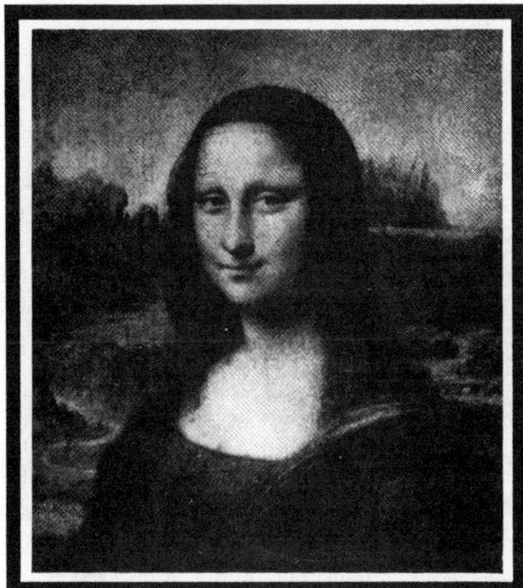

LEONARDO DA VINCI'S *Mona Lisa*

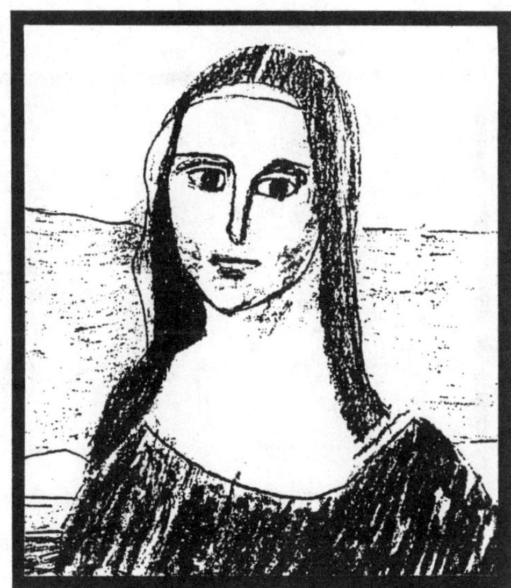

THOMAS MERRELL'S *Mona Lisa* (5TH GRADE)

2) Students are inspired to create their own images after studying great masterpieces.

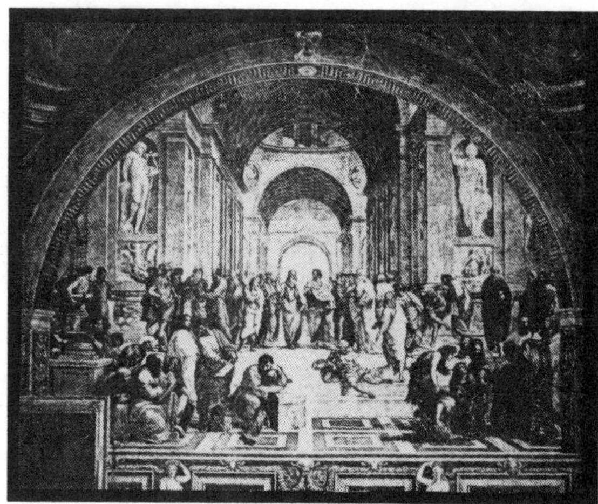

RAPHAEL'S *School of Athens*

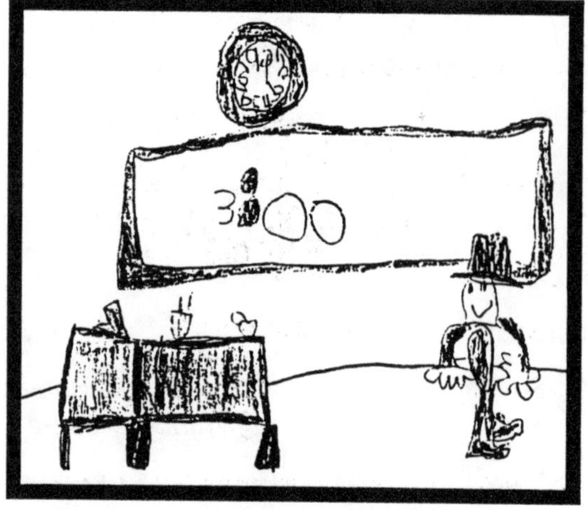

BENJI'S *School of StoneBridge* (KINDERGARTEN)

C. Another method of drawing, inspired by Albrecht Dürer, is to use a divided view finder. This allows the student to divide the composition in order to study and reproduce it easily.

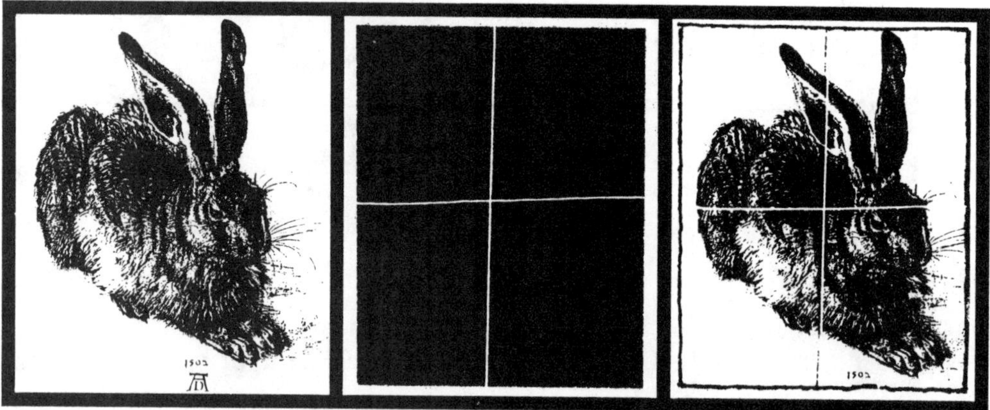

D. Drawing instruction may be done in a step-by-step method.

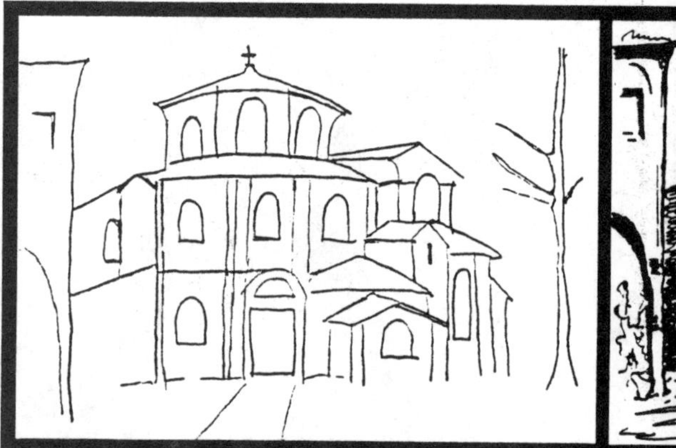

This drawing was done from a photograph of an early Christian church.

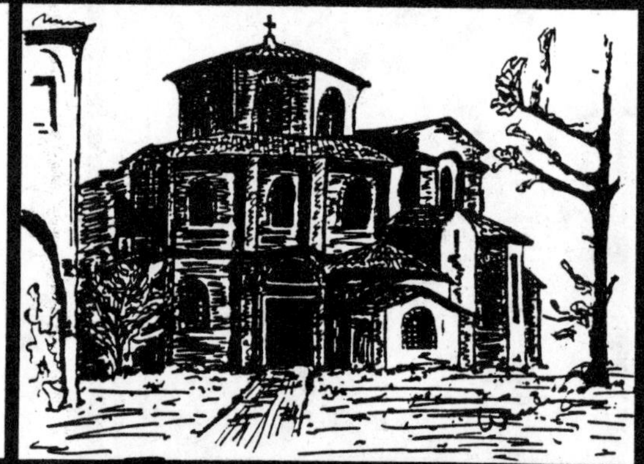

Major shapes and spaces are outlined first. Students are taught to define the whole space before beginning detail work.

III. EXPERIENCE

A. In preparation for a drawing assignment, students experiment with textures and values.

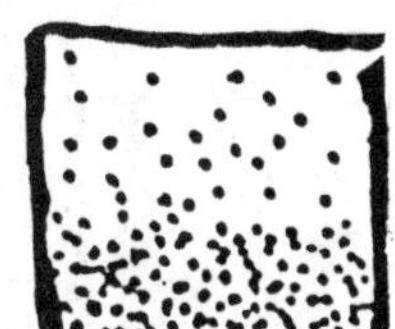

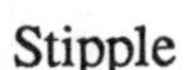

Stipple

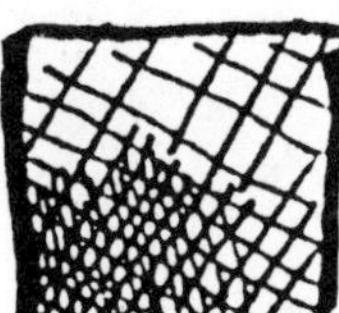

Crosshatch

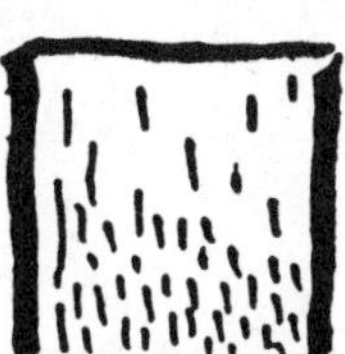

Short broken strokes

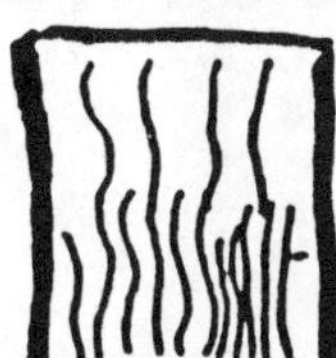

Long wavy lines

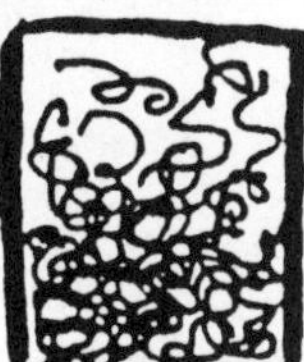

Other

TEXTURE and VALUE

Students must observe textures and values and how they change with distance.

Young children can be taught how to create texture or value on a coloring page, while at the same time training their "artists' eyes" with masterpieces. Coloring sheets for preschool or primary-aged students can be quickly done from masterpieces by the art teacher simply by tracing a masterpiece using a window or a light box and duplicating copies for the students. (See pp. 38 and 39 for an example.)

FRA ANGELICO STUDY

B. In studying Fra Angelico, older students can become scribes and design illuminated letters or pen selected Scripture in calligraphy. With their study of Fra Angelico, whose name means "brother angel," younger students can draw or make construction paper angels, as illustrated in the kindergarten examples below.

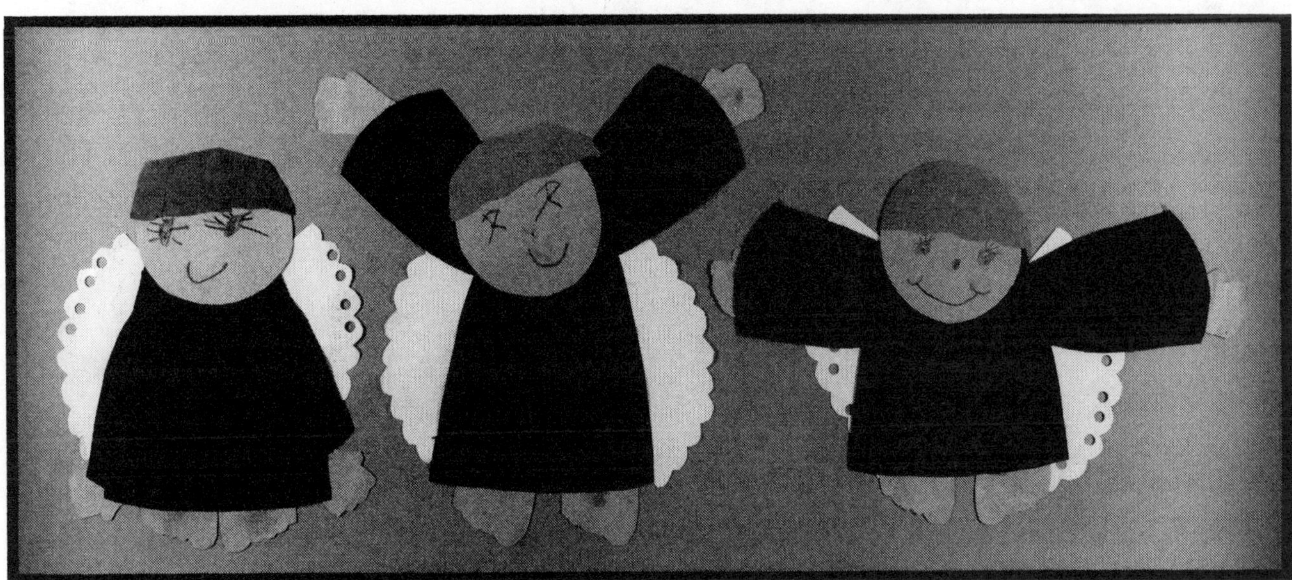

When teaching a class in which skill levels are widely varied, it is often beneficial to "apprentice" some students to other students whose skills are more highly developed.

Fra Angelico

1395 – 1455

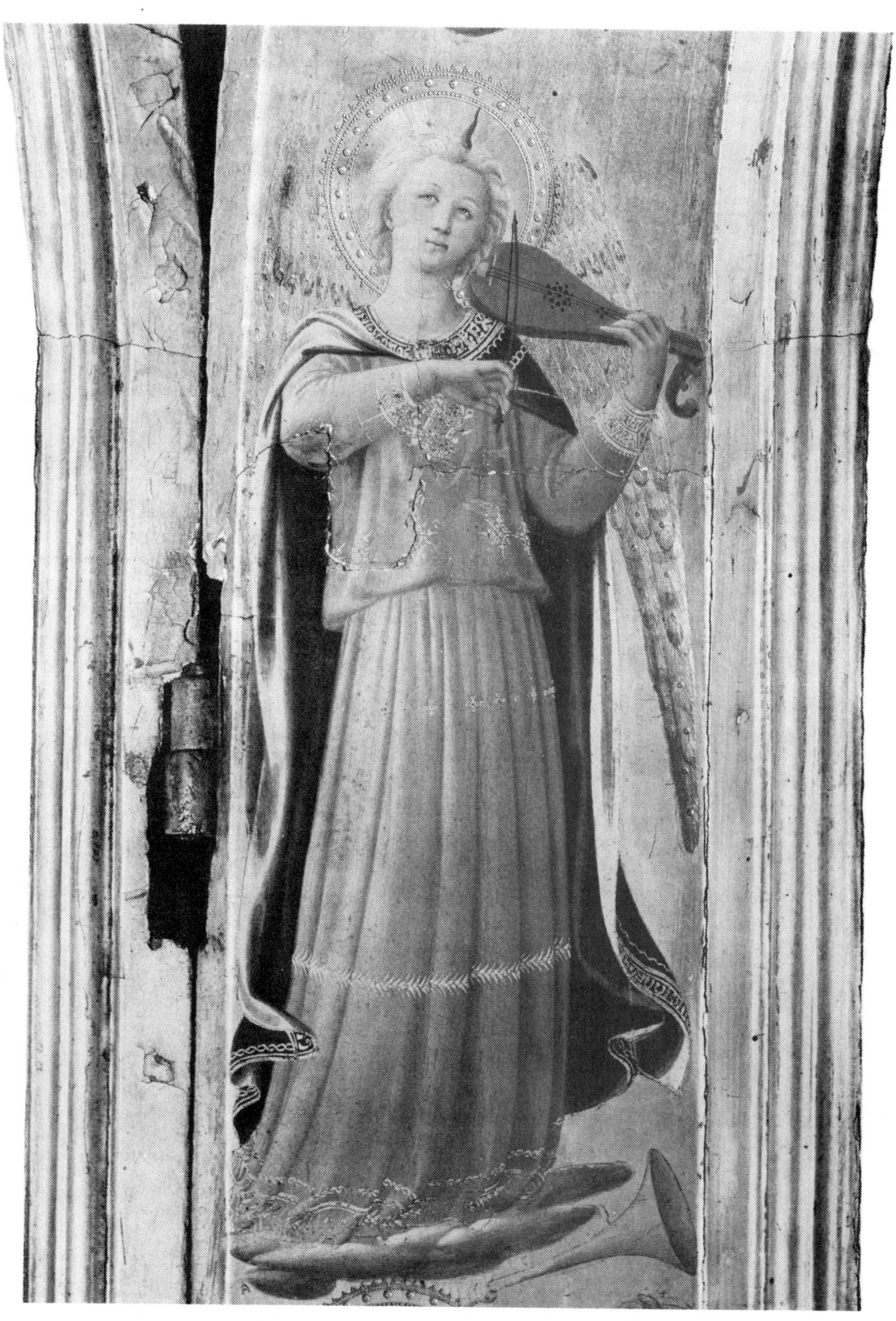

Fra Angelico

1395 – 1455

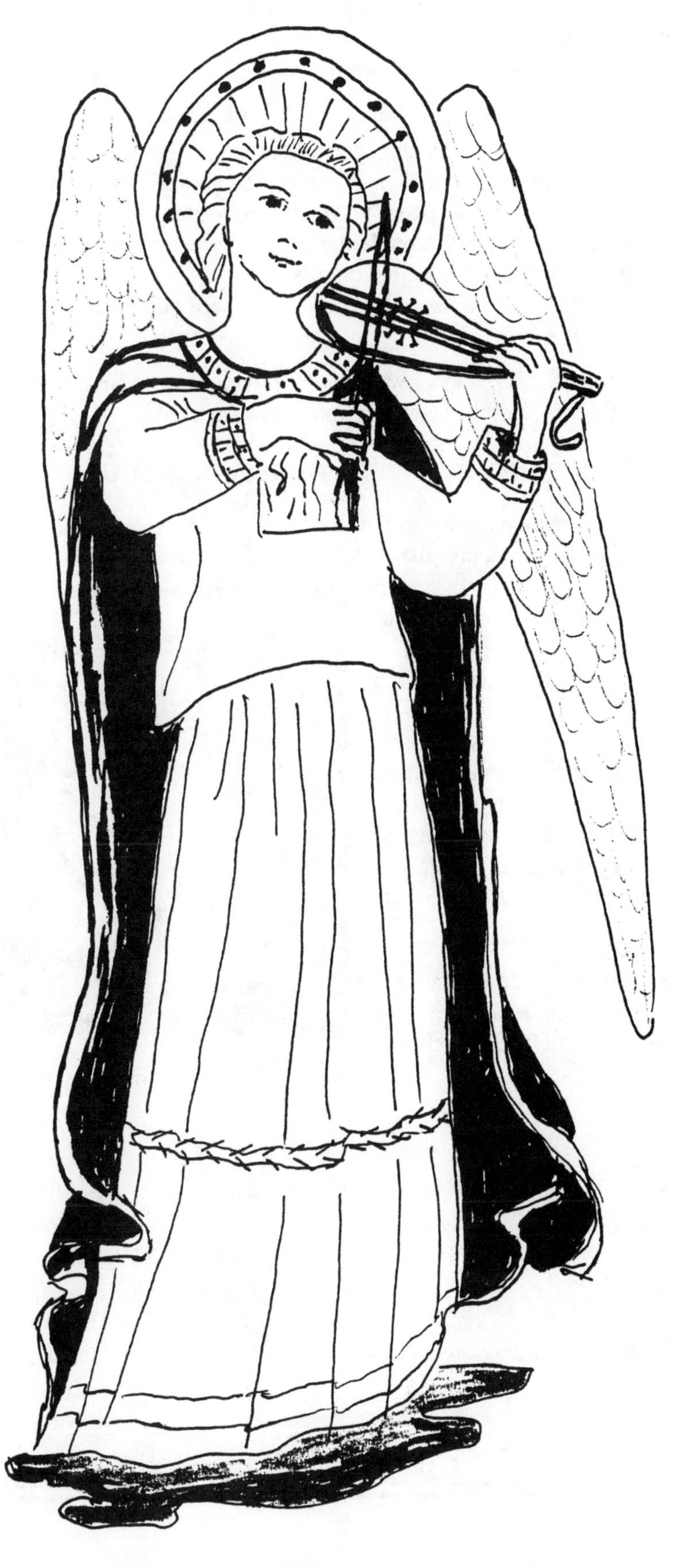

IV. VISUAL DEMONSTRATIONS

Visual demonstrations or dramatizations increase student interest and develop wider understanding. Inviting a locally or nationally acclaimed artist to the school to sketch, paint, or sculpt provides a wonderful learning experience for the whole school family and builds interest in art.

V. OTHER METHODS

In the curriculum when students become portrait artists, inspired by the multitalented American artist Charles Willson Peale, they compose their portraits in an oval shape instead of the usual 8½- by 11-inch rectangular paper. The shape of the paper poses different compositional challenges and relates to Peale's background as a miniaturist. Fourth through eighth grade students use mirrors to observe the shapes of and the spaces between their facial features. Colonial-style signs are designed on posterboard and painted with markers in the study of Joshua Johnson. Johnson was a sign painter before becoming a portrait painter, as were other colonial artists.

While teaching about frescoes and how artists' drawings are transferred to a newly plastered wall, a tracing wheel designed for clothing construction could be used.

MEETING THE NEEDS OF THE INDIVIDUAL ARTIST

It is the art instructor's responsibility to nurture and encourage each student. It is up to the instructor to take steps to avoid possible problems ahead of time. The teacher needs to know the students and their challenge areas. If a student is struggling with the class project, the instructor may want to adapt the project to create more interest and to allow the student to experience success. One method of giving individual direction that is especially successful in a large class is to attach brief notes of instruction and positive comments to students' work. After general instruction has been given, period music may be played quietly. This adds another dimension to the **whole approach** of learning in the art studio.

Dallas Anderson, a contemporary sculptor from Utah who has sculpted many Biblical themes, spent a day at StoneBridge Schools sculpting one of our students.

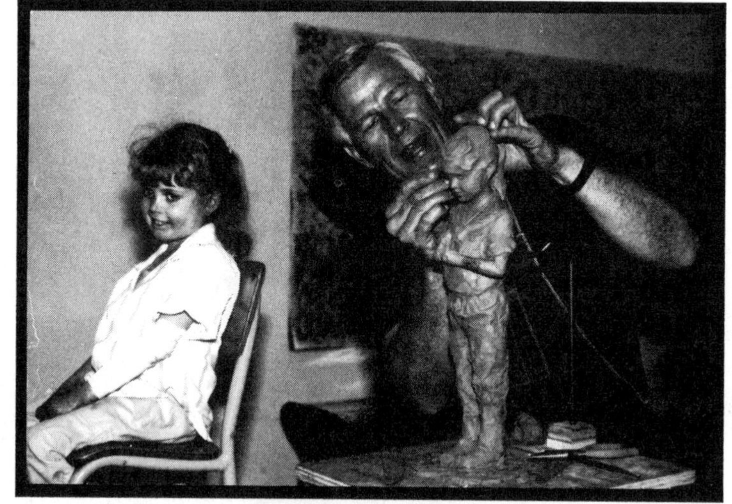

DALLAS ANDERSON
SCULPTING JESSICA SIMPSON

Other methods described in this Guide are:

Page xiii	Benjamin West paintbrush, inspired by literature
Page 15	Value, student work inspired by Rembrandt
Page 34	Observation skills
Page 42	"Bubbling," an alternative method
Pages 43–52	Michelangelo sample lessons
Page 67	Crafts
Pages 68–70	Bulletin board displays
Pages 71–76	Encouraging a spirit of excellence
Pages 77–80	Teaching the Faculty, inspired by Dürer
Pages 84–86	Field Study Tours and game
Page 87	Art detectives, inspired by literature

THE STUDENT RECORD IN THE ART CURRICULUM

TITLE PAGE INSPIRED BY SYMBOLIC LINE DRAWINGS OF EARLY CHRISTIANS
8TH GRADE STUDENT

THE WRITTEN RECORD

The Notebook Method in art has been modified because of the limited time students spend in the art class. The students are not required to take notes in order to have as much time as possible to interact with the art project. The teacher writes Art "His" Story notes and distributes copies to each student, so that the student will have a written record of his learning. The students underline or highlight important concepts and may also be directed to illustrate certain thoughts or ideas on the notes.

STUDENT ART NOTEBOOKS ARE SET UP AS FOLLOWS:

- **TITLE PAGE** (designed by the student)
- **CLASSROOM CONSTITUTION** (signed by the teacher and the student); see p. 82.
- **ART OVERVIEW**
- **PRINCIPLES OF ART**
- **ART "HIS" STORY TIME LINE**
- **NOTES AND ILLUSTRATIONS**

THE VISUAL RECORD

Individual portfolios are made and decorated by each student. The portfolios are maintained to preserve a visual record of student progress. These are kept in the art room during the school year and go home with the student at the end of the year.

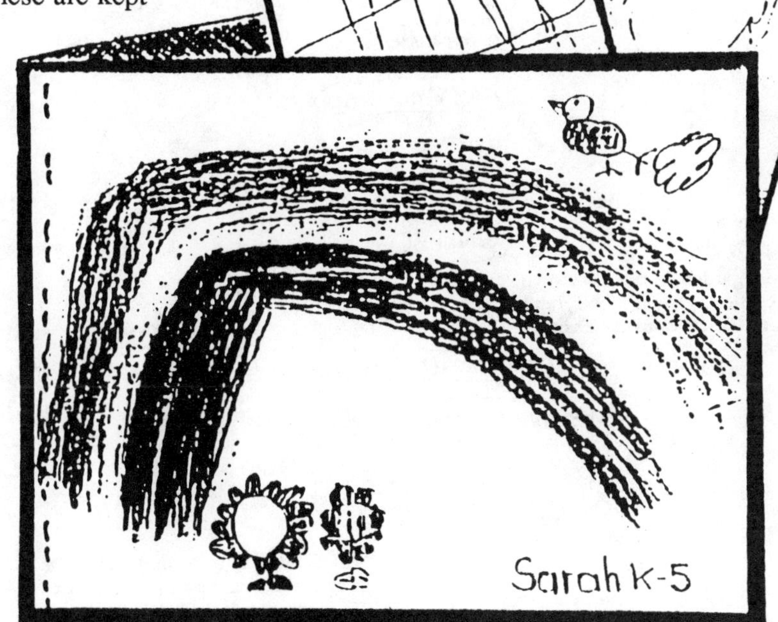

ART PORTFOLIO
KINDERGARTEN STUDENT

SAMPLE STUDENT RECORD OF A BIOGRAPHICAL SKETCH

"Bubbling" is an alternate method of note taking frequently used by the art instructor with older students to conserve class time for art practice. As the art teacher shares her knowledge of a master artist, the student quickly records phrases or key words on the provided page. When the study of the master artist is completed, the student has a simple record of the biographical data presented in the study.

CLAUDE MONET
(1840–1926)

"I perhaps owe having become a painter to flowers."

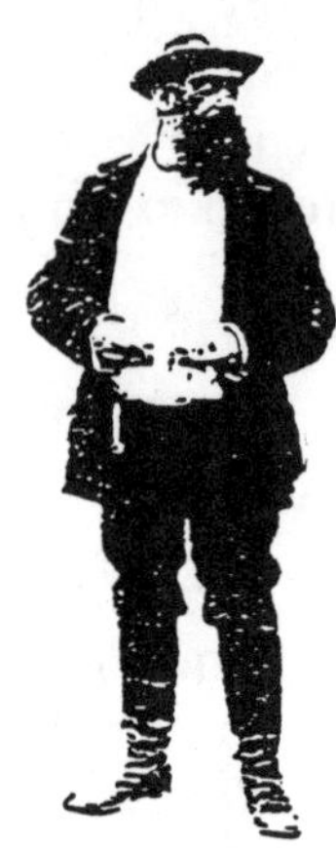

"My garden is my very own creation, grown slowly and tended with never-ceasing love."

"All I did was to look at what the universe showed me, to let my brush bear witness to it."

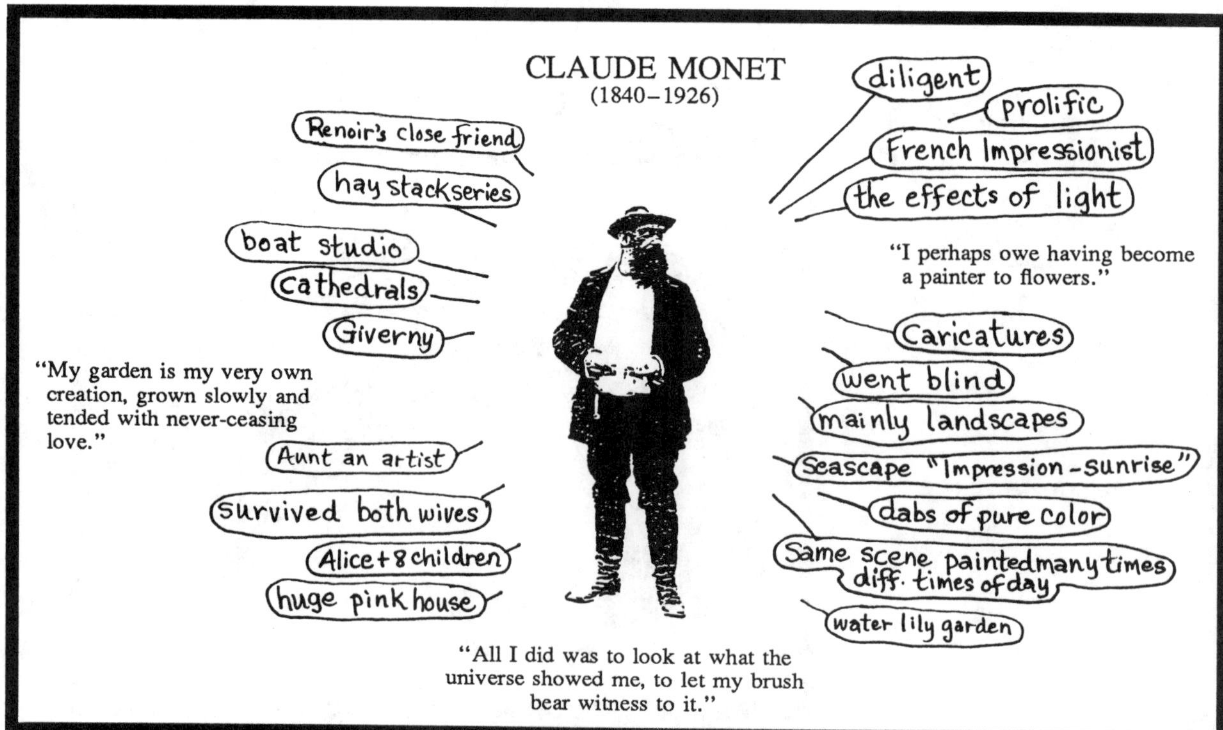

MODEL ART LESSON PLAN

SUBJECT: Art DATE: 3-2-91 TIME: 10:30 GRADE: 1st TEACHER: Giancoli

TITLE DESCRIPTION: ***Ceiling Drawings Inspired By a Study of Michelangelo***

BIBLICAL REFERENCE: *"Remember the former things of old: For I am God, and there is none else, I am God, and there is none like me, declaring the end from the beginning, and from ancient times the things that are not yet done. . . ."*
[ISAIAH 40:9,10]

LEADING IDEA & EXPRESSION: Michelangelo's God-given talent was used to visually spread "His" Story; Contour Drawings.

COMPONENTS OF A LESSON

INTRODUCE LEADING IDEA	REVIEW
Show a visual of the the Sistine Chapel Ceiling.	Fra Angelico's role of spreading the Gospel visually through frescoes

PRESENT NEW PRINCIPLES AND CONTENT

Content:	Visual Aid Tools:
1) Present biographical sketch of Michelangelo with a focus on his frescoes in the Sistine Chapel and his character qualities. 2) Contour drawings and outline drawings 3) Bible stories	Poster of ceiling of the Sistine Chapel Pictures of Michelangelo's sculpture and architecture Tools Needed for Lesson: Manila Paper, Pencils, Erasers Masking Tape, Mats for Floor

METHOD OF INTERACTING WITH STUDENT	CONCLUDE WITH A SUMMARY AND REVIEW
Tell the story. Show visual representation of Chapel ceiling. Demonstrate and instruct contour drawing. Give student copy of notes. Walk through classroom to encourage every child.	Display student work on ceiling of the classroom (see sample on pp. 45–46). **EVALUATION OF LESSON EFFECTIVENESS** This was a very successful lesson with high student interest and response.

NARRATIVE OF LESSON PLAN

1. Compile illustrated notes (see sample on pp. 47–48) to be used as student written record. Be sure to include a portrait of Michelangelo.

2. Duplicate or obtain a copy of the ceiling of the Sistine Chapel in its entirety, the larger the better. Secure this reproduction to the classroom ceiling.

3. Compile visuals of Michelangelo's sculpture, painting, and architecture to display in the classroom and to refer to while reading notes.

4. Do a sample contour drawing to show students.

5. Draw a □ or △ on each paper to be used as a border for student drawings. Tape one of these papers **under** each desk.

6. Collect the following supplies for the art practice: carpet squares or mats (one for each child), pencils, erasers, extra paper, and tape.

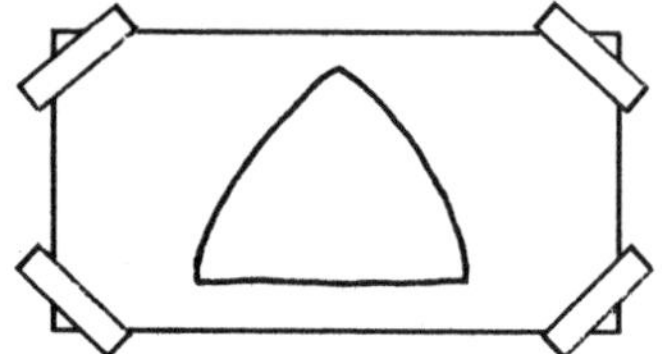

Many times the regular classroom must be used for art instruction. If so, that classroom becomes the "art studio" the moment the art lesson begins. All young artists should sit up straight and have their eyes on the teacher before instruction begins.

It is important to begin every lesson with enthusiasm, perhaps even a bit of drama, and with something that is of interest to the age level being taught. For example, tell the students, "Close your eyes and imagine lying flat on your back on a wooden platform high above the ground – six times higher than this classroom! – to paint a ceiling. Michelangelo was an Italian sculptor who was asked to paint Biblical prophets and the creation of man on a curved ceiling of a chapel. Today we will learn about Michelangelo and you, too, will create a drawing while lying on your back."

As you read notes pertaining to the life and works of the artist, ask the children to follow along on their own copies. The students may be asked to underline important thoughts or words or asked to illustrate something on their notes. This is done to reinforce thoughts and to keep the students' attention. To keep the interest of your students, ask questions both during the lecture and while students are working on their art projects. "Sally, what do you think would happen if Michelangelo put too much paint on his brush while painting the ceiling?"

Student notes are filed in their notebooks. To save time in the lower grades, the teacher may want to have students put their names on notes to be collected and filed by the teacher at a later time. To begin the practical part of the lesson, the instructor visually reviews with the class how to create a contour or an outline drawing.

Students delight in looking at the reproduction of Michelangelo's ceiling that you have placed on the classroom ceiling for them.

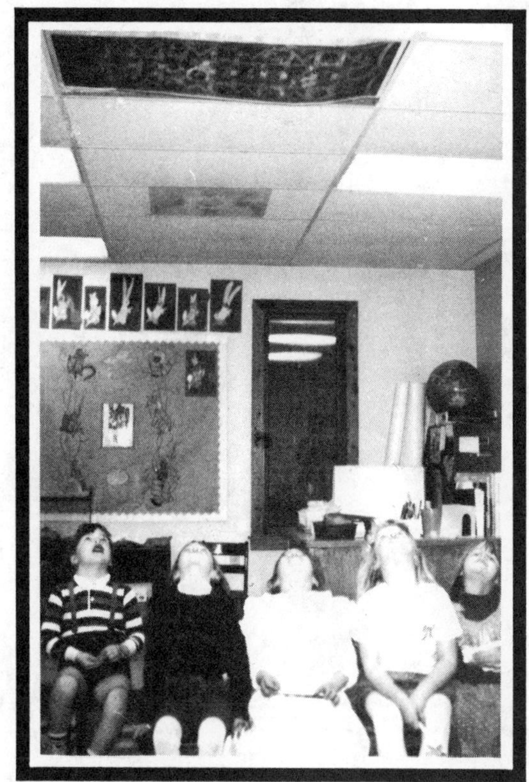

Have students think about their favorite Old Testament story in keeping with Michelangelo's ceiling. "Zachary, which story are you going to draw?" "Sara, what is your favorite story in the Old Testament?"

Now the fun begins as students engage in their own "ceiling" drawings.

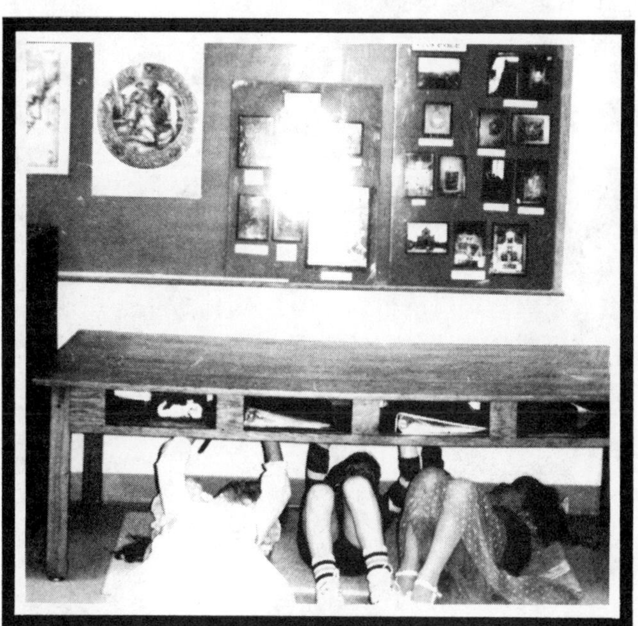

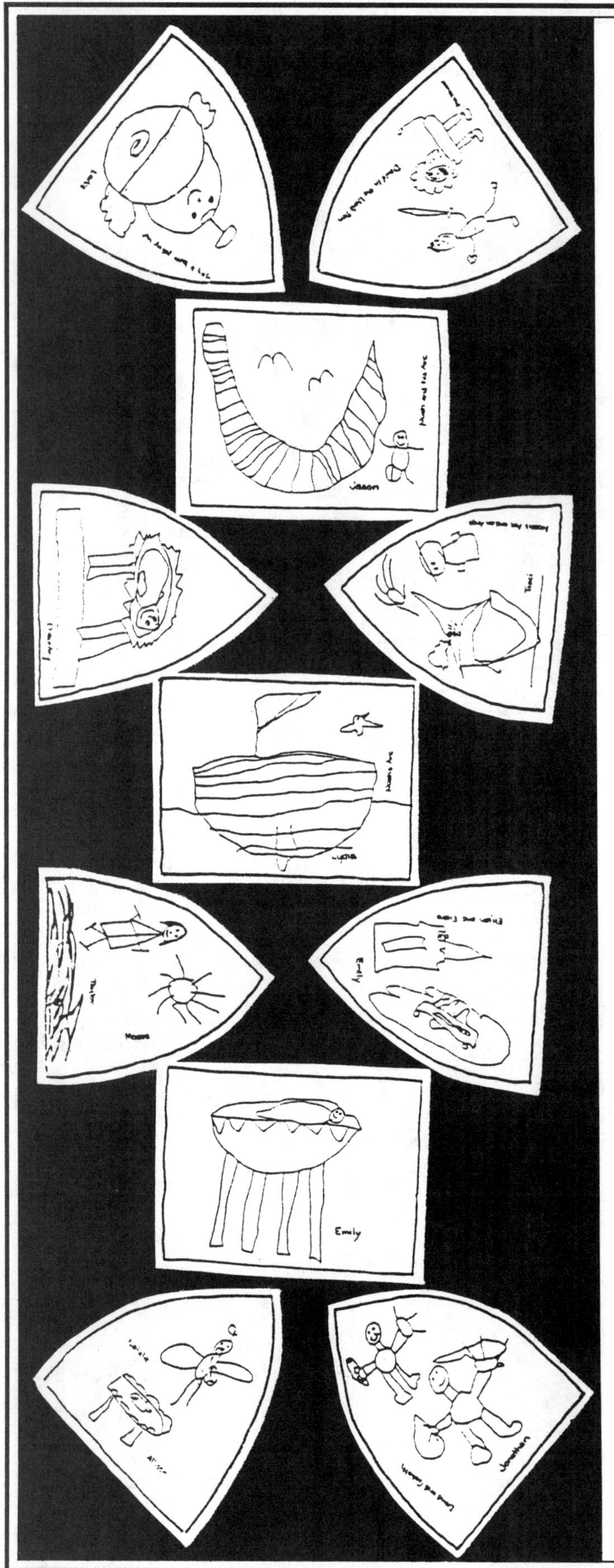

When drawings are completed the students should carefully remove the masking tape, put their names on their drawings, and hand them in.

Students always enjoy seeing their work displayed. They are especially excited to see their ceiling drawings displayed on the ceiling of their classroom.

CLASSROOM CEILING 1990
MRS. CARTIER'S FIRST GRADE
(Patterned after Michelangelo's fresco on the Sistine Chapel ceiling.)

SAMPLE WRITTEN RECORD FOR 1ST THROUGH 3RD GRADES
PREPARED BY THE ART TEACHER*

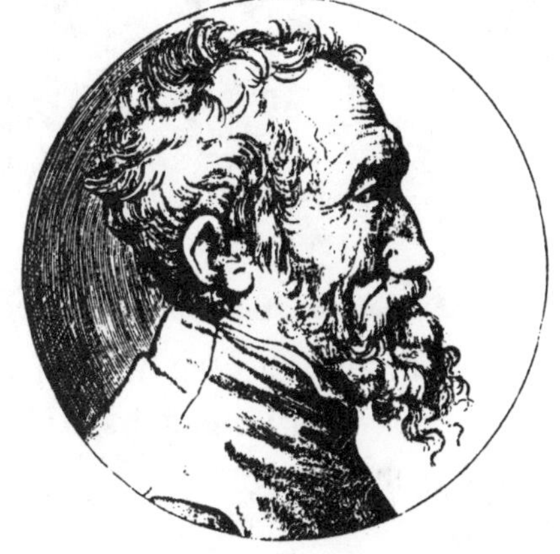

MICHELANGELO

(1475 – 1564)

A Sculptor Who Painted a Ceiling And Who Loved God

Around the time when Columbus discovered the New World, a young boy named Michelangelo, to whom God gave an abundant amount of creativity and natural artistic skill, was born in Italy. His mind was always filled with pictures and he drew all the time! Sometimes his father punished him for drawing when he should have been studying his school lessons.

When Michelangelo was about fourteen years old, he studied in the workshop of a famous local artist. As an ***apprentice*** he learned to mix colors, paint, and do many other things. This was the only training Michelangelo was to receive in his life. He had to teach himself most of the skills of art.

Michelangelo became a famous ***sculptor*** and carved huge figures in ***marble*** for many popes and other church leaders.

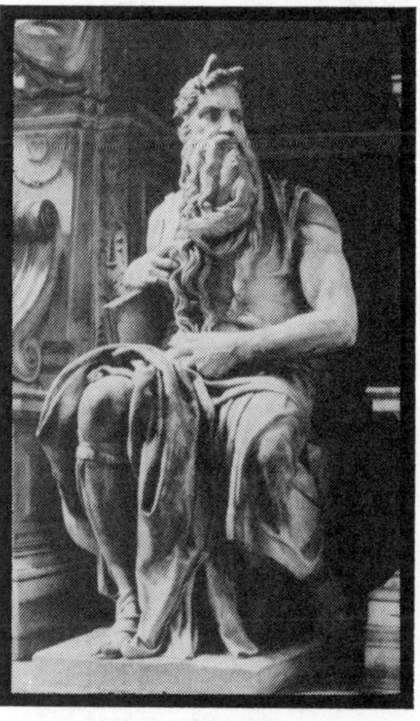

MOSES

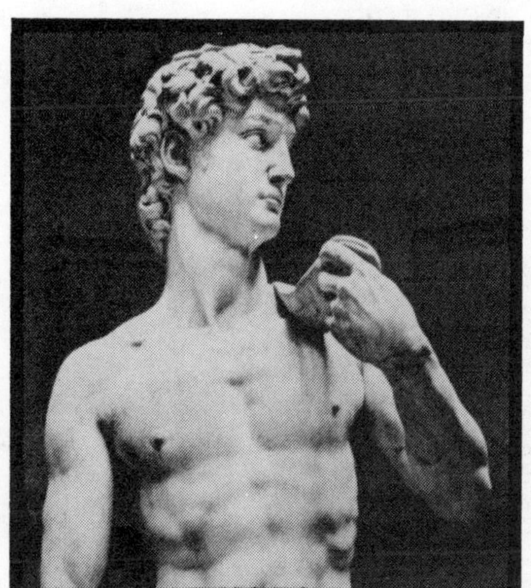

DAVID

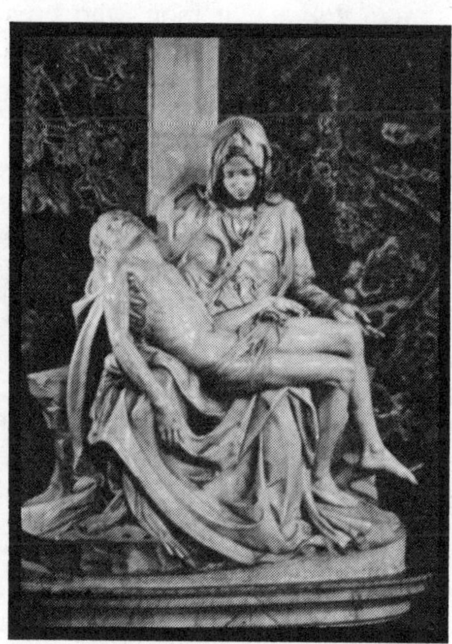

THE VATICAN PIETÀ

*When studying the life of an artist, students in the art class are not required to take notes. In order to have as much time as possible for the students to interact with the project, this art teacher types up a brief summary of the biographical sketch and has the students file these notes in the art section of their notebooks. The average length of an art period is 35-40 minutes. In that time Art "His" Story is highlighted, an art project is taught, and the art teacher must distribute and clean up all the tools and materials needed for the project.

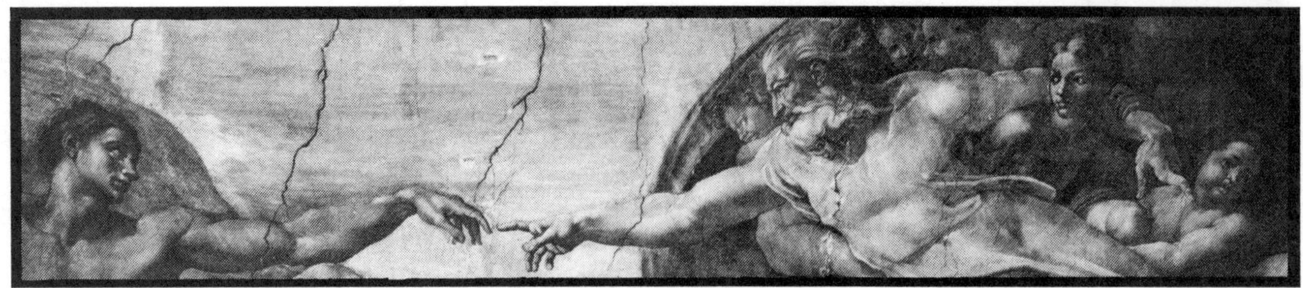

One day the head of the church asked him to paint figures from the Bible on a very high curved ceiling in the Sistine Chapel. Michelangelo had to lay on his back on a ***scaffold*** erected sixty-five feet to paint the ceiling. He painted Creation, Noah and the Flood, and many Old Testament prophets. The figures he painted had to be very large so that people could see them from the floor below. His magnificent talent made the figures look almost like statues. He had no help and it took him four years to complete the huge painting. Michelangelo's strong Christian character enabled him to complete this enormous project. He had some of the same character qualities as the Pilgrims such as diligence, industry, and steadfastness.

Michelangelo Buonarroti lived to be nearly ninety years old. He worked until the day he died! He used his God-given talents and skills for the glory of God as seen in his sculpture, his paintings, his architecture, and his poetry. His knowledge of Scripture and his love for God were expressed in all that he did!

VOCABULARY:

apprentice – one who is learning the trade and skills of the master artist

sculptor – a person who creates a work of art by chiseling three-dimensional figures from stone or marble

marble – a limestone, often colored or streaked, used for sculpting pieces of art

scaffold – a raised platform used by an artist while painting frescoes on walls or ceilings

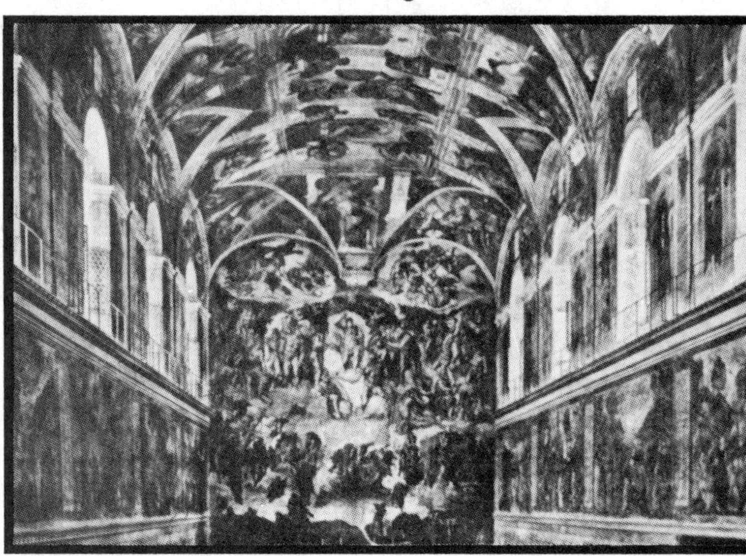

THE SISTINE CHAPEL CEILING

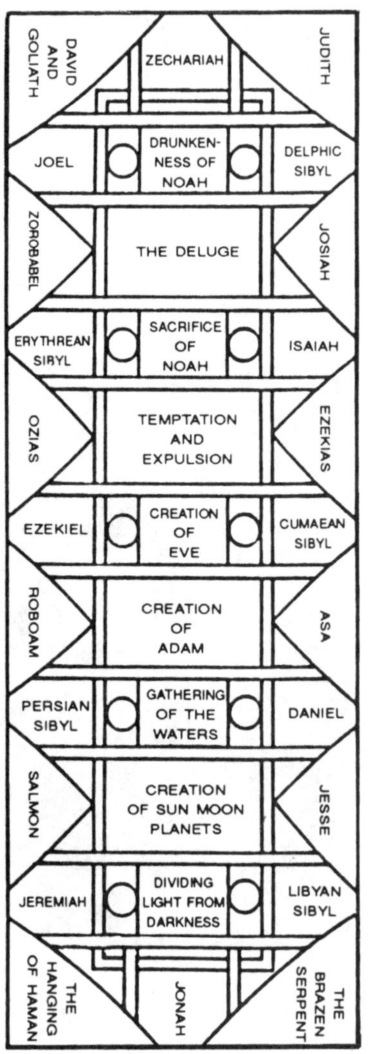

LAYOUT OF BIBLICAL THEMES ON SISTINE CHAPEL CEILING

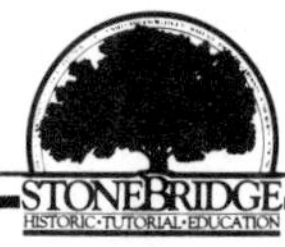

WENDY GIANCOLI
1991–1992

LESSON ENRICHMENT FOR
MICHELANGELO STUDY

Leading ideas, biographical information, or questions can be interspersed throughout the art lesson to inspire and hold the interest of the students, such as:

- Michelangelo means "Michael, the archangel" and is still a common name in Italy today. In the sixteenth century it was spelled Michelagnolo or Michelagniolo.
- Michelangelo went to the marble quarries himself and chose his own "marbles." The marble was transported down river by ship to Rome or Florence.
- Leonardo da Vinci wanted the eighteen-foot block of damaged marble that was awarded to Michelangelo. It was the marble that he sculpted into "David."
- The Rome "Pietà" is the only work Michelangelo ever signed. He signed it after he overheard someone credit his work to another sculptor.
- The Sistine Chapel was about thirty years old when Michelangelo painted it. He had to clean the ceiling before he was able to paint it.
- Michelangelo used only seven colors when he painted the ceiling of the Sistine Chapel.
- Michelangelo painted the entire ceiling himself.
- If it is done well, a fresco can last thousands of years.
- Michelangelo would often awaken in the middle of the night and work. He would make himself a thick paper cap and put a lighted candle in it so he could see and at the same time have the use of both hands.
- He delighted in reading and writing poetry. Michelangelo's beautiful sonnets reveal his deep love for the Lord. (See poem on p. 50.)
- Michelangelo outlived thirteen popes and served under seven. He also worked for many cardinals and bishops.
- Although he was rich he lived a very frugal life and had few luxuries. From the time he was twenty-two until he died, Michelangelo helped support his father and brothers.

CLAY NATIVITIES
Inspired By the Study of
Michelangelo

Meditate on this poem in preparation for sculpting

For Inspiration
by Michelangelo
Translated by William Wordsworth

The prayers I make will then be sweet indeed,
If Thou the spirit give by which I pray;
My unassisted heart is barren clay,
Which of its native self can nothing feed;
Of good and pious works Thou art the seed.
Which quickens where Thou say'st it may;
Unless Thou show us then Thine own true way,
No man can find it! Father, Thou must lead!
Do Thou, then, breathe those thoughts into my mind
By which such virtue may in me be bred
That in Thy holy footsteps I may tread:
The fetters of my tongue do Thou unbind,
That I may have the power to sing of Thee
And sound Thy praises everlastingly.

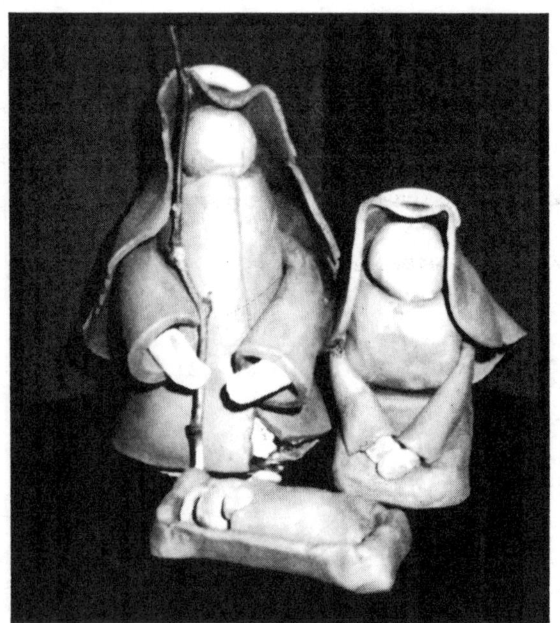

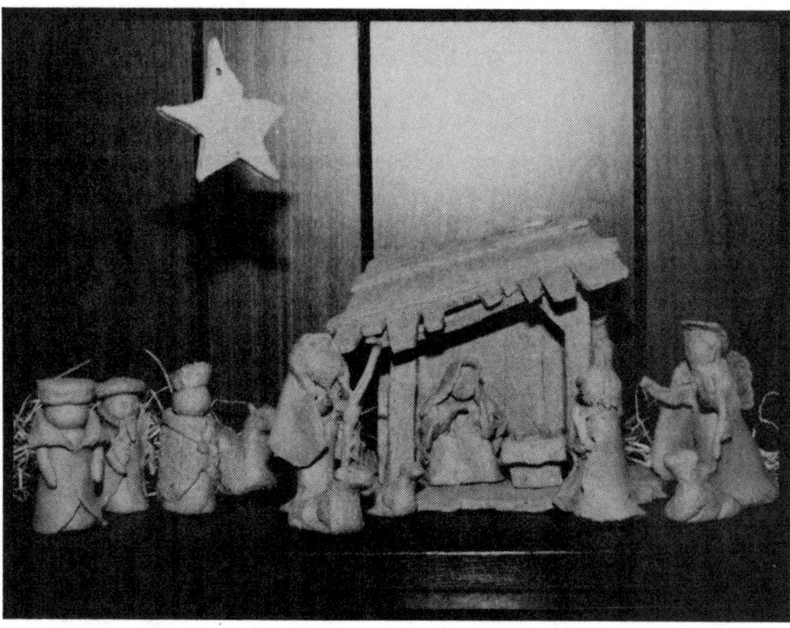

He was a genius, gifted in many areas, painting, poetry, architecture, but he called himself a sculptor.

PENCIL DRAWINGS Inspired By the Study of *Michelangelo*

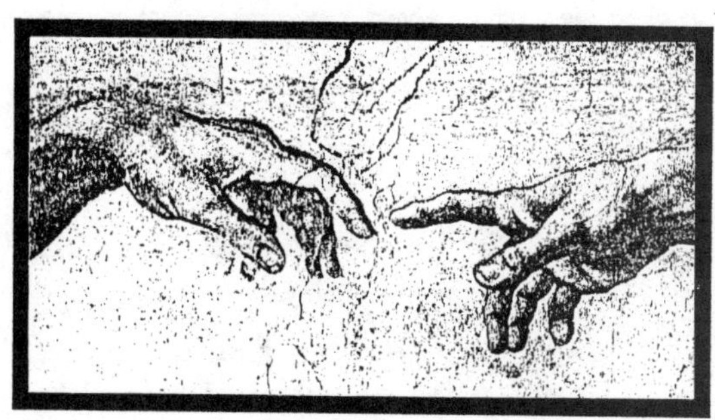

THE CREATION OF MAN
ENLARGEMENT FROM THE FRESCO ON THE CEILING OF THE SISTINE CHAPEL

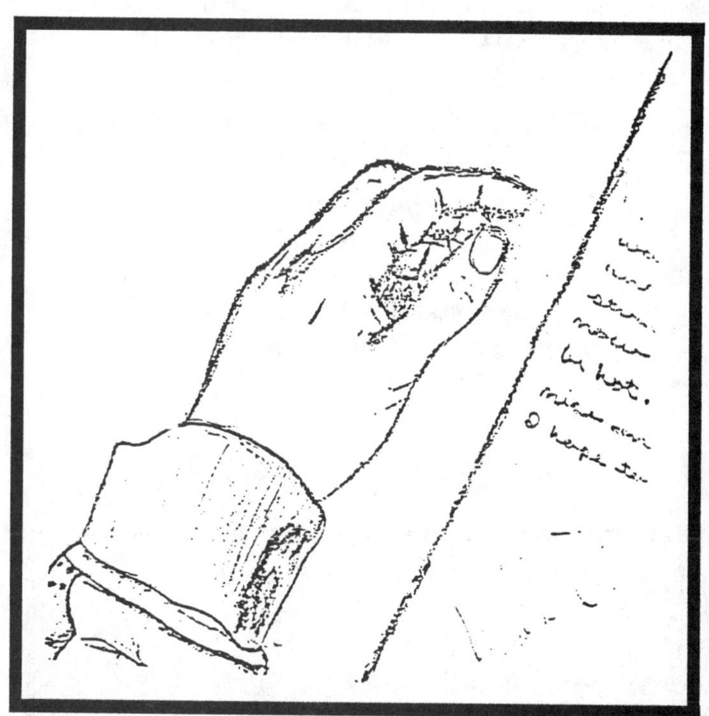

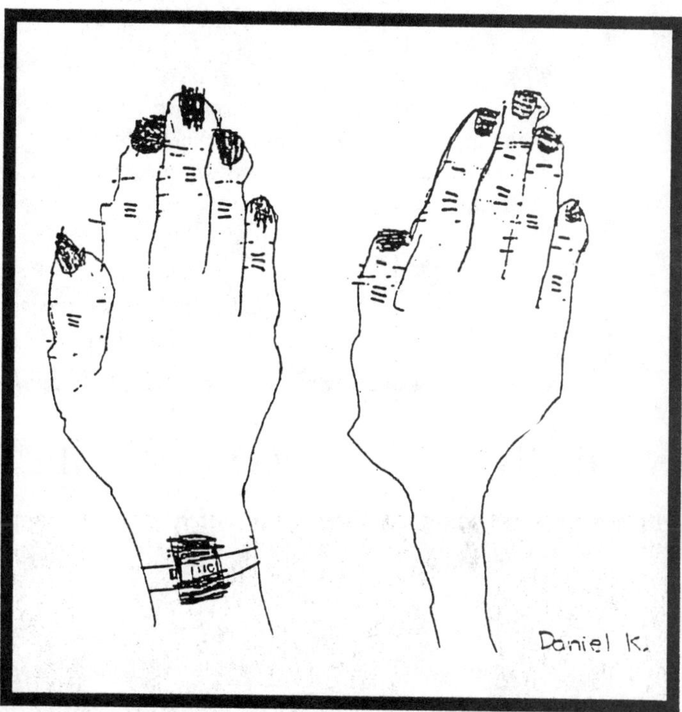

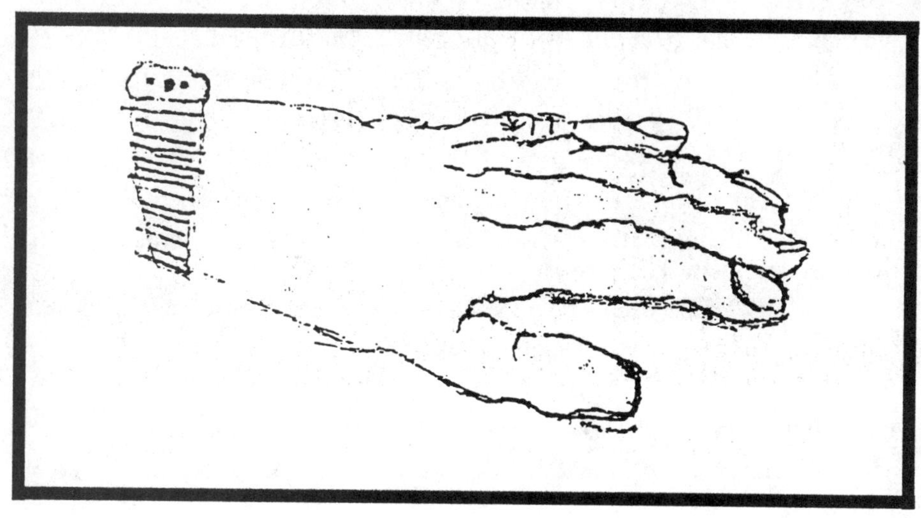

A SCHOOL-WIDE CELEBRATION OF MICHELANGELO'S BIRTHDAY

Happy Birthday Michelangelo
March 6

Dear StoneBridge Teachers,

To conclude a schoolwide study of Michelangelo, the art department will celebrate his birthday on March 6th. Hall bulletin boards are displayed with reproductions of this great artist's masterpieces. In art class the students have been studying his techniques and sculpting clay creations. After reflecting on the character and works of Michelangelo and being quizzed, "Scholarship and Behavior Badges" will be awarded. The winners will select ice cream for their class from an assortment donated by a local grocer. This should be a most successful celebration!

Thank you for your support.

Mrs. Giancoli, Art Department

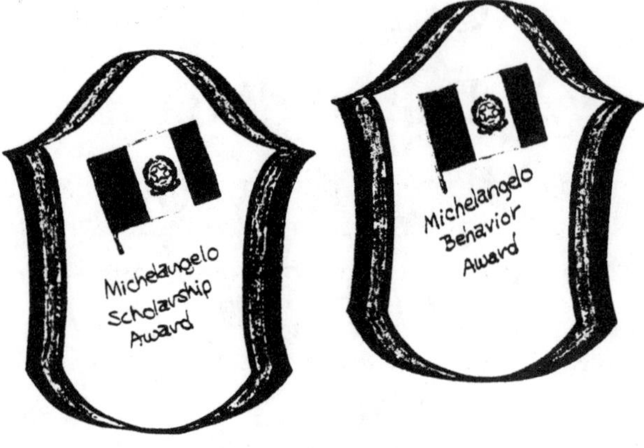

MUSIC THAT COULD BE USED DURING LESSON ON MICHELANGELO

Fine Young Madrigals
New Jersey Shakespeare Festival 1990
Kopaesthetics, New York

Princess Royal
Carrie Crompton
Renaissance & Traditional Music on Dulcimer
Tape produced by Bob Baker
Sutton Sound Studio, Atascadero, CA

BIBLIOGRAPHY FOR MICHELANGELO RESEARCH AND STUDY

Art and Man Magazine, "Michelangelo," Sept./Oct., Vol. 15, No. 1.

Coughlan, Robert, and the *Time-Life Books* Editors, *The World of Michelangelo*. Time Incorporated, New York (1966).

Hillyer, V. M. and E. G. Huey, *A Child's History of Art*. Appleton: New York (1934).

Janson, H. W., *History of Art for Young People*. Harry Abrams, Inc.: New York (1987).

Janson, H. W., *History of Art*. Prentice-Hall, Inc.: Englewood, New Jersey; & Harry Abrams, Inc.: New York (1986).

Murray, Linda, *Michelanglo: His Life, Work and Times*. Thamses and Hudson: New York (1984).

Rabott, Ernest, *Michelangelo: Art for Children*. Harper & Row: New York (1988).

Rodriguez, Susan, *Art Smart*. Prentice Hall: New Jersey (1988).

Schaeffer, Francis, *How Should We Then Live?* Fleming H. Revell Co.: New Jersey (1976).

Stone, Irving, *The Agony and the Ecstasy* (biographical novel). Doubleday: New York (1961).

Stone, Irving and Jean Stone, *I, Michelangelo, Sculptor* (autobiography through letters). The New American Library: New York (1962).

Stone, Irving, *The Story of Michelangelo's Pietà*. Doubleday: Garden City, New York (1964).

Vasari, Giorgio, *Lives of the Artists*. Penguin Books: New York (1984).

Ventura, Piero, *Great Painters*. G. P. Putnam's Sons: New York (1984).

Ventura, Piero, *Michelangelo's World*. G. P. Putnam's Sons: New York (1988).

Wadley, Nicholas, *Michelangelo*. The Colour Library of Art (53 plates in full color); Hamlyn: London (1965).

ART OVERVIEW

Kindergarten (age five years)

PURPOSES:

To develop the knowledge of God's character in Creation through the visual arts

To teach the Biblical principles of art and to build Christian character through their applied use

To instill a love for art history, the visual record of the Gospel, through a study of the individual lives of master artists

To develop the disciplined use of each child's God-given talent to produce visual art for the glory of God

To draw from *every* child his fullest potential in creative expression, thereby building self-esteem

To develop a lifetime habit of good stewardship of time, talent, and tools

To develop and sharpen observation and problem-solving skills

To explore a wide variety of art media with an emphasis on the fine arts

The goal of art in the kindergarten curriculum is to plant the seeds of the whole program. Creativity, fine motor coordination, observation skills, and resourcefulness are developed and nurtured.

I. ART PRACTICE
   - A. Introduction to God's elements of design through the study of Creation
   - B. Introduction to drawing
   - C. Introduction to painting
   - D. Introduction to pastels

II. CRAFTS
   - A. Leaf rubbings
   - B. Papercutting
   - C. Chalk paintings
   - D. Mixed media projects

III. ART "HIS" STORY
   - A. Looking at the whole of art history with an art time line from a Christian perspective
   - B. Noah's Ark
   - C. Individual artists and their masterpieces:
     1. Fra Angelico (1400–1458)
     2. Michelangelo (1475–1564)
     3. John James Audubon (1785–1851)
     4. Walt Disney (1901–1966)
     5. StoneBridge Students (1991–1992)

". . . whatever you do, do all to the glory of God."
[I Corinthians 10:31]

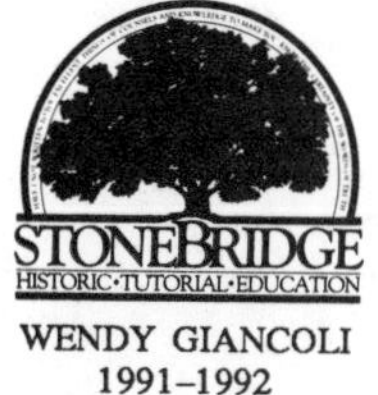

WENDY GIANCOLI
1991–1992

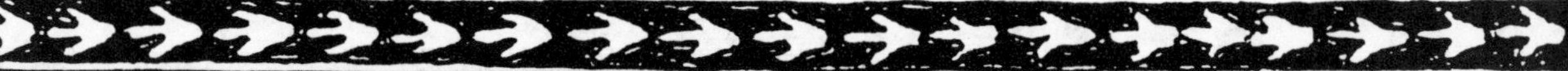

ART OVERVIEW

First, Second, and Third Grades

PURPOSES:

To develop the knowledge of God's character in Creation through the visual arts
To teach the Biblical principles of art and to build Christian character through their applied use
To instill a love for art history, the visual record of the Gospel through a study of the individual lives of master artists
To develop the disciplined use of each child's God-given talent to produce visual art for the glory of God
To draw from *every* child his fullest potential in creative expression, thereby building self-esteem
To develop a lifetime habit of good stewardship of time, talent, and tools
To develop and sharpen observation and problem-solving skills
To explore a wide variety of art media with an emphasis on the fine arts
The goal of art in the lower school curriculum is to lay a firm foundation for the development of individual creative potential. Creativity, fine motor coordination, observation skills, resourcefulness, and self-confidence are developed and encouraged.

I. ART PRACTICE
   - A. Introduction to God's elements of design through the study of Creation (color, value, line, texture, shape, space)
   - B. The basics in drawing
   - C. The basics of color and value in painting
   - D. The basics of color and value in pastels

II. CRAFTS
   - A. Clay projects
   - B. Printing
   - C. Mixed media
   - D. Miscellaneous projects

III. ART "HIS" STORY
   - A. Looking at the whole of art history with an art time line from a Christian perspective
   - B. Early Christian art
   - C. Individual artists and their masterpieces:
     1. Fra Angelico (1400–1458)
     2. Albrecht Dürer (1471–1528)
     3. Michelangelo (1475–1564)
     4. John James Audubon (1785–1851)
     5. Claude Monet (1840–1926)
     6. Walt Disney (1901–1966)
     7. StoneBridge Students (1991–1992)

"... whatever you do, do all to the glory of God."
[I Corinthians 10:31]

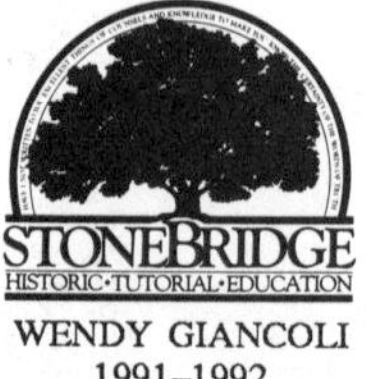

WENDY GIANCOLI
1991–1992

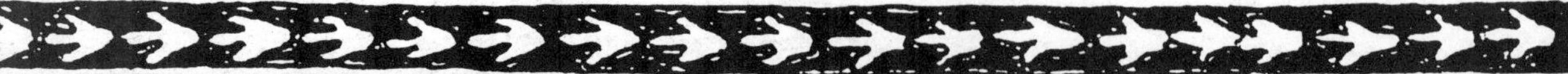

ART OVERVIEW

Fourth, Fifth, and Sixth Grades

PURPOSES:

To develop the knowledge of God's character in Creation through the visual arts

To teach the Biblical principles of art and to build Christian character through their applied use

To instill a love for art history, the visual record of the Gospel through a study of the individual lives of master artists

To develop the disciplined use of each child's God-given talent to produce visual art for the glory of God

To draw from *every* child his fullest potential in creative expression, thereby building self-esteem

To develop a lifetime habit of good stewardship of time, talent, and tools

To develop and sharpen observation and problem-solving skills

To explore a wide variety of art media with an emphasis on the fine arts

The goal of art in the middle school curriculum is to build on the foundation already laid in God's elements of design and the techniques of production.

I. ART PRACTICE
   - A. Laying the foundation as seen in **Creation** with God's elements of design – color, value, line, texture, shape, and space
   - B. The basics of sketching and drawing
   - C. Introducing balance, emphasis, harmony, variety, graduation, movement/rhythm, and proportion as seen in Creation
   - D. The basics of color and value in pastel and tempera painting

II. CRAFTS
   - A. Clay projects
   - B. Printing
   - C. Mixed media
   - D. Miscellaneous projects

III. ART "HIS" STORY
   - A. Looking at the whole of art history with an art time line from a Christian perspective
   - B. Early Christian art
   - C. Individual artists and their masterpieces:
     1. Fra Angelico (1400–1458)
     2. Albrecht Dürer (1471–1528)
     3. Michelangelo (1475–1564)
     4. John James Audubon (1785–1851)
     5. Claude Monet (1840–1926)
     6. Walt Disney (1901–1966)
     7. StoneBridge Students (1991–1992)

". . . whatever you do, do all to the glory of God."
[I Corinthians 10:31]

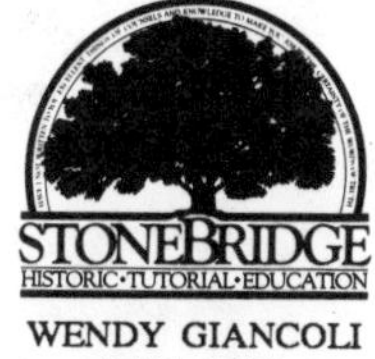

WENDY GIANCOLI
1991–1992

ART OVERVIEW

SEVENTH AND EIGHTH GRADES

PURPOSES:

To develop the knowledge of God's character in Creation through the visual arts

To teach the Biblical principles of art and to build Christian character through their applied use

To instill a love for art history, the visual record of the Gospel through a study of the individual lives of master artists

To develop the disciplined use of each child's God-given talent to produce visual art for the glory of God

To draw from *every* child his fullest potential in creative expression, thereby building self-esteem

To develop a lifetime habit of good stewardship of time, talent, and tools

To develop and sharpen observation and problem-solving skills

To explore a wide variety of art media with an emphasis on the fine arts

The goal of art in the upper school curriculum is to expand the student's knowledge of the elements of design and techniques of production.

I. ART PRACTICE
   - A. God's elements of design as seen in Creation – color, value, line, texture, shape, space
   - B. The application of balance, emphasis, harmony, variety, graduation, movement/rhythm, and proportion of art as seen in Creation
   - C. Color and value in pastel and tempera painting
   - D. The basics of color and value in pastels

II. CRAFTS
   - A. Clay projects
   - B. Printing
   - C. Mixed media
   - D. Miscellaneous projects

III. ART "HIS" STORY
   - A. Looking at the whole of art history with an art time line from a Christian perspective
   - B. Early Christian art
   - C. Individual artists and their masterpieces:
     1. Fra Angelico (1400–1458)
     2. Albrecht Dürer (1471–1528)
     3. Michelangelo (1475–1564)
     4. John James Audubon (1785–1851)
     5. Claude Monet (1840–1926)
     6. Walt Disney (1901–1966)
     7. StoneBridge Students (1991–1992)

"... whatever you do, do all to the glory of God."
[I Corinthians 10:31]

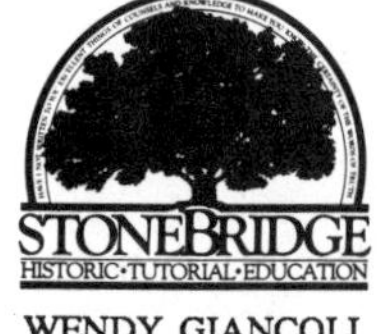

WENDY GIANCOLI
1991–1992

GRADING STUDENT ART WORK

The teacher's responsibility is to assure success in every child. Art is a subject in which no student should experience failure. Grading in all levels is done to make the student accountable in the classroom and in his or her work. Grades are given to promote a spirit of cooperation in the classroom and to encourage every student to become actively involved in the lesson to the best of his or her ability.

K4 – 3rd The grades in these grade levels are given for overall performance as follows:

✓ -	✓	✓ +
Below Grade Level	Good	Above Grade Level

✓ - would rarely be given and parents would be notified of any problem long before grading period ends.

4th – 8th In order to encourage success, students generally receive A's and B's. If a student is having a problem in art class, parents would be notified long before grades are given.

The grading system is as follows:

60% Character: Stewardship of time, talent, and tools
- Interest
- Diligence
- Participation
- Completion*

40% Projects & Field Trips: Spirit of the work (expression of beauty)
- Use of talent
- Neatness
- Following directions
- Applying past lessons
- Creativity used
- Use of media

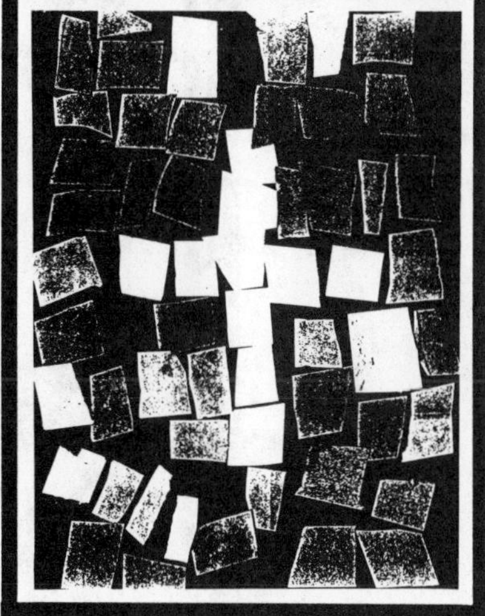

Grades can be modified at the teacher's discretion to allow for differences in individuals.

* Students should be encouraged to persevere and complete their work. The teacher may need to make extra time available for slower students; however, student art work is never completed at home.

"Blessed is the man that endureth temptation: for when he is tried, he shall receive the crown of life, which the Lord hath promised to them that love him."
[James 1:12]

CHAPTER 6

DEVELOPMENT OF INDIVIDUAL TALENT THROUGH ART PRACTICE

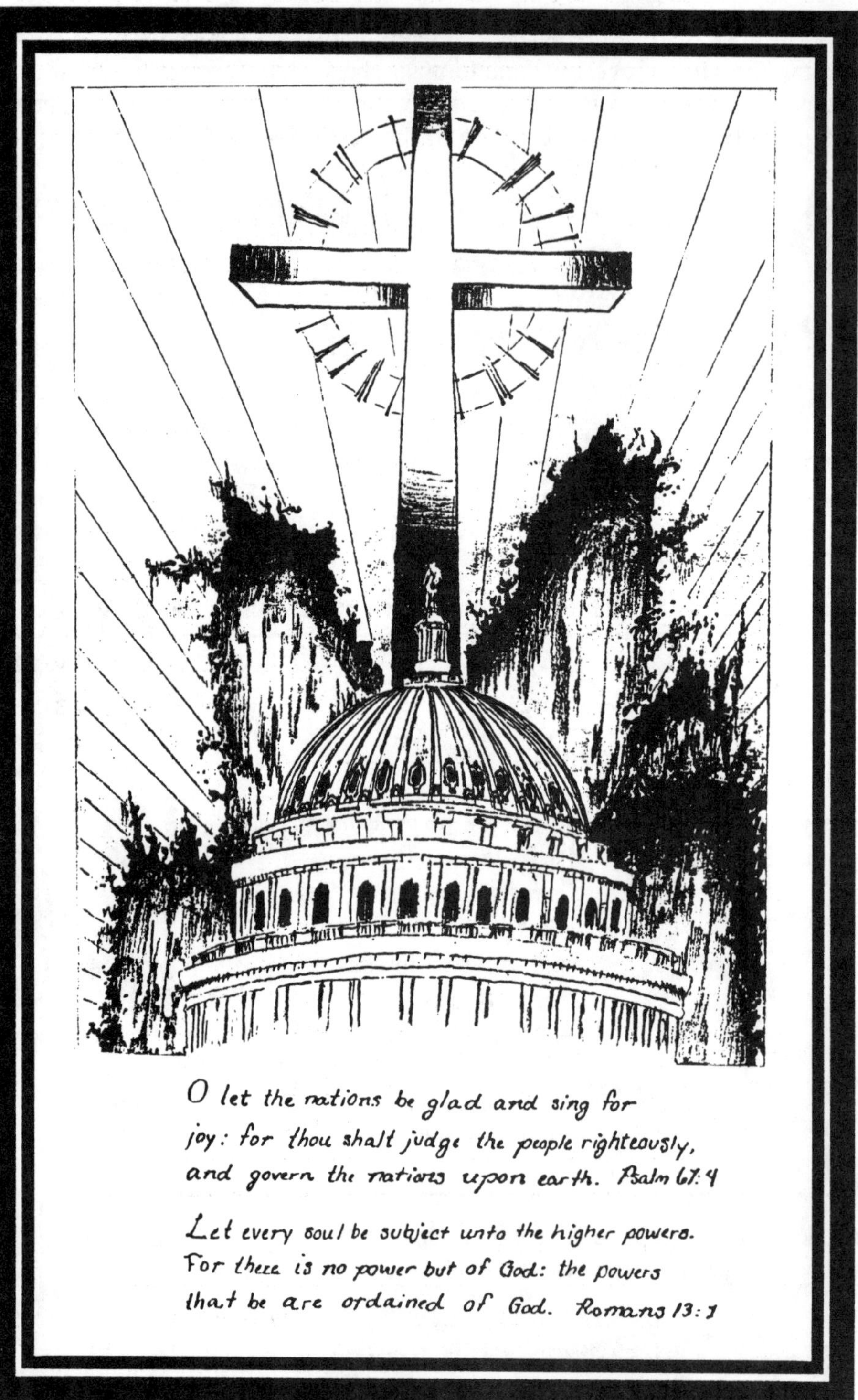

MICHAEL DAULTON, 10TH GRADE
1991 WINNER OF NATIONAL STUDENT ART CONTEST
SPONSORED BY THE PLYMOUTH ROCK FOUNDATION

KINDERGARTEN ART SCOPE & SEQUENCE

GOD'S ELEMENTS OF DESIGN

VALUE

Introduce students to two values through pencil drawing.

COLOR

(1) Identify the "God given" primary colors – red, yellow, and blue. They are the only colors that cannot be made by mixing other colors. (2) Using play dough, show and have students mix equal amounts of two primary colors to make a secondary color, (3) Using crayons to decorate portfolios, identify and create God's rainbow colors, beginning outside to inside – red, orange, yellow, green, blue, violet.

SPACE

All space in an art composition should be considered. Flat or two-dimensional space has only height and width.

SHAPE

Identify and draw the three basic geometric shapes (● ■ ▲), and their variations (⬬ ▬ ▲). Recognize the top, bottom, and sides of these. Using leaf shapes in drawings and rubbings, expose students to the organic shapes seen in creation. Distinguish between flat and solid form.

LINE

Introduce straight and curved lines and the combination of both. Introduce vertical, horizontal, diagonal, and parallel lines. Observe lines in nature such as in spiderwebs, trees, etc.

TEXTURE

Using the sense of touch, distinguish between rough and smooth, soft, and hard. Suggested methods: a "touch & guess" box, leaf rubbings, sponge painting

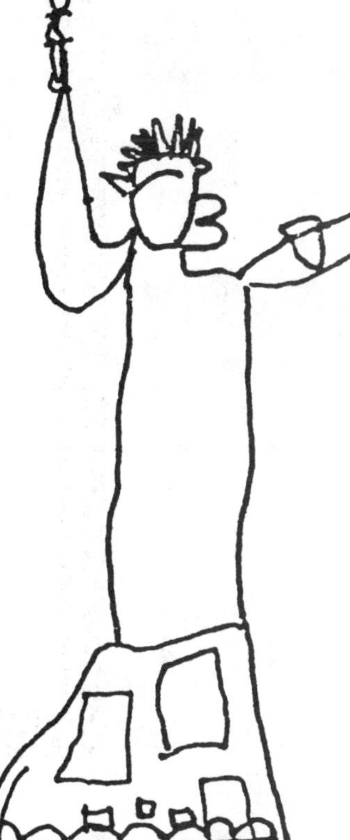

ART PRACTICE

ART MEDIA	PENCIL, CRAYON, CHALK, CLAY, TEMPERA PAINT, FINGER PAINT, TORN PAPER
CRAFTS	CRAYON RESIST, PINCH POTS, PAPER WEAVING, THUMB PRINTS, STYROFOAM PRINTING, SIMPLE PAPER MOSAICS

FIRST GRADE ART SCOPE & SEQUENCE

GOD'S ELEMENTS OF DESIGN

VALUE	Recognize variations of darkness and lightness in pencil drawing and in colors. Mixing black and white with a color to produce variation in the value of that color.
COLOR	Identify primary *and* secondary colors; mix colors to make new colors.
SPACE	All space in an art composition should be considered. Measure the size of an object by comparing it to other things, such as the student's hand or foot. Observe that the sky reaches all the way down to the earth or sea.
SHAPE	Identify and cut out the three basic geometric shapes and organic shapes such as leaves.
LINE	Introduce horizon line, where sky meets land or sea. Observe and use variation in the width of lines. Introduce slanted and diagonal lines. Introduce repetition of lines to create texture, such as waves in water.
TEXTURE	Distinguish between rough and smooth texture. Create texture in clay, play dough, and torn paper.

ART PRACTICE

ART MEDIA	Pencil (No. 2's), chalk, crayon, clay, styrofoam printing, tempera paint, torn paper, mixed media
CRAFTS	Paper weaving, mosaics

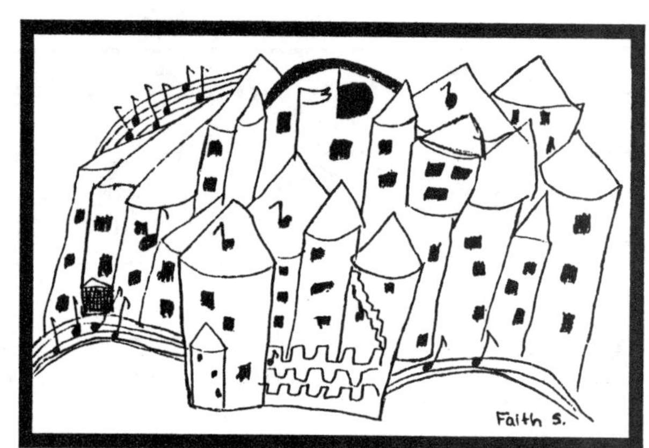

SECOND GRADE ART SCOPE & SEQUENCE

GOD'S ELEMENTS OF DESIGN

VALUE	BLACK AND WHITE CAN BE USED TO CHANGE THE VALUE OF ANY COLOR. THE ABSENCE OF DIRECT LIGHT INFLUENCES THE WAY A CERTAIN SUBJECT MAY APPEAR, SUCH AS IN THE FOG, TWILIGHT, OR EARLY MORNING.
COLOR	INTRODUCE AND IDENTIFY WARM AND COOL COLORS.
SPACE	ALL SPACE IN AN ART COMPOSITION SHOULD BE THOUGHT OUT IN AN ORDERLY MANNER. INTRODUCE BACKGROUND, MIDDLE GROUND, FOREGROUND, AND OVERLAPPING OBJECTS. INTRODUCE SIZE RELATIONSHIPS, SUCH AS THE SIZE OF A BOY NEXT TO HIS DAD.
SHAPE	WHEN SHAPES ARE REPEATED IN A REGULAR OR IRREGULAR SEQUENCE, A PATTERN IS FORMED.
LINE	THE "HORIZON LINE" IS AT THE EYE LEVEL OF THE VIEWER. LINES CAN BE USED TO SEPARATE ONE OBJECT FROM ANOTHER.
TEXTURE	STUDENTS DRAW TEXTURE THAT THEY DO NOT LIKE AND TEXTURE THAT THEY *DO* LIKE.

ART PRACTICE

ART MEDIA	PENCIL (NO. 2'S), TEMPERA PAINT, CLAY, MIXED MEDIA, PRINTING, CHALK
CRAFTS	PAPER WEAVING, MOSAICS

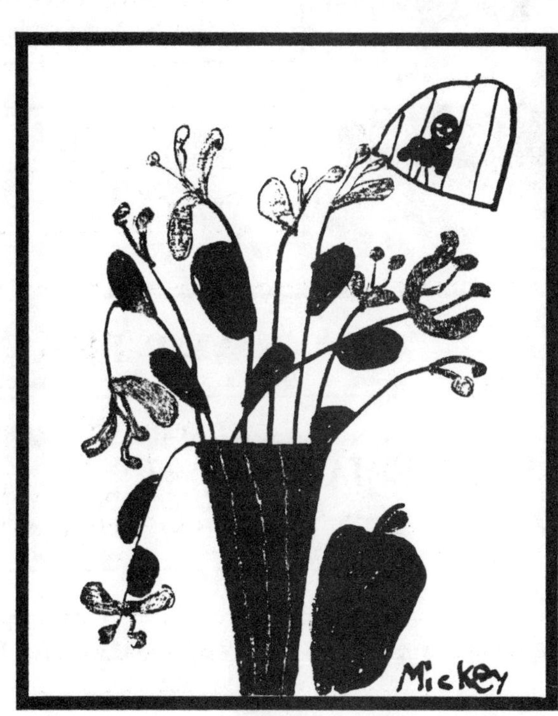

THIRD GRADE ART SCOPE & SEQUENCE

GOD'S ELEMENTS OF DESIGN

VALUE	DARK VALUES SEEM HEAVIER THAN LIGHT VALUES; LIGHT VALUES APPEAR LARGER. AN OBJECT IN THE PATH OF LIGHT CASTS A SHADOW AND CAST SHADOWS FALL AWAY FROM THE LIGHT SOURCE.
COLOR	PURE COLOR DOMINATES GRAY AND BRIGHT COLORS DOMINATE DARK ONES; LIGHT COLORS ADVANCE. COLOR IS AFFECTED BY ITS SURROUNDINGS. EMPHASIZE BLENDING COLORS.
SPACE	DIMINISHED SIZE AND DETAILS CREATES DEPTH. THE POSITION OF OBJECTS ON A PAGE: LOWER SEEMS CLOSER; HIGHER SEEMS FARTHER AWAY. ALL VIEWS OF A THREE-DIMENSIONAL FORM SHOULD BE CONSIDERED. PEOPLE AND OBJECTS APPEAR SMALLER AS THEY GET FARTHER AWAY. OBJECTS IN THE DISTANCE APPEAR IN MASS WITH NO DETAIL; OBJECTS THAT ARE CLOSER SHOW DETAIL. WHEN SHAPES CONTRAST WITH THEIR BACKGROUND A SENSE OF DEPTH IS CREATED.
SHAPE	ALL FORMS (SHAPE) ARE VARIATIONS OF CONE, CUBE, CYLINDER, SPHERE, OR PYRAMID.
LINE	LINES CAN BE USED TO DESCRIBE THE CONTOUR OF AN OBJECT. OBSERVE THAT SOME OBJECTS HAVE A LINEAR APPEARANCE.
TEXTURE	CREATE THE ILLUSION OF TEXTURE THROUGH REPETITION OF LINE OR SHAPE. PAINT A TREE FOUR TO SIX DIFFERENT WAYS, DEMONSTRATING TEXTURE.

ART PRACTICE

ART MEDIA	PENCIL, TEMPERA PAINT, CLAY, PASTELS – DRY AND OIL, MIXED MEDIA, PRINTING
CRAFTS	PAPIER-MÂCHÉ, MARBLED PAPER

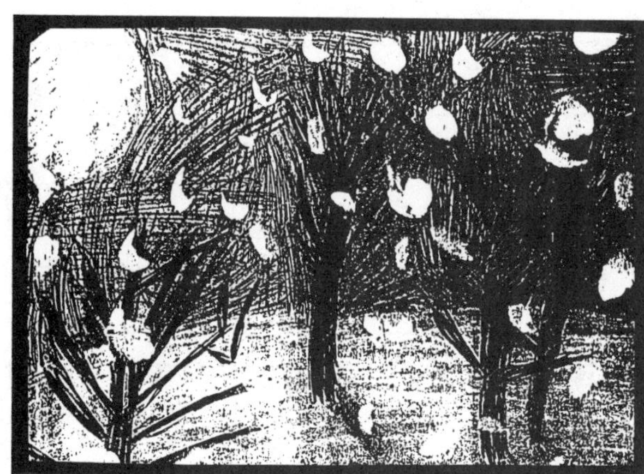

FOURTH GRADE ART SCOPE & SEQUENCE

GOD'S ELEMENTS OF DESIGN

VALUE

MASTER DRAWING OBJECTS WITH A LIGHT SIDE AND A SHADOW SIDE. INTRODUCE VALUE SCALE WITH FOUR VALUES; SQUINT THE EYES TO SEE VALUES MORE CLEARLY. THE EYE IS A MORE COMPLEX VERSION OF A CAMERA LENS IN ITS CAPACITY TO CONTROL LIGHT.

COLOR

THE INTENSITY OF ANY COLOR CAN BE CHANGED BY ADDING GRAY. REPETITION OF COLOR CAN CREATE THE ILLUSION OF MOVEMENT IN DESIGN.

SPACE

OBJECTS PLACED ON THE LOWER HALF OF THE PICTURE SEEM HEAVIER AND CLOSER TO THE VIEWER THAN THOSE ON THE TOP HALF. FORMS CAN BE CONVEX OR CONCAVE. SPACE CAN BE CREATED IN THEM AND THEY CAN OCCUPY SPACE. DIMINISHING OBJECTS CREATE SPACE. THREE-DIMENSIONAL SPACE CAN BE CREATED BY USING VALUE.

SHAPE

THE SHAPE OF SHADOWS CAN APPEAR DIFFERENT FROM THE SHAPE OF THE OBJECT CASTING THEM. STUDENTS CREATE PARTIAL PICTURES, WHERE SHAPES "BLEED OFF" OF THE PAGE.

LINE

LINE CAN CREATE MOVEMENT.

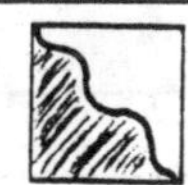

TEXTURE

STUDENTS ADD DECORATIVE TEXTURES TO OBJECTS.

ART PRACTICE

ART MEDIA	PENCIL (B'S), TEMPERA PAINT, PASTELS, CLAY, MIXED MEDIA, PRINTING
CRAFTS	PAPIER-MÂCHÉ, MARBLED PAPER

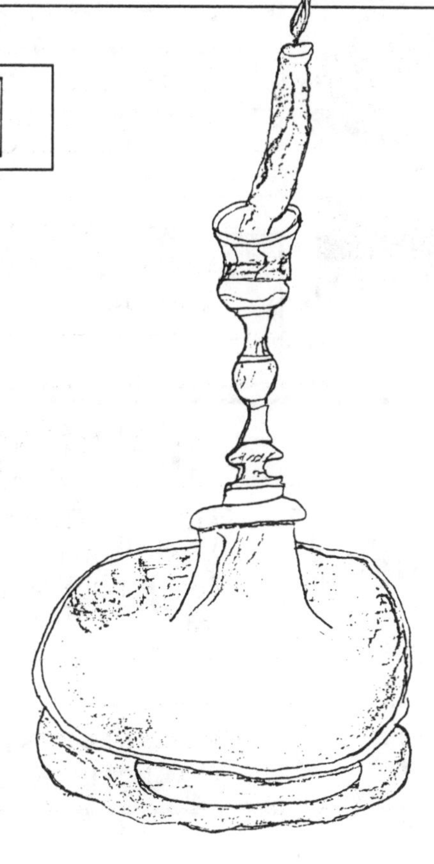

FIFTH GRADE SCOPE & SEQUENCE

GOD'S ELEMENTS OF DESIGN

VALUE	Shadows help observe the passage of time. Shadows are darker, grayer versions of whatever color they rest on; use washes. Using value accurately creates realism.
COLOR	Mixing and blending colors: complementary colors are those directly across from each other on the color wheel (yellow–violet; red–green; orange–blue) and are used together as a point of emphasis. Objects in the distance usually appear bluer, grayer and lighter, such as mountains.
SPACE	Relationships between things are measured by the pencil-eye method. Space can be organized symmetrically or asymmetrically, to achieve balance. Three-dimensional space is created from triangle to cone, square to box, circle to sphere. One-point perspective. Introduce proportion in figure drawing.
SHAPE	Many forms can be identified by their silhouettes or contours. Grouping shapes instead of lining them up is more interesting.
LINE	One-point perspective; detailed drawings.
TEXTURE	Repetition of line to create illusion of texture, such as for wood and marble.

ART PRACTICE

ART MEDIA	Pencil (B's), pastels, clay, mixed media, tempera paint
CRAFTS	Mosaics, stenciling, marbled paper

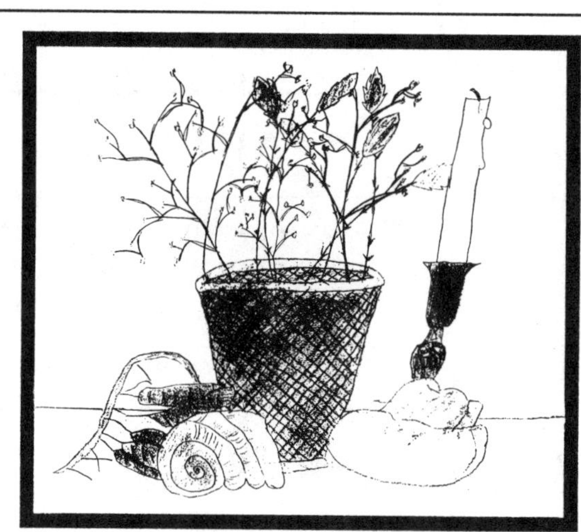

SIXTH GRADE SCOPE & SEQUENCE

GOD'S ELEMENTS OF DESIGN

VALUE	SHARP CONTRASTS OF VALUE (BLACK NEXT TO WHITE) DRAWS ATTENTION OR DOMINATES. GRADUAL CHANGE IN VALUE WILL LEAD THE EYE PROGRESSIVELY FROM ONE OBJECT TO ANOTHER. SHADOWS ARE DARKEST IMMEDIATELY UNDER AN OBJECT AND GRADUALLY GET LIGHTER AS THEY MOVE AWAY FROM THE OBJECT.
COLOR	INTERMEDIATE COLORS. ADVANCING AND RECEDING COLORS. COLORS CAN BALANCE THE COMPOSITION AND/OR CREATE A FOCAL POINT.
SPACE	ORDERLY VISUAL THINKING! STABILES VERSUS MOBILES.
SHAPE	SHAPE CAN BE USED TO CREATE THE ILLUSION OF RHYTHM OR MOTION (OPTICAL ILLUSION).
LINE	LINES CAN BE USED TO CREATE THE ILLUSION OF RHYTHM OR MOTION (OPTICAL ILLUSION).
TEXTURE	YARN WEAVING ON CARDBOARD LOOMS YIELDS THREE-DIMENSIONAL TEXTURE.

ART PRACTICE

ART MEDIA	PENCIL (B'S), CLAY, LINOLEUM BLOCK PRINTS, WATERCOLORS, PASTELS – OIL OR DRY, TEMPERA PAINT
CRAFTS	PAPIER-MÂCHÉ, STRING ART ON WOOD BLOCKS WITH NAILS, YARN WEAVING, STENCILS, MOBILES

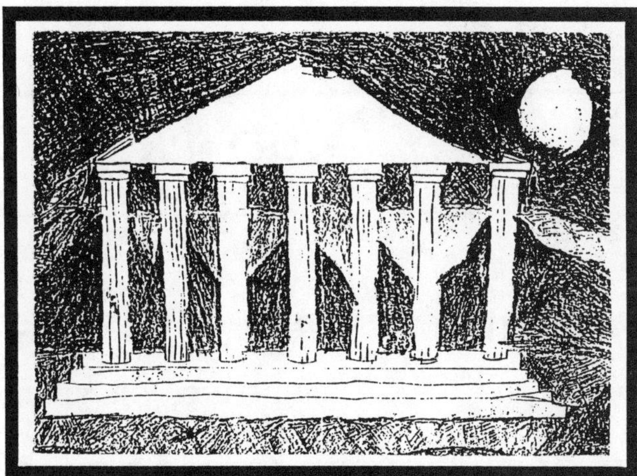

"The young student should learn about perspective, so that he will be able to give each object its proper placement."
– Leonardo da Vinci

SEVENTH & EIGHTH GRADE SCOPE & SEQUENCE

GOD'S ELEMENTS OF DESIGN

VALUE	Create value with pencil by crosshatching, stippling, and shading. Students should aim for mastery. See chart on p. 37.
COLOR	Small amounts of one hue can be used to vary darkness or lightness of another hue. Complements mixed together gray one another and used next to each other emphasize one another.
SPACE	Focal point or point of emphasis is created by contrast, isolation, and placement. Off-center placement creates informal focal point.
SHAPE	Function of man-made forms directly affects their shape.
LINE	"Reading your own line" – personality expressed in signature just as in art work. Two-point perspective.
TEXTURE	Details (tree trunk drawing). Textures created by variation and repetition of line patterns.

ART PRACTICE

ART MEDIA	Pencil (B's & H's), tempera paint, watercolors, pastels – oil and dry, clay sculpture, linoleum block printing, or silkscreen printing
CRAFTS	Yarn weaving

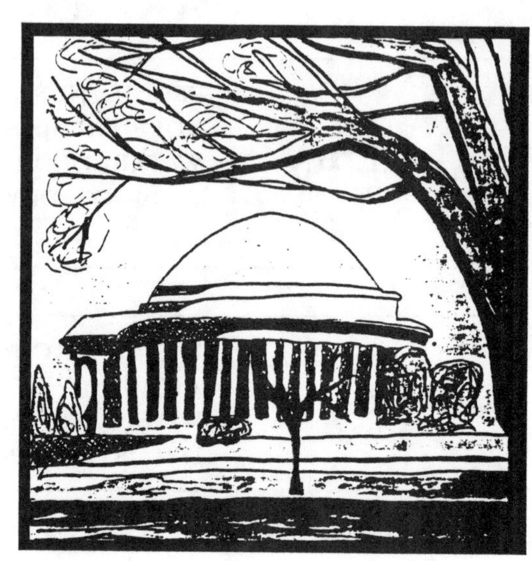

Crafts or "Useful Trades"

"Then Moses said to the Israelites, 'See, the Lord has chosen Bezalel son of Uri, the son of Hur, of the tribe of Judah, and he has filled him with the Spirit of God, with skill, ability and knowledge in all kinds of ***crafts*** *– to make artistic designs for work in gold, silver and bronze, to cut and set stones, to work in wood and to engage in all kinds of craftsmanship.'"* [EXODUS 35:30–33]

In Noah Webster's 1828 definition of art, arts are divided into liberal or polite and useful or mechanic. The mechanic arts, or trades, are those in which the hands and body are more concerned than the mind. Crafts provide the opportunity to learn different skills and are important to include in a well rounded program. Crafts often make lovely parent gifts. Students may need more teacher assistance with crafts in order to maintain a standard of excellence. Often students who have difficulty in drawing and painting excel when creating a craft.

MARBLED PICTURE FRAME

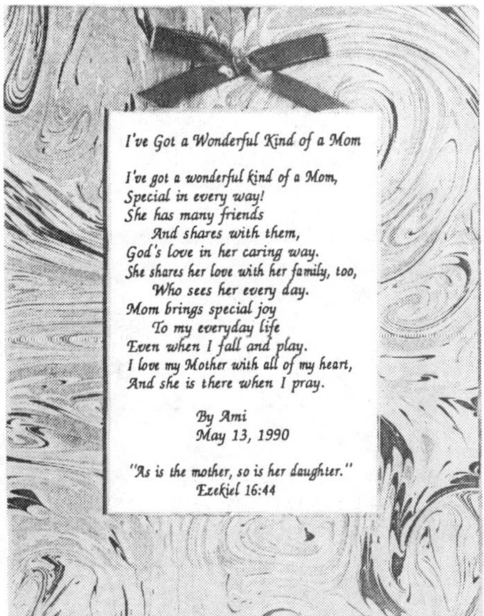

STUDENT POEM FROM ENGLISH CLASS

FABRIC PICTURE FRAME

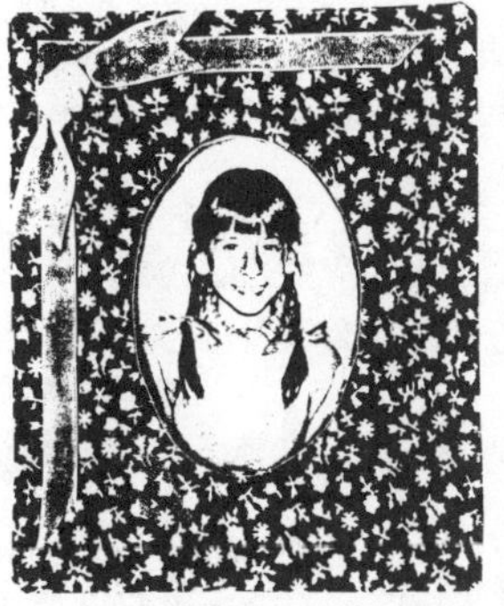

FRONT

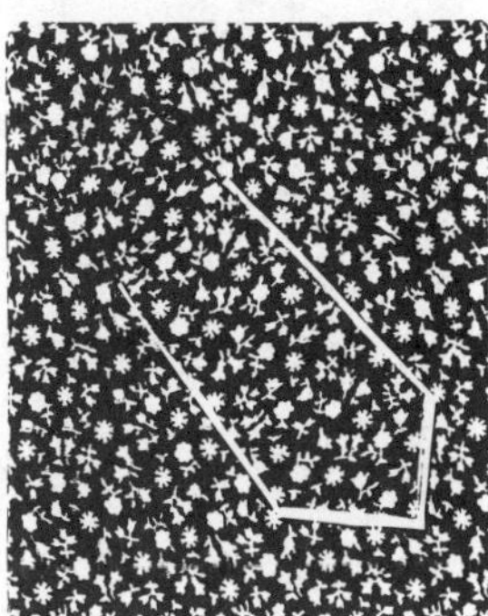

BACK

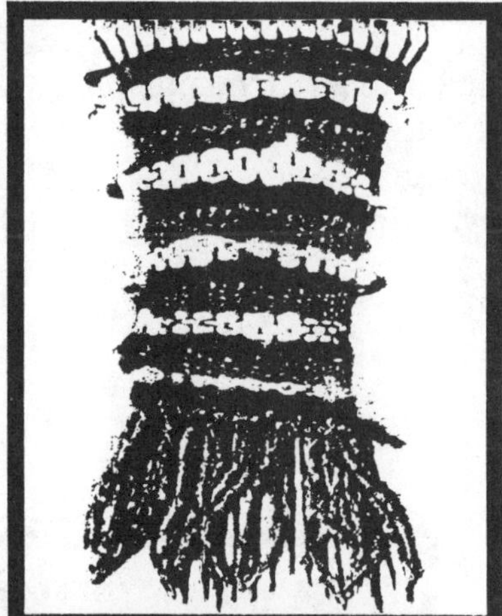

WOVEN WALL HANGING

LIFE-SIZE TEEPEE
DECORATED BY 7TH & 8TH GRADERS

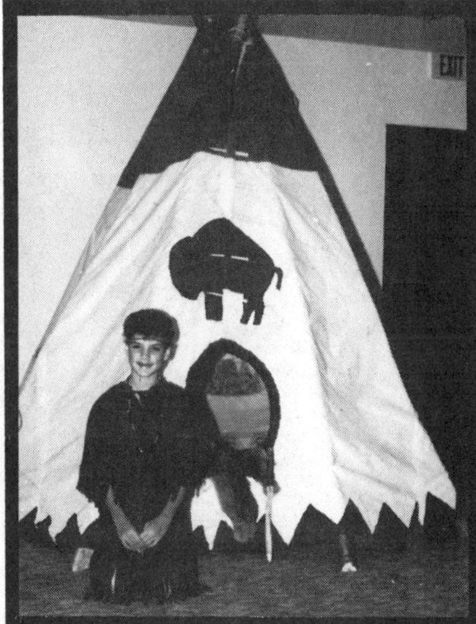

JANIE CARDOZA, 8TH GRADE

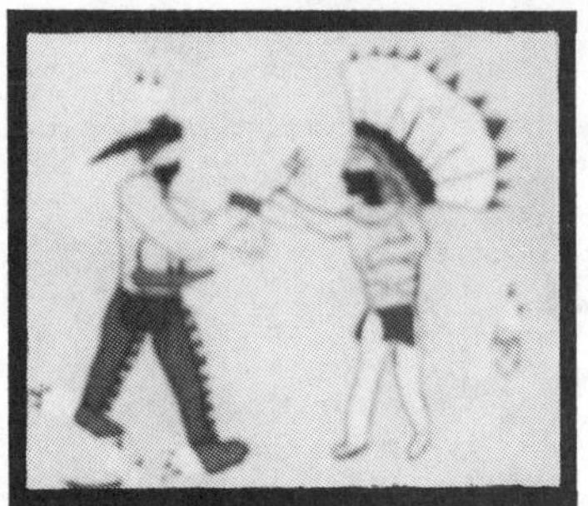

TEEPEE DECORATION DETAIL

Recognition of Individual Expression in Art

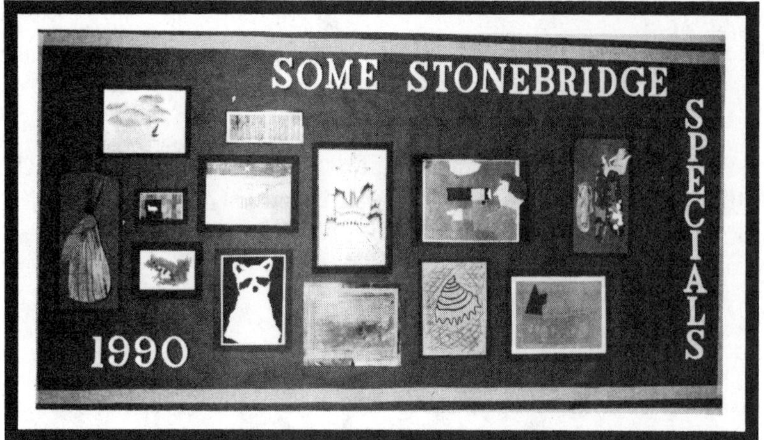

At the beginning of the school year bulletin boards are ever so bare. It is a perfect time to display a sampling of work done the previous year. These are copies of student art work from all grade levels.

STUDENT ART WORK SHOULD BE DISPLAYED WITH CARE

ANCIENT EGYPT

HER ART, HER PEOPLE, HER ROLE IN CHRISTIAN HISTORY

Three-dimensional pyramids, created by fourth grade architects, are displayed as one "great pyramid."

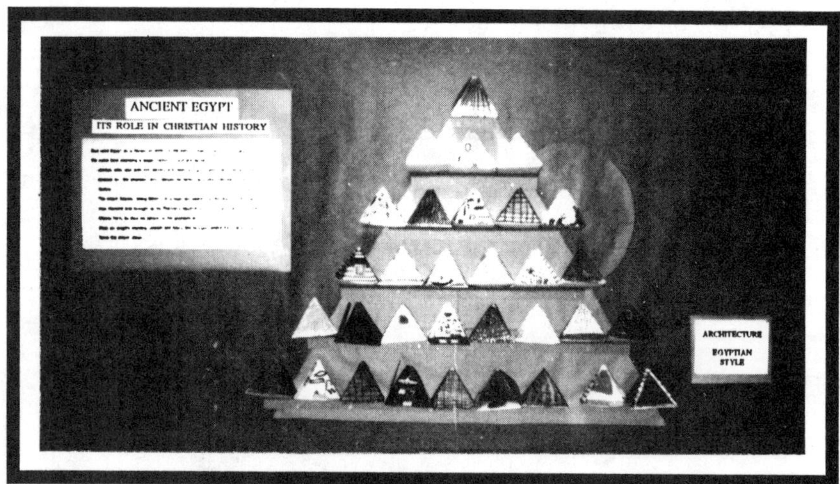

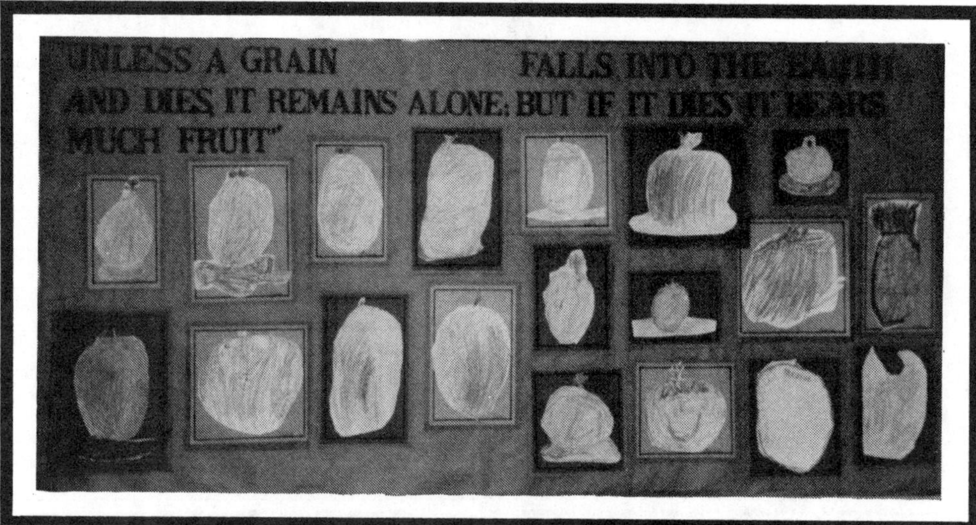

Pumpkins inspired by God's Creation; pastels, first grade

Bulletin Boards Should Inspire and Instruct

In the Beginning God Created

The Elements of Design
Value and Color
Space and Shape
Line and Texture

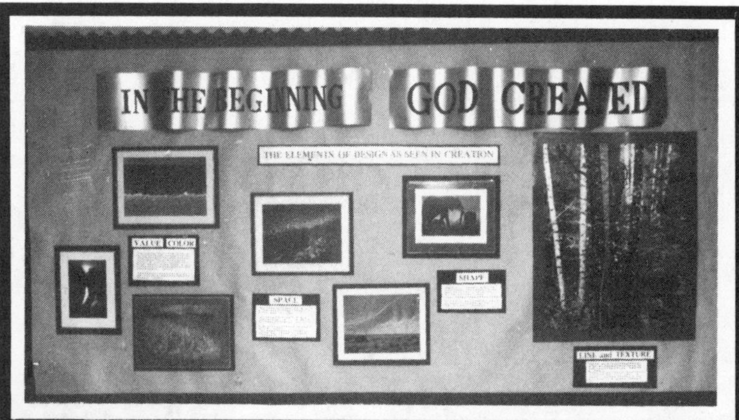

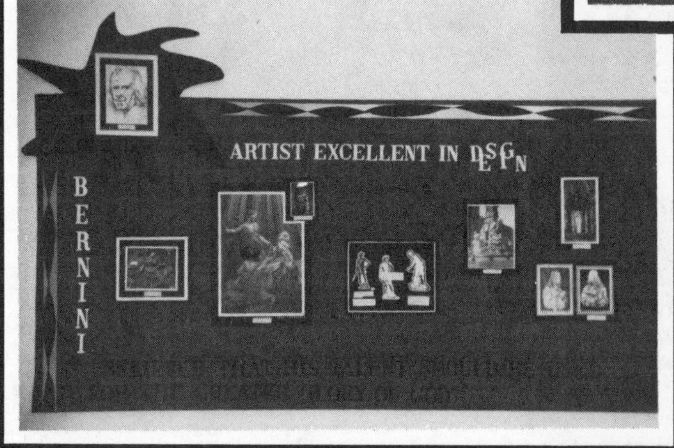

BERNINI
An Artist
Excellent in
DESIGN
Believed his talent
should be used for the
greater glory of God

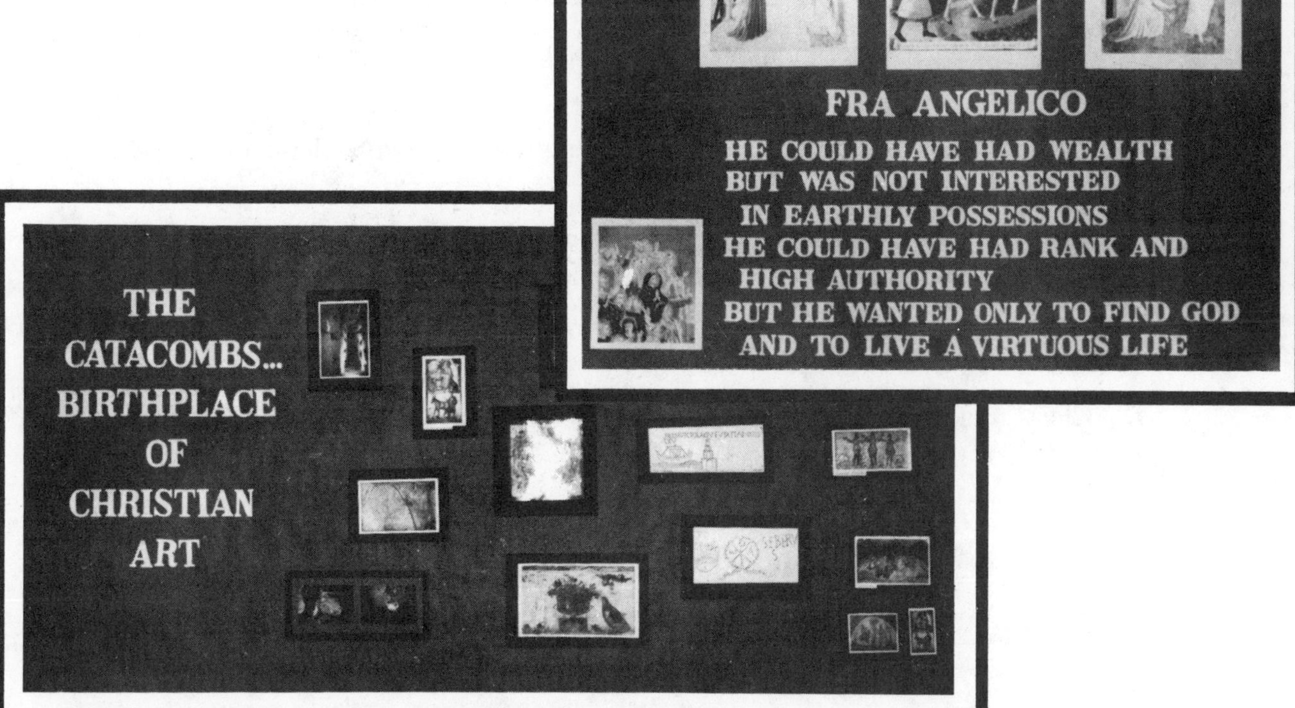

THE STANDARD FOR DESIGNING BULLETIN BOARDS

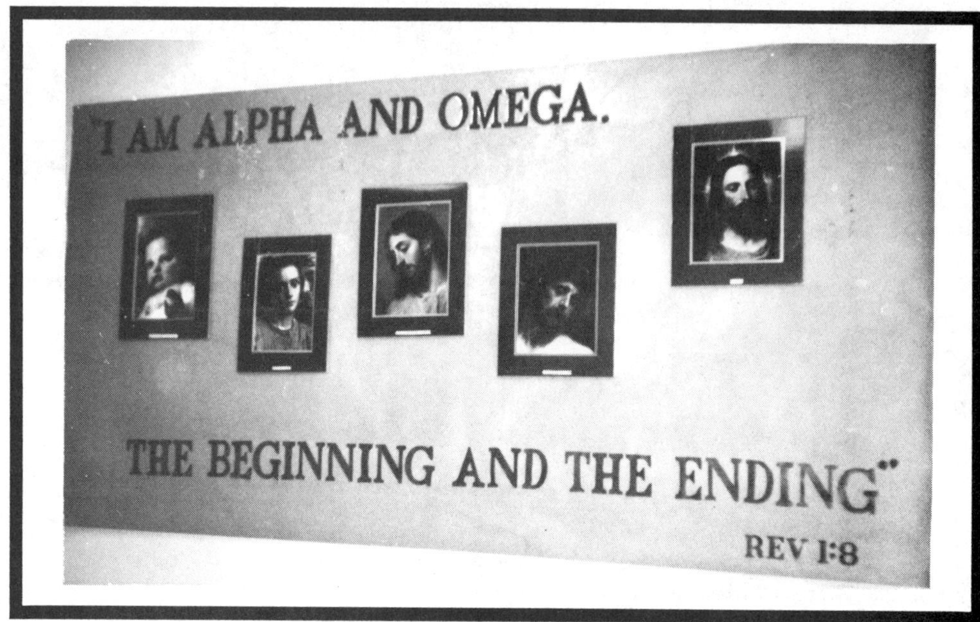

1. Bulletin boards serve as a valuable teaching tool and a visual ministry. They reflect the life of the classroom, the curriculum, and the school!
2. The bulletin board background should be chosen in a color that compliments the art work but does not detract from it. Dark blue or dark violet shows drawings nicely.
3. Each piece of art work is matted to frame it or is displayed in such a way that each individual piece of art is highlighted while a unified whole is maintained.
4. Borders may be added to the board or drawn on with chalk or oil pastel if needed to unify.
5. Lettering may be cut out, drawn directly onto the bulletin board paper, or drawn on a separate paper and attached in an attractive manner.
6. Names are uniformly placed on the lower right-hand corner of art work.
7. Class grade level is labeled on bulletin boards with student work.
8. Student work inspired by a master artist is designated accordingly.

STUDENT ART IN SCHOOL PUBLICATIONS

Student art can enhance school publications and at the same time work by individual students is recognized.

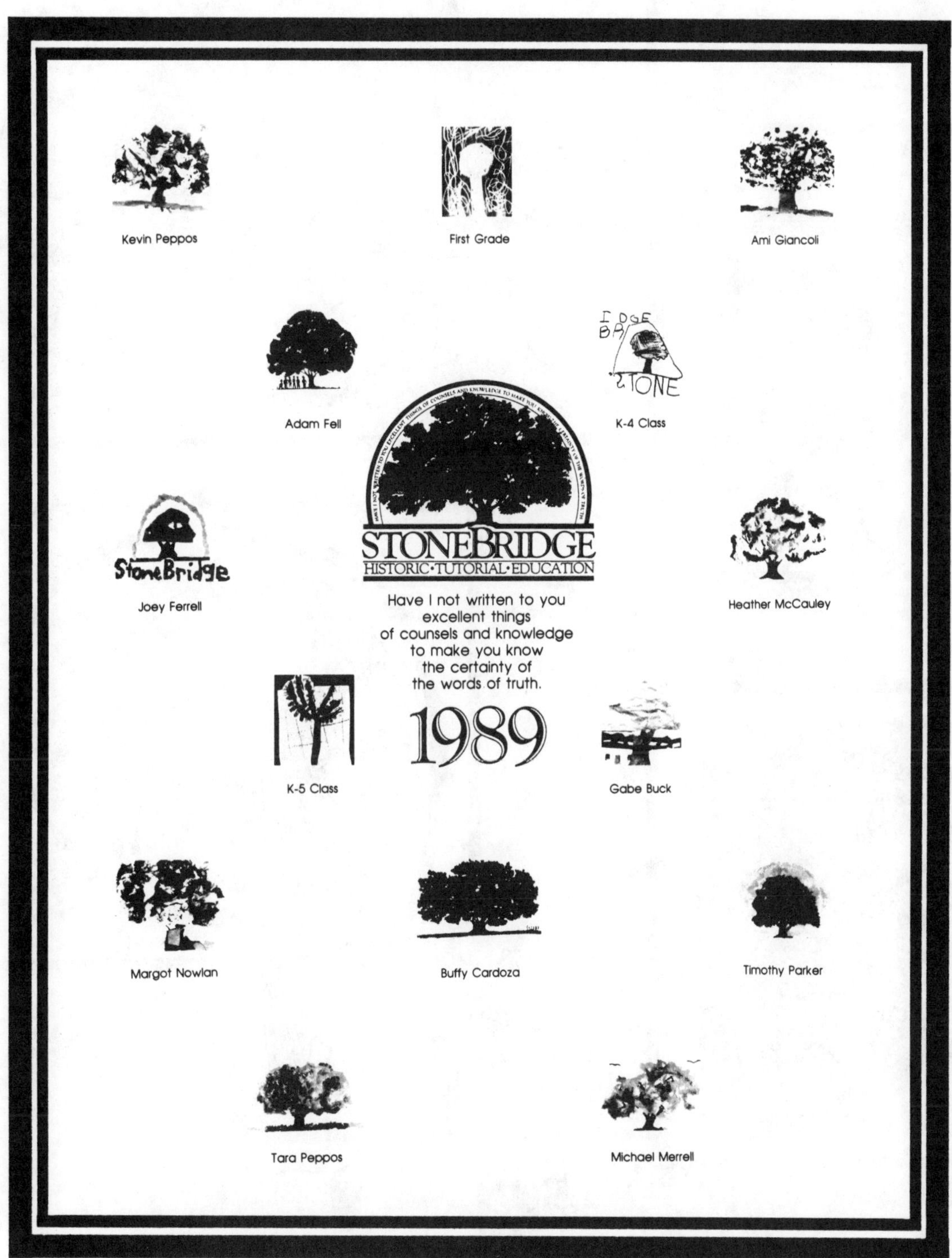

A StoneBridge Yearbook frontispiece was designed with the logo tree as seen through the eyes of the students and created in a variety of media. One tree from each grade level was selected.

StoneBridge

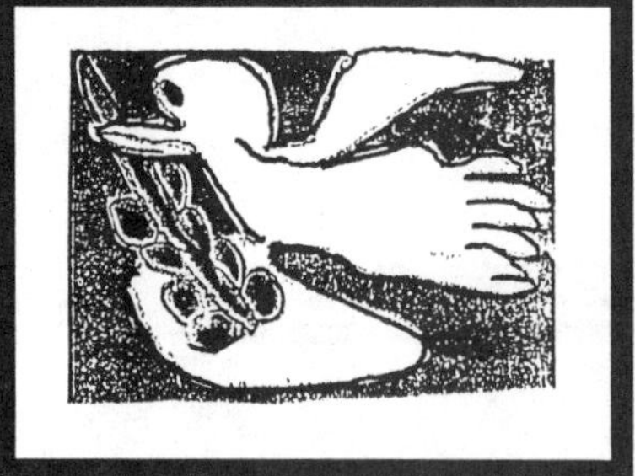

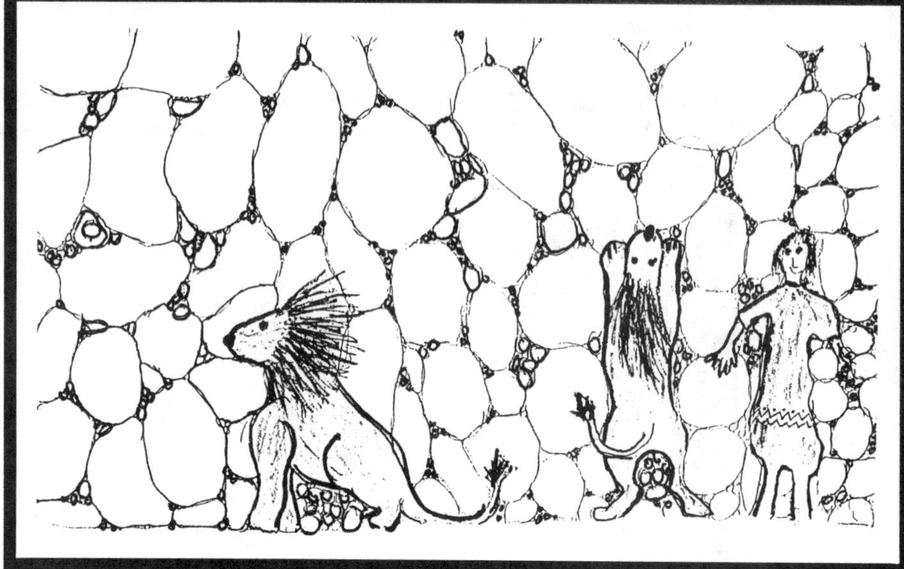

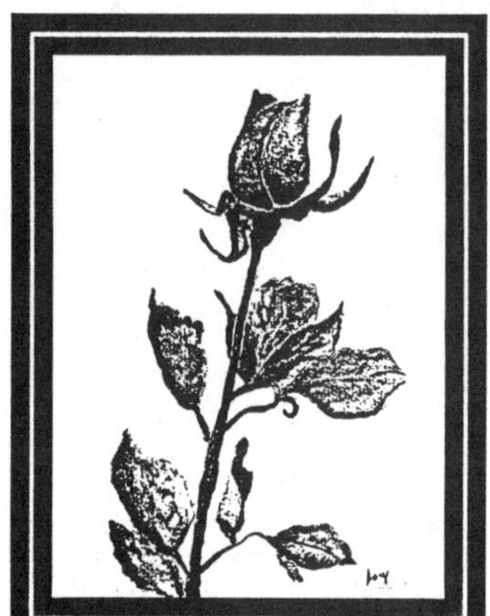

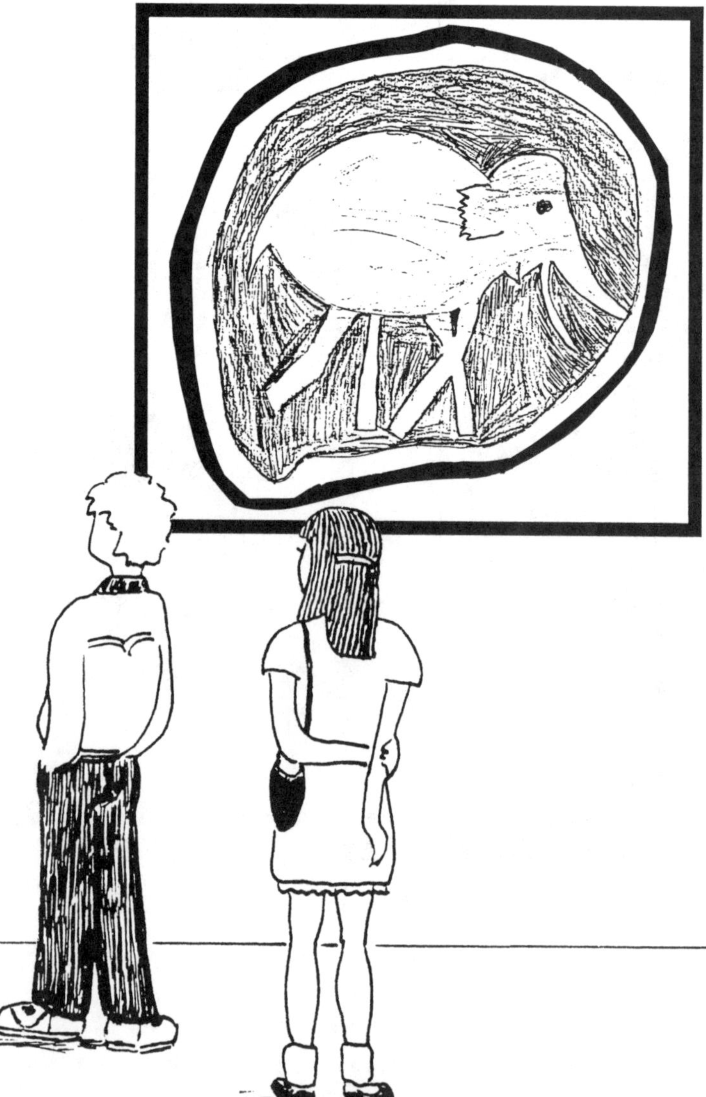

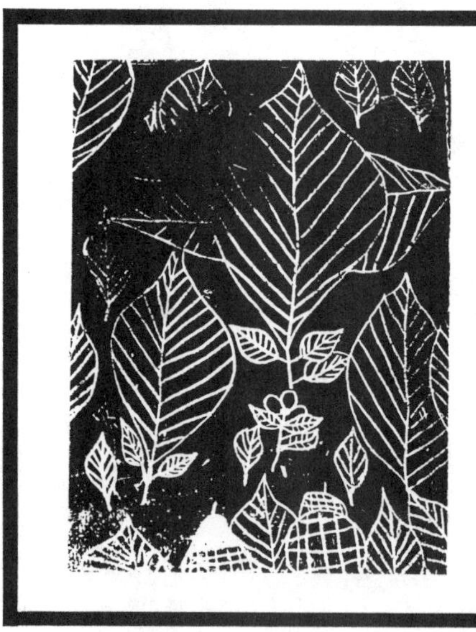

MASTERPIECES

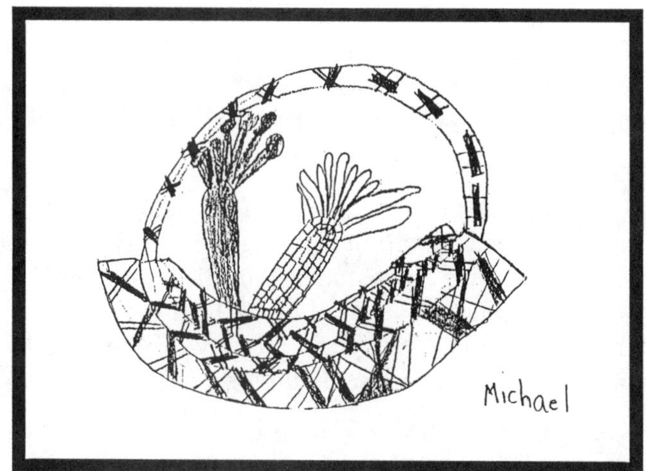

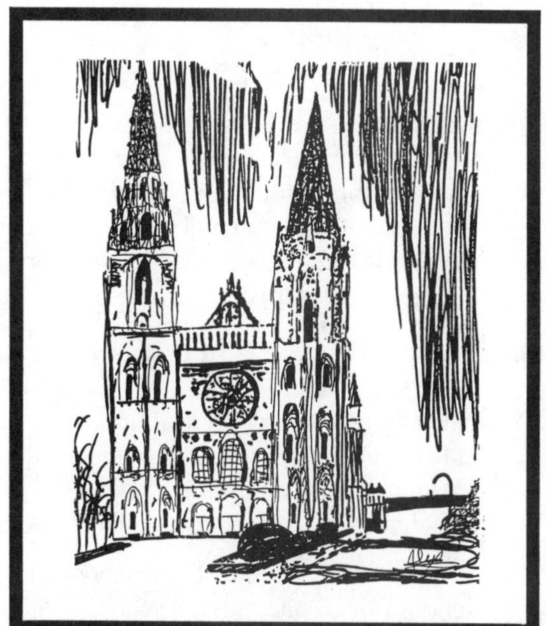

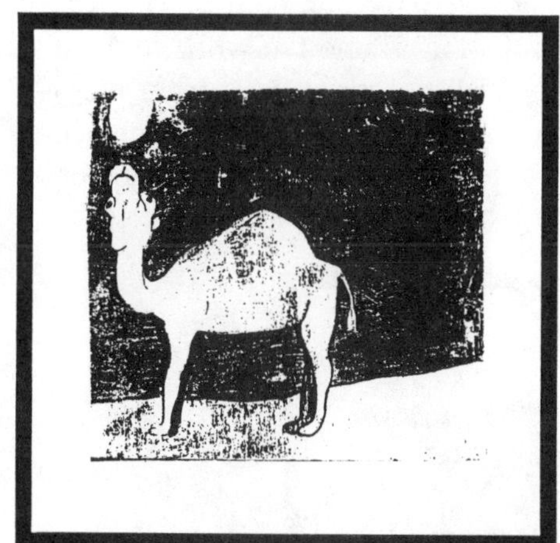

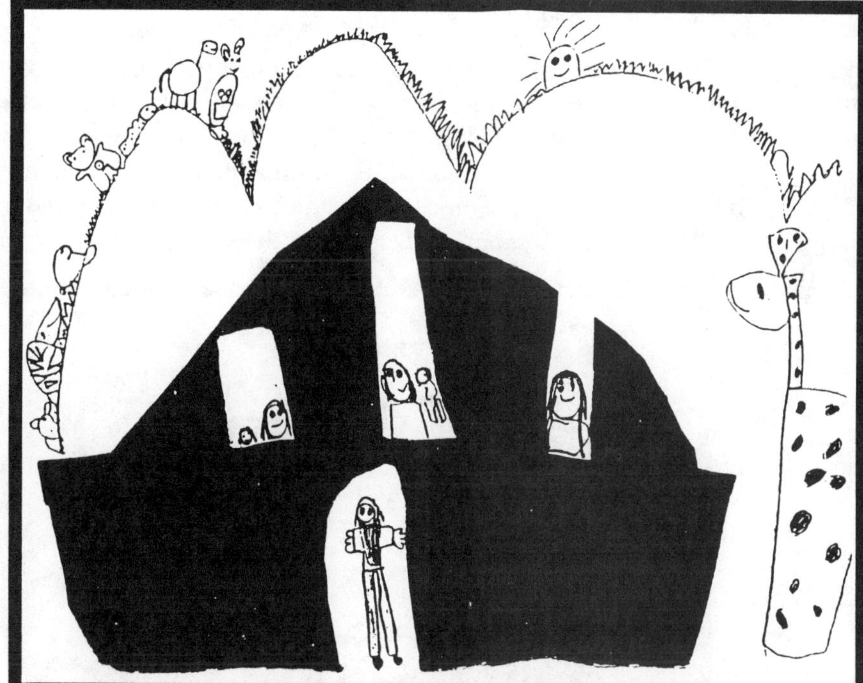

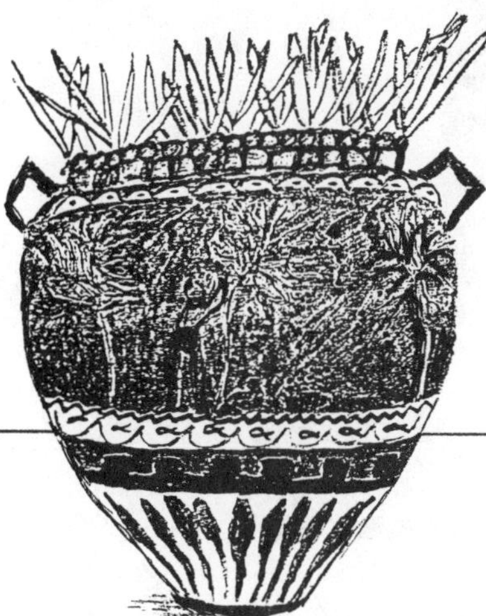

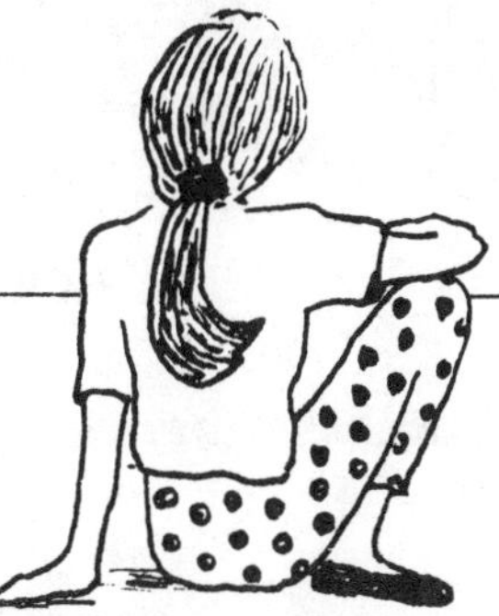

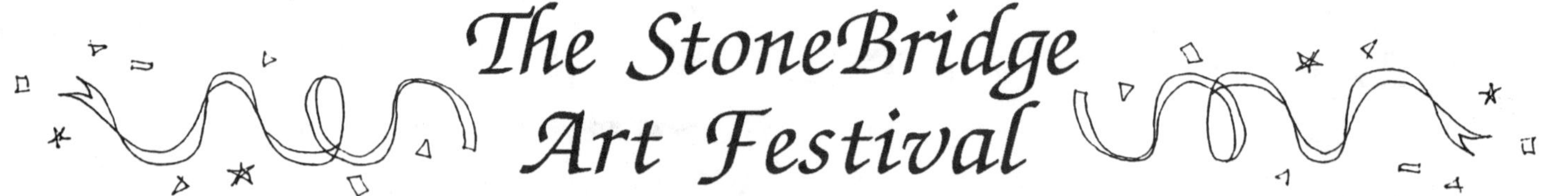

The StoneBridge Art Festival

PURPOSE: The annual spring Art Festival is one of the enriching highlights of the StoneBridge school year for the students, faculty, and parents as well. Its purpose is to cultivate and nurture excellence in the fine arts through creative expressions that glorify God. This is achieved more through the internal response of the students to the Biblically principled art curriculum than by merely choosing religious subject matter. The festival provides the opportunity to celebrate **every** student's creative effort and stewardship of time and ability.

REQUIREMENTS: All students from kindergarten through the eighth grade enter art work and may submit two selections. If the child has two entries, they must be entered in different catagories, such as a painting and a piece of sculpture. If time allows, it is beneficial for older students to select their own entries. The selection is made with the instructor's supervision and is based on skill in the use of various media, on creativity, and on the spirit of the work. Kindergarten and primary-aged entries are chosen by the instructor, but students may discuss their preferences with the teacher.

An aspiration for excellence should be evident in the work submitted. All entries must be done in school during the current school year and must have the student's full name identified in the lower right-hand corner.

The categories of art work are determined by the projects done in the art program for the current school year. Suggested categories are: drawing, painting, prints, crafts, calligraphy, mixed media, pastels, clay, and sculpture.

DISPLAY: Three-dimensional work is displayed on top of a piece of mat board or poster board. All two-dimensional work is single or double matted. The teacher selects mats that frame the work so as to draw the eye of the viewer into the work, not to detract from it. Dark colors (gray, black, blue) generally look best to frame drawings and many works done in color. Matted work is then displayed by grade level in categories according to media. Each piece of art entered in every category is then numbered. The number is placed over the student's name until the judging is completed.

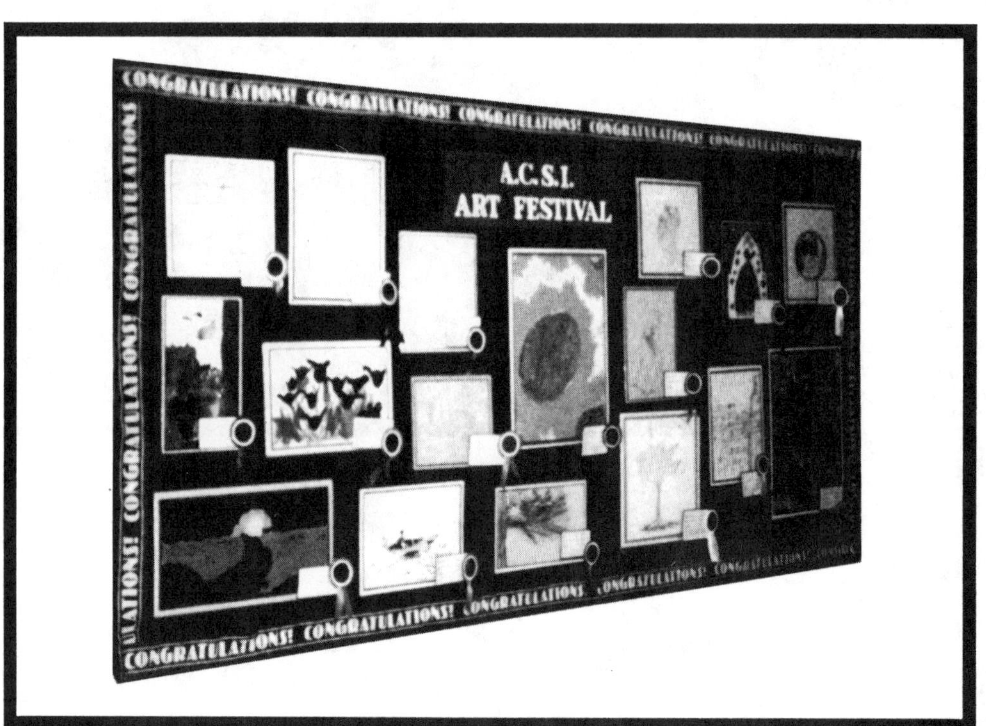

JUDGES: It is advantageous to invite three judges to provide a variety of opinions. If possible, ask those who have had experience working with children's art. Art teachers from other elementary schools, college art professors, and individuals from a local art organization are good choices for judges. A small honorarium may be given to cover transportation or babysitting costs. Judges should be directed to observe craftsmanship, design, creativity, and the spirit reflected in the work. Supply each judge with a clipboard, paper, and pencil to record choices. A beverage and snack is a gracious way to show appreciation for the difficult task of judging children's work.

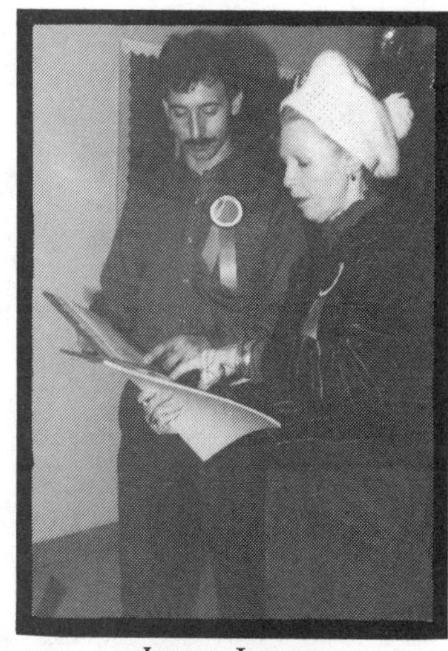

LOCAL JUDGES

AWARDS: Recognition is given for the quality of excellence achieved, not for competition with others' works. Therefore, three first place ribbons might be given in one category and no second or third given in that category, or perhaps no first place awards given in a category.

Designated achievement for awards is:

1. Blue ribbons are given for superior work (work done above grade level).
2. Red ribbons are given for excellent work.
3. White ribbons are given for good work.
4. Violet ribbons are given for honorable mentions.

Awards Ceremony and Reception

A school-wide ceremony is held to present the awards for the winners of the Art Festival. The date is pre-announced through school publications to enable parents to attend. The art director is the master of ceremonies and opens with prayer and the singing of the school song, *Eternal Excellence*. The school director is invited to deliver a short address centered around the subject of the visual arts. The presentation of ribbons begins with direction on how to properly receive an award. The students are instructed to come forward, shake hands with the presenter, receive the award by saying "Thank you," and return to their seats. As each award is presented, an appointed assistant displays the winning art work for a visual feast for the audience. With the completion of the ceremony, the winners and their parents are invited to enjoy refreshments at a reception.

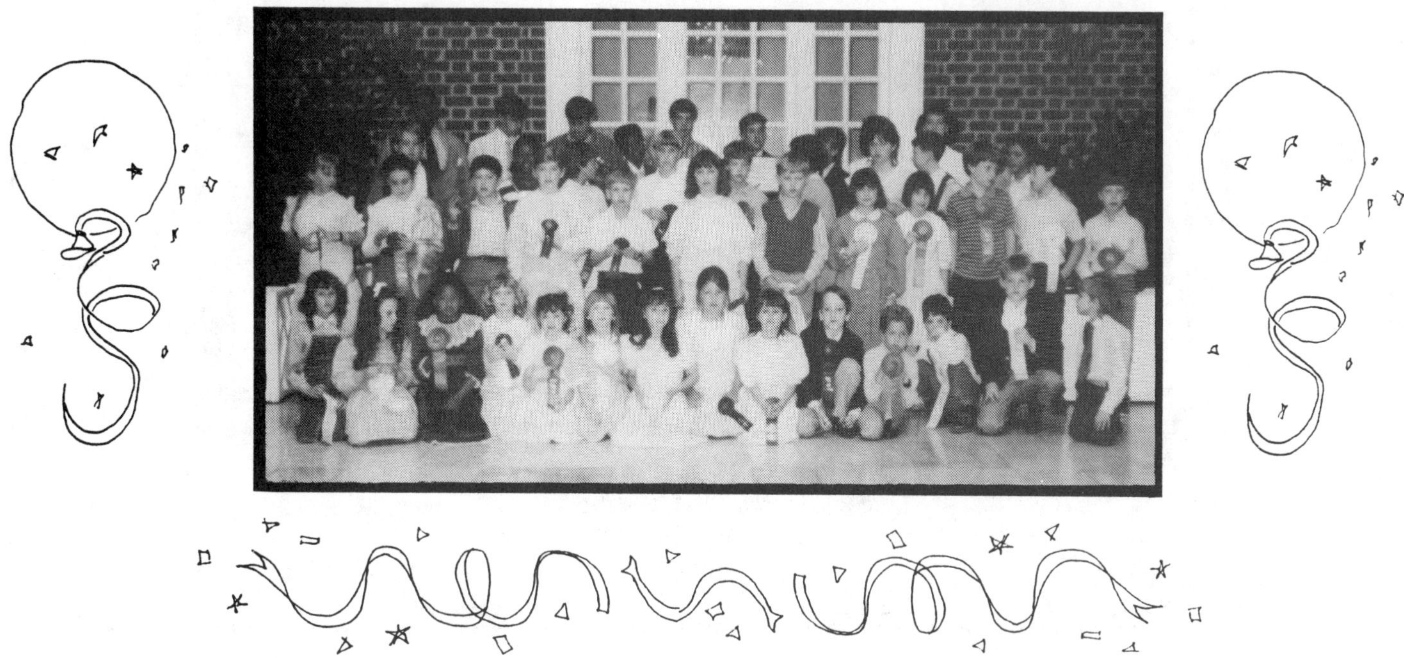

THE JOHN MOFFET MEMORIAL AWARD AND GALLERY

The *John Moffet Memorial Award* is a scholarship fund that was established by one of our StoneBridge Schools' founding families in honor of a parent. It is awarded annually to a graduating eighth grade Art Festival winner whose character consistently demonstrates diligence and industry and whose art work reflects creativity and a spirit of excellence over the years. The student receives a scholarship to participate in a local summer fine arts program, his or her name is placed on a plaque, and the winning piece of art work is matted, framed, and permanently hung in the *John Moffet Art Gallery.*

The *John Moffet Art Gallery,* located in the main hallway of the elementary school, is a collection of attractively framed student "masterpieces" that were StoneBridge Art Festival award winners over the years. A committee, comprised of the schools' director and the art department, chooses the selections each year at the Art Festival. The student and his parents are contacted for permission to either hang the original piece of art or a color-duplicated copy.

Permanently exhibiting student art work and masterpieces of the great artists that are studied in the curriculum daily bathe the hearts and minds of the children in beauty that glorifies God. The masterpieces become intimate friends of the children and nourish their sensibilities for Christ. This is one way to cultivate an elevated standard and a value system that will guide their aesthetic tastes for life and future leadership.

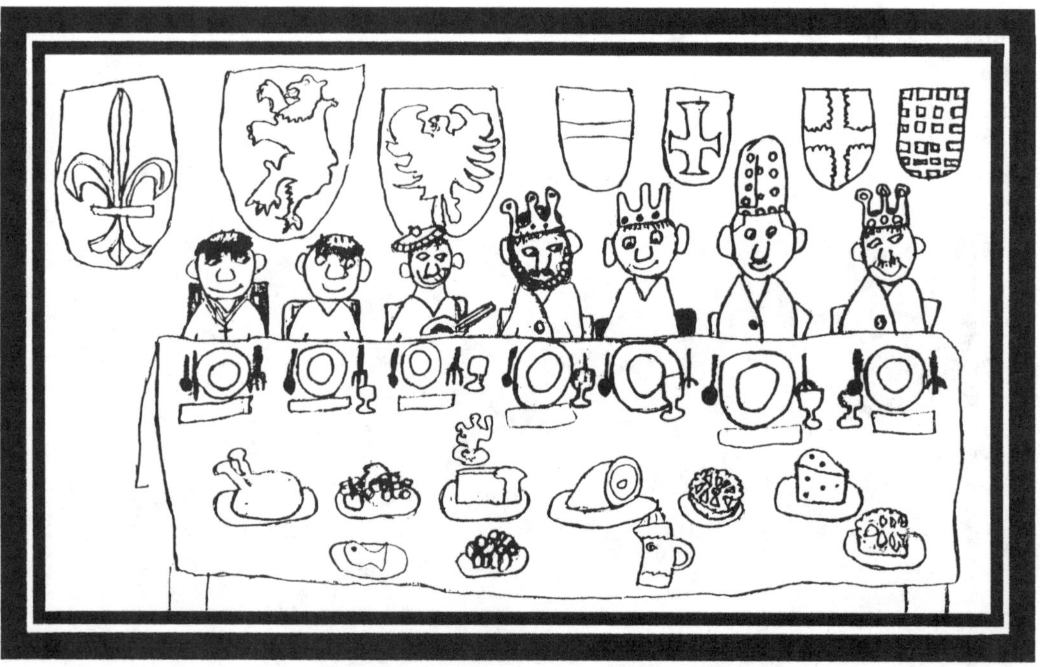

"Seest thou a man diligent in his business?
he shall stand before kings."
[PROVERBS 22:29]

TEACHING ART TO THE FACULTY

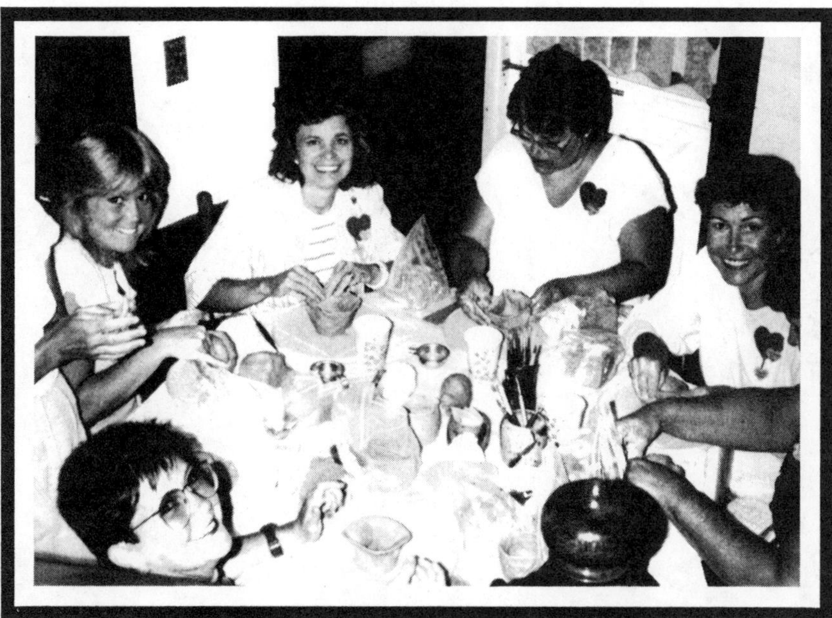

SCULPTURE PROJECT INSPIRED BY MICHELANGELO
1988 STONEBRIDGE FACULTY RETREAT

Research has proven that the visual image is remembered far longer than the spoken word and, in the area of learning styles, that many individuals learn best through their visual channel. Therefore, in the whole scope of the elementary educational process, each classroom teacher, as well as the art department, share the responsibility for nurturing aesthetic tastes and creative expression through the visual arts and to teach to the visual learners. Masterful teaching includes the use of visual aids, maps, charts, chalkboard illustrations, color-coded information, and masterpieces and requires the students to illustrate their notebook work and assignments (see Chapter 9). However, many teachers have received little or no art education and are reluctant to employ many of these methods, so the art staff must assume the leadership to inspire and equip classroom teachers.

The Annual StoneBridge Faculty Retreat, in the seclusion of a beautiful Virginia summer setting, provides the opportunity and the environment for inspiring and instructing teachers. The first day of the Retreat, among other scheduled classes, an art class is taught to the whole faculty. The faculty members become "art students" and the art director employs the same methods of instruction as the children receive in art class. Choosing a master artist, the director inspires with a biographical sketch and introduces an art project to be completed by each faculty member during the remainder of the Retreat. The necessary art practice skills are taught and demonstrated and the lesson is highlighted with the master artist's reproductions. These skills, coupled with the knowledge that all have been endowed with God-given abilities, ensure each faculty member a successful project. Adults need to be encouraged just as much as young students. Following the session, all faculty masterpieces are displayed and each member's effort and creativity are celebrated! It is through such a session that teachers experience the joys and frustrations that their students experience in the art studio.

At the 1991 Faculty Retreat, *The Lady of the Lake* by Sir Walter Scott was the centerpiece of all Retreat teaching. The art instructor used Albrecht Dürer and his love of nature to teach *value* as the element of design in still life drawings of Scottish wildflowers. On the following pages are sample hand-outs that the art instructor used with the faculty. The inclusion of art is always a highlight of the Retreat and a very liberating and enriching experience for teachers!

PENCIL DRAWINGS FROM THE 1991 STONEBRIDGE FACULTY RETREAT

Inspired by the Study of *The Lady of the Lake* and Scottish Wildflowers

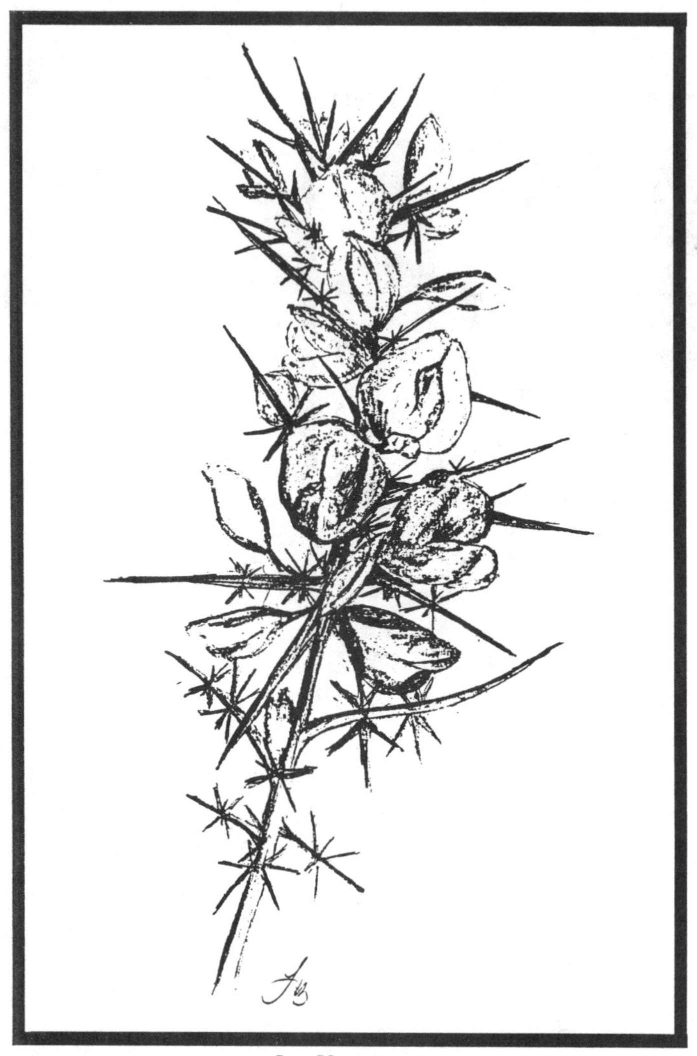

LIZ VANSICKLE
(CLASSROOM TEACHER)

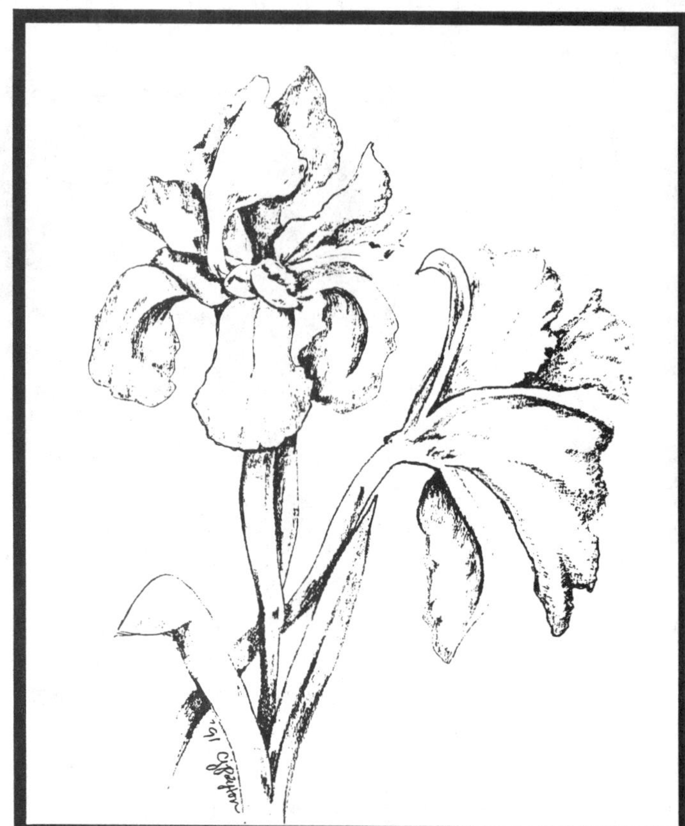

CAROLE PAYTON
(ART TEACHER)

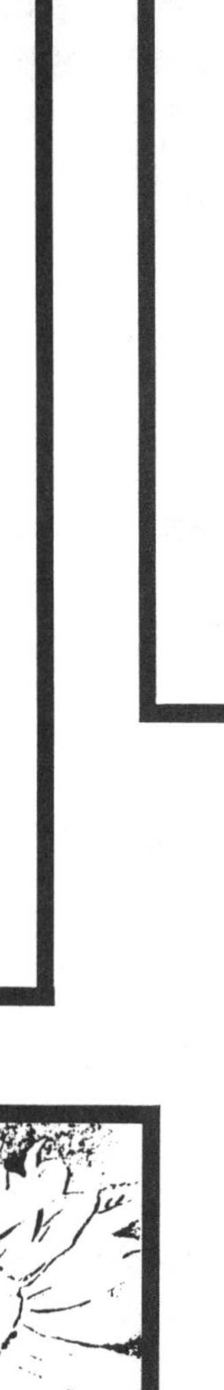

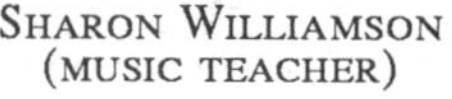

SHARON WILLIAMSON
(MUSIC TEACHER)

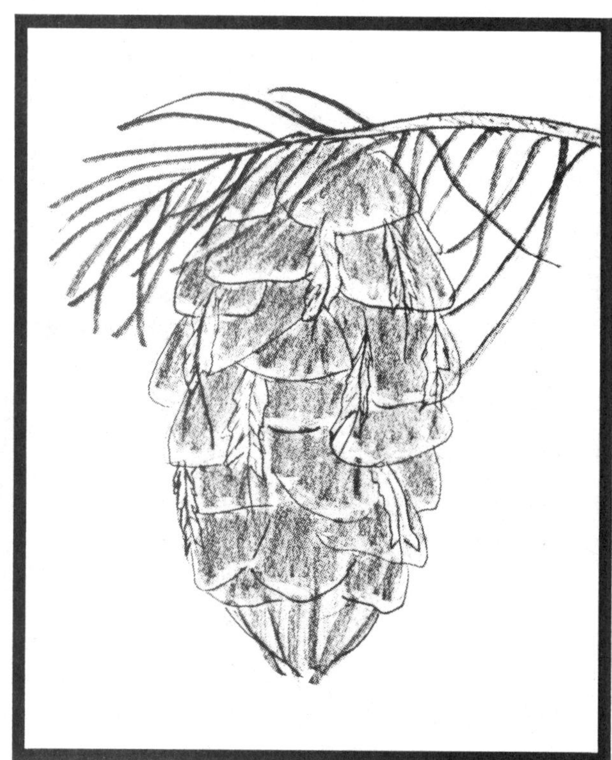

DIANA GONZALEZ
(DRAMA COACH)

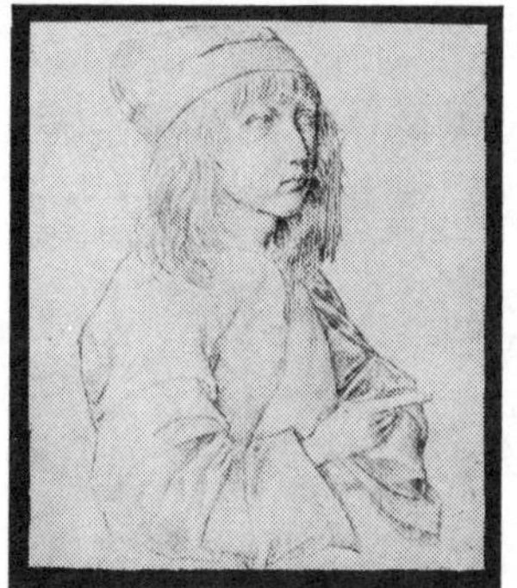

ALBRECHT DÜRER

(1471 – 1528)

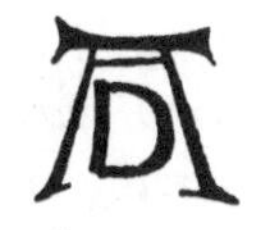

(DÜRER'S MONOGRAM)

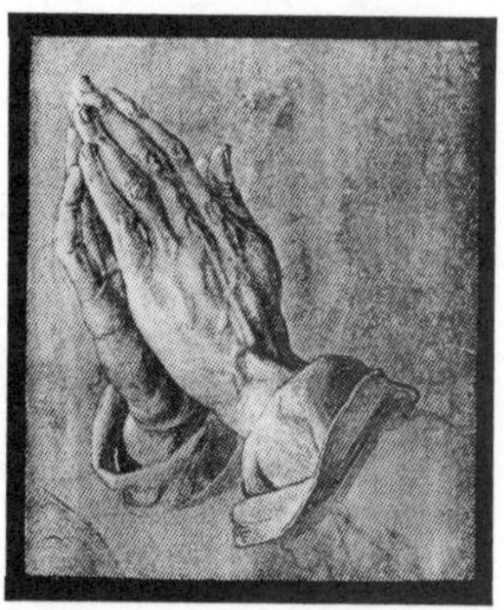

Albrecht Dürer is considered the greatest German artist of the Reformation. Born in the bustling commercial town of Nüremberg in 1471, Dürer lived and painted at the same time as Raphael, Michelangelo, and Leonardo da Vinci. Gutenburg had just invented movable type in Germany. This, in combination with the invention of the printing press and inexpensive paper, made it possible for illustrated books to be reproduced in mass.

Like his father and ancestors before him, young Albrecht was trained as a goldsmith. Albrecht, however, found his greatest joy in drawing. He drew a remarkable self-portrait when he was just thirteen which shows his amazing ability to express himself through line (see above). It is one of the earliest self-portraits in Western Art. Observing his son's talent, Dürer's father allowed Albrecht to apprentice under an accomplished Nüremberg artist.

Albrecht was one of seventeen children born to devout Christian parents. The strong faith in God that was developed in him is seen in his art and his writings. He was constantly recording, keeping journals of his travels, a family chronicle, and his thoughts on the "Divine Origin of Art." He states that "Art comes from God," and that "God created all forms of art." In one of his diaries, his words led into spontaneous prayer for Martin Luther for whom he had high respect.

He had a strong desire to draw a portrait of Luther but never had the opportunity. However, he did give Luther's features to his portrait of St. John, who was Luther's favorite evangelist. Dürer was a man of pure morals and as stated in his epitaph, he was a "good man in Christ."

Albrecht Dürer was a painter, an engraver, a printer, a publisher, and a master of woodcuts and independent drawings. He valued his drawings and placed his famous monogram in his pictures. He often made it a part of the composition. He was perhaps the first to realize the full potential of drawing, making it worthy of being considered a finished work of art. Dürer's keen observation skills and his accuracy produced detailed drawings with wonderful expression. The emphasis on outline seen in his work reflects his early training as an engraver. Two of his most famous drawings are the *Young Hare* (done with a brush) and the *Praying Hands*. These were unusual subjects for artists of Dürer's day. Others of this period were painting altarpieces, formal portraits, and religious scenes.

One of history's greatest graphic artists, Dürer was extremely diligent and was always striving to learn everything relating to his art. He is a link between the "artistic achievement" and "academic ideas" of the Renaissance in southern Europe and the "spiritual awakening" of the Reformation in northern Europe.

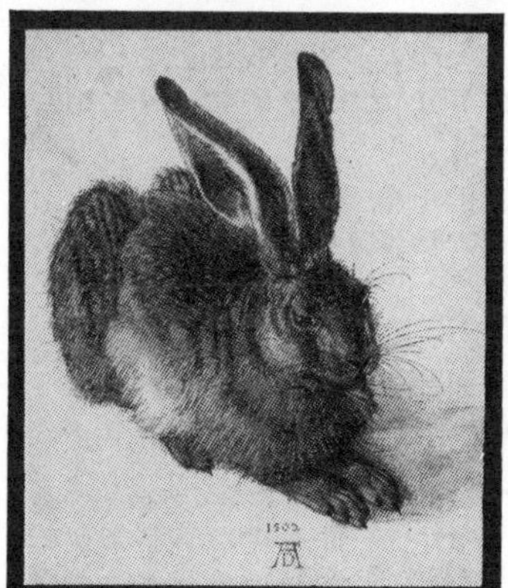

YOUNG HARE

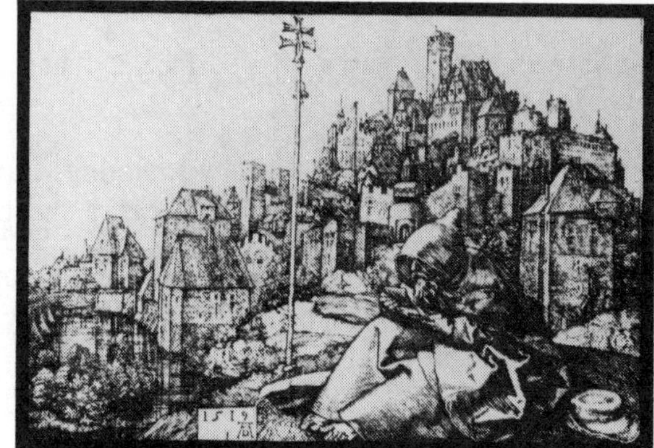

ST. ANTHONY (1519 ENGRAVING)

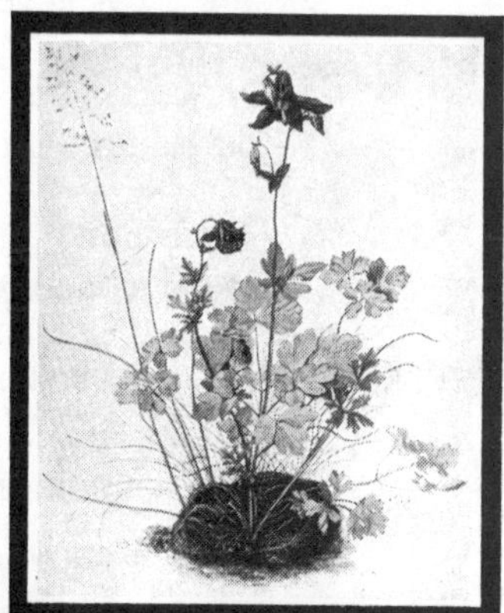

COLUMBINE

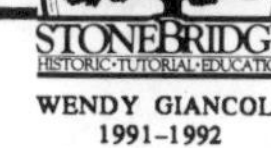

WENDY GIANCOLI
1991–1992

HAND-OUT #2

VALUE

THE DEGREE OF LIGHTNESS OR DARKNESS OF AN OBJECT

"In the beginning God created the heavens and the earth.
And the earth was formless and void, and darkness was over the surface of the deep;
and the Spirit of God was moving over the surface of the waters.
Then God said, 'Let there be light,' and there was light.
And God saw that the light was good;
and God separated the light from the darkness."
[Genesis 1:1–5]

"Then God made two great lights;
the greater light to rule the day
and the lesser light to rule the night."
[Genesis 1:16]

A PENCIL DRAWING FROM NATURE INSPIRED BY ALBRECHT DÜRER

Step #1 Before you begin, plan your composition, or the placement of your plant on your paper.

Step #2 OBSERVE WITH AN ARTIST'S EYE!

Observe is defined: To see or sense especially through careful attention.

"Stand still, and consider the wondrous works of God." [Job 37:14]

Is the bottom of the vase straight or does it curve slightly? How tall is the vase in relation to the height of the palm?

Step #3 Make a contour drawing or a silhouette. For an accurate, realistic drawing, your eyes should be primarily on the still life, glancing briefly down at your paper for placement. When drawing a foreshortened leaf, think of it as a shape, not as a leaf. Focus on one shape and how it relates to the other shapes and spaces.

Step #4 Hold the drawing away from you. Look at it from a distance to check proportions and then make any corrections. This step may be repeated throughout the drawing process. To help estimate proportions, you may use a pencil for a measuring device. Remember to hold it at an arm's length and at eye level, shut one eye, and then measure.

Step #5 Draw in details. Your vase should be placed on a surface so that it does not appear to be floating. Indicate the table in your drawing.

Step #6 Observe the lights and the darks in the "still life" by squinting your eyes as you look at it. Which side is your light source coming from? Does the plant cast a shadow on the table beneath it?

Step #7 Now add shading to your composition, beginning lightly and building up the values. If you use several values you will create a more realistic rendering. You may soften a tone by smudging it with your finger, a smudge stick, or a tissue.

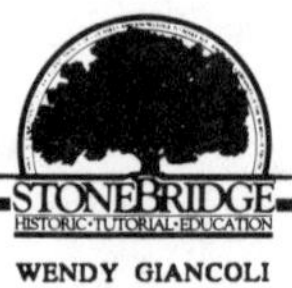

WENDY GIANCOLI
1991–1992

CHAPTER 7

THE ART STUDIO

The art studio may be a separate art room where the art director conducts the art classes and stores art tools and supplies, or it may be in individual classrooms to which the art director must carry art tools and supplies, leaving the room clean for the next academic class. Regardless, an assigned seating arrangement for art instruction should be used to maximize each artist's diligence and industry. The seating arrangement should enable the art teacher to move freely throughout the studio to spend time at each student's work area.

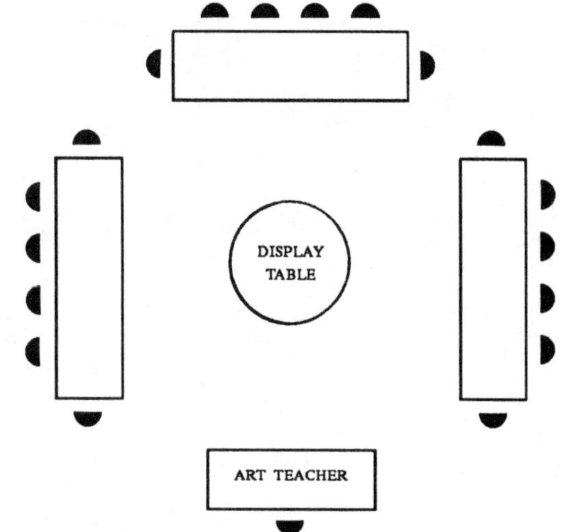

IDEAL PHYSICAL LAYOUT FOR AN ART STUDIO

Art studio etiquette is based on the principle of Christian self-government with law. The **Art Classroom Constitution** (see sample on the following page) states the basic rules that govern the art studio. The art director reviews the Constitution the first art period, signs the Constitution, and gives a copy to each student to be signed and filed in the art notebook. The student's consent to abide by the "law" then becomes the basis for any necessary discipline in the future, which is accomplished privately with the student and in a positive manner.

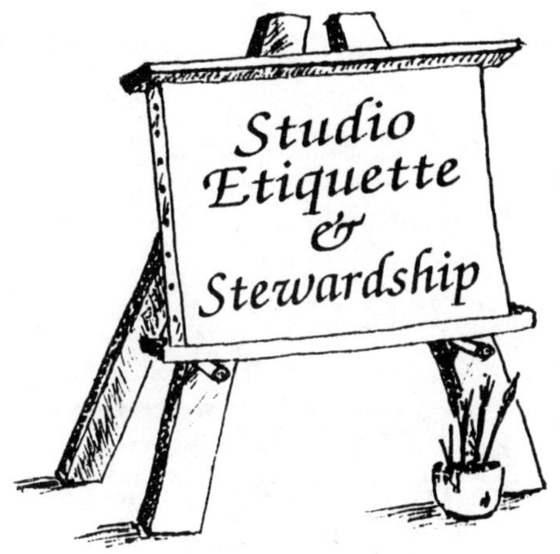

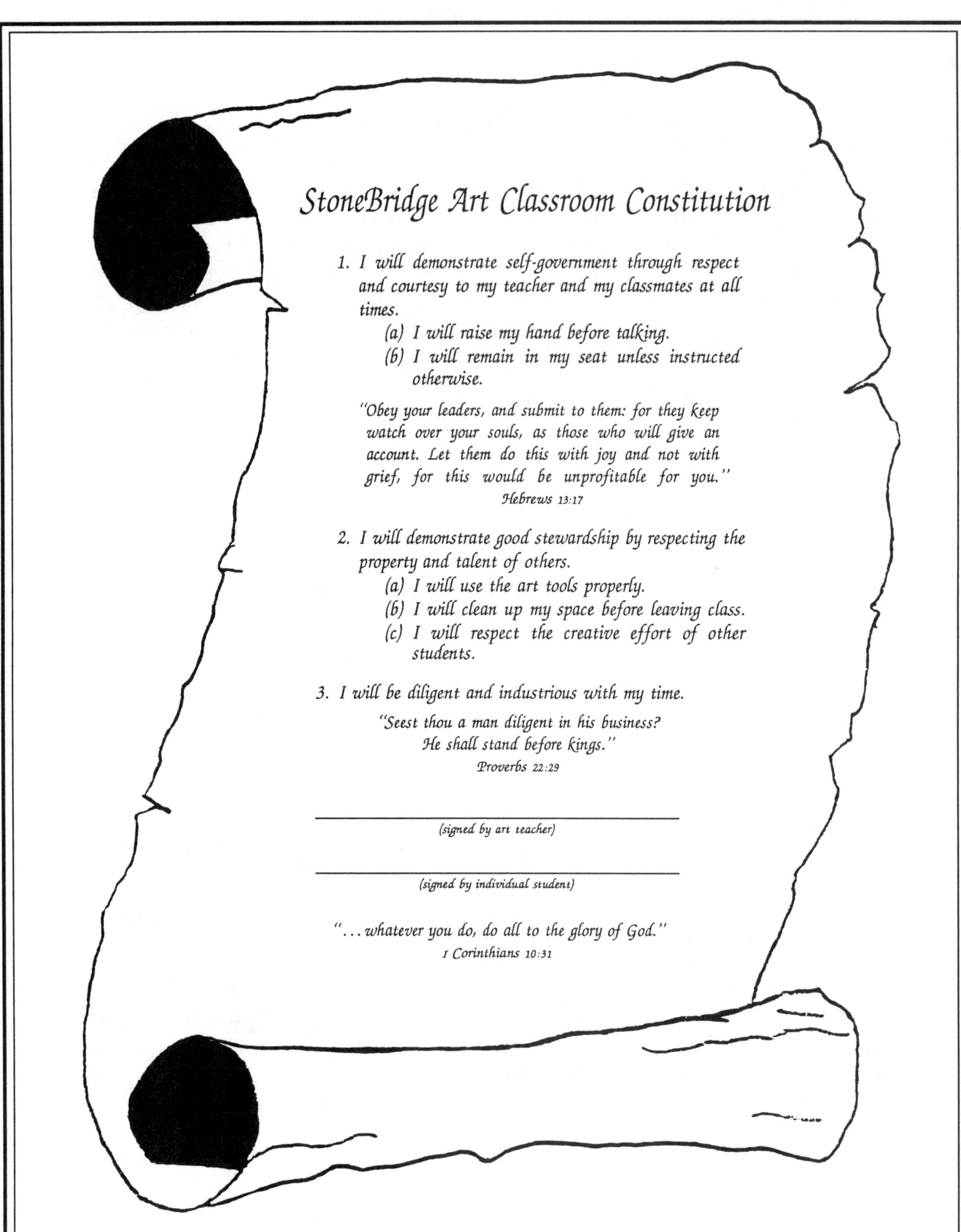

StoneBridge Art Classroom Constitution

1. *I will demonstrate self-government through respect and courtesy to my teacher and my classmates at all times.*
   - *(a) I will raise my hand before talking.*
   - *(b) I will remain in my seat unless instructed otherwise.*

"Obey your leaders, and submit to them: for they keep watch over your souls, as those who will give an account. Let them do this with joy and not with grief, for this would be unprofitable for you."
Hebrews 13:17

2. *I will demonstrate good stewardship by respecting the property and talent of others.*
   - *(a) I will use the art tools properly.*
   - *(b) I will clean up my space before leaving class.*
   - *(c) I will respect the creative effort of other students.*

3. *I will be diligent and industrious with my time.*

"Seest thou a man diligent in his business? He shall stand before kings."
Proverbs 22:29

____

(signed by art teacher)

____

(signed by individual student)

"...whatever you do, do all to the glory of God."
I Corinthians 10:31

BASIC ART TOOLS AND SUPPLIES REQUIRED FOR AN ELEMENTARY ART PROGRAM

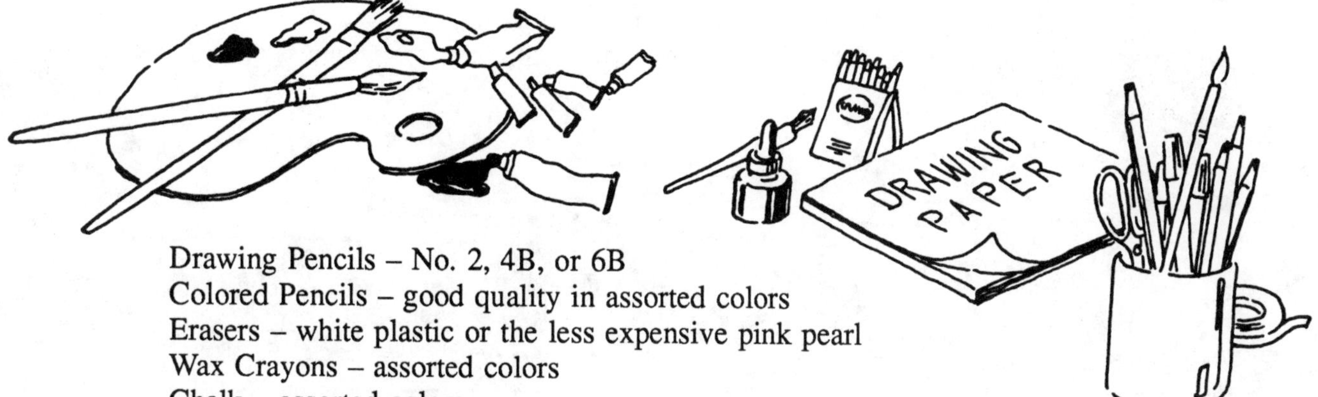

Drawing Pencils – No. 2, 4B, or 6B
Colored Pencils – good quality in assorted colors
Erasers – white plastic or the less expensive pink pearl
Wax Crayons – assorted colors
Chalk – assorted colors
Dry and Oil Pastels – assorted colors
Tempera Paints – red, blue, yellow, orange, green, violet, white, black, & brown
Tube Water Colors – assorted colors
Acrylic Paints – optional
Paint Brushes – large and small; rounds and flats; soft hair unless painting on boards; and inexpensive ones for primary-aged children
Felt-Tip Markers – more wide-tip than thin-tip are needed
India Ink and Pens – for 7th & 8th grades

Manila Paper – oversized needed for younger children
White Drawing Paper
Construction Paper – assorted colors; larger black for matting
Water-color Paper – medium grade
Poster Board ("tag board") – for portfolios
Bulletin Board Paper – dark blue, violet, brown, and green used most often

Low-Fire Clay – red or white
Linoleum Blocks – optional
Linoleum Block Tools – optional

Scissors – sharp pairs needed for older students
Masking Tape
Elmer's Glue – one small bottle for each child
Glue Sticks – provided by parents at the first of the year
Rubber Cement – for teacher's use in matting art work

Plastic Water Containers
Paper Plates or Styrofoam Meat Trays – used for paint palettes
Paper Towels
Smocks – provided by parents at the first of the year (T-shirts are best because they slip on and off easily)

CHAPTER 8

FIELD STUDY TOURS

NATIONAL GALLERY OF ART, WASHINGTON, D.C.

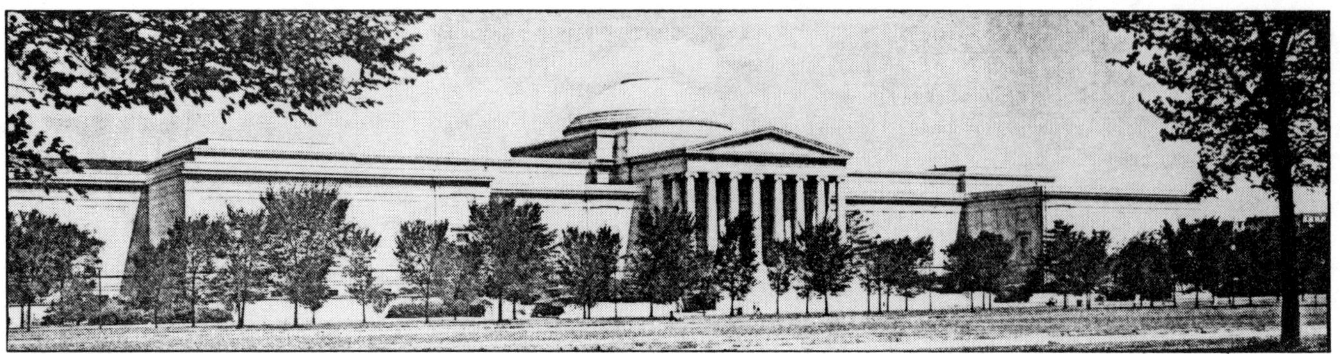

When asked where one should learn to paint, Renoir replied, "In the museum, of course!" Near the end of his life when Renoir was unable to walk, he traversed in his wheel chair down the long halls of the Louvre to see the masterpieces he loved.

A field study tour is a marvelous gateway to divergent learning experiences for students. Because it is a valuable learning experience, the teacher should always take classroom time to prepare the students for what will be seen and experienced, to have students write out questions they would like to ask the tour guide, and then to record their learning experience after the field study tour. The teacher should always telephone or write ahead and request that the tour guide or docent focus on the particular aspects of the curriculum that have been studied in class. Learning begins the moment the students leave the school building. Depending upon the length of travel time, a wise teacher will plan coordinated activities for the students while traveling. Frequently, students are requested to bring their sketch pads and pencils to use during the day. Follow up the field study tour with a written assignment and request that the students illustrate their work. A grade should be given the assignment and thank you notes should be written by each student to express appreciation to the tour guide.

VISITING THE ART MUSEUM IS AN IMPORTANT LINK TO LEARNING

1. Call ahead and ask that an individualized tour be arranged to include those artists on the time line for the current school year.

2. Prepare students ahead so they know what to expect and what to look for. Perhaps they could be "art detectives" and investigate how various artists used specific elements of design.

3. Instruct students to be courteous and respectful of the museum docent by listening, asking questions, and by following with their docent as directed.

4. Teach students proper museum etiquette, such as "low voices," "touching with eyes only, please."

5. Have students write letters of appreciation to their docent.

6. Directly following the museum visit, reinforce learning by asking students questions that make them think about the art they viewed. Second grade students expressed these thoughts when asked which painting impressed them most and why.

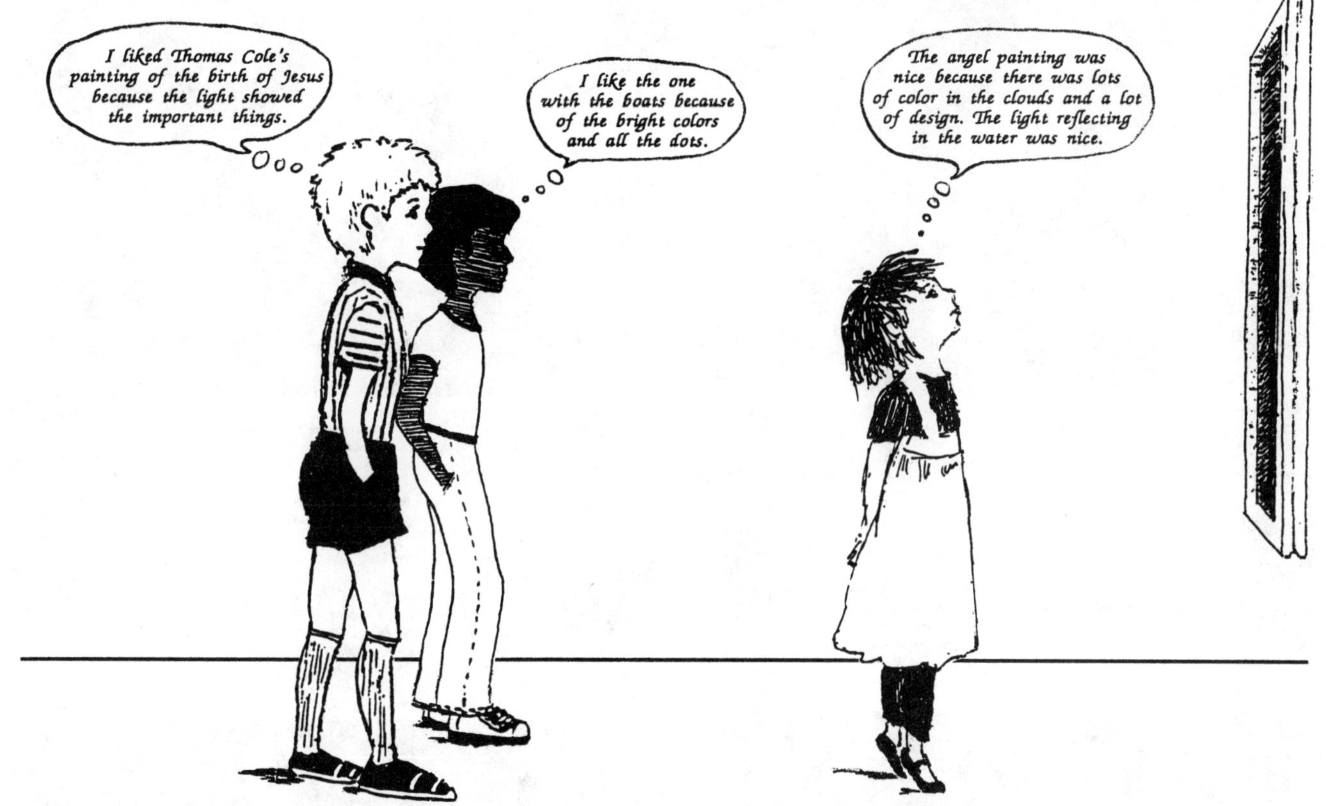

Create Your Own

"Identify the Masterpiece" Game

Playing educational games is an enjoyable way for students to use traveling time when going to the museum. *Identify the Masterpiece* is a game that was created for just such an outing. In addition to spending quality time with the master artists and their work, it provides reinforcement for what they have studied in class. There are several ways to organize the game:

1. Assemble a mixture of masterpieces on postcards or colored reprints that have been studied, or other works by artists in the curriculum. Place in folders that have inside pouches and be certain the name of the masterpiece and its artist is on the back. Working in groups of two to four, the students discuss the subject matter and style and identify the artists.
2. Place a biographical sketch on the folder. Insert an assortment of artists' masterpieces, including several by the artist in the sketch. The students then identify the masterpieces by the artist described, and also try to identify the other masterpieces.

Prepare several folders that can be passed from group to group.

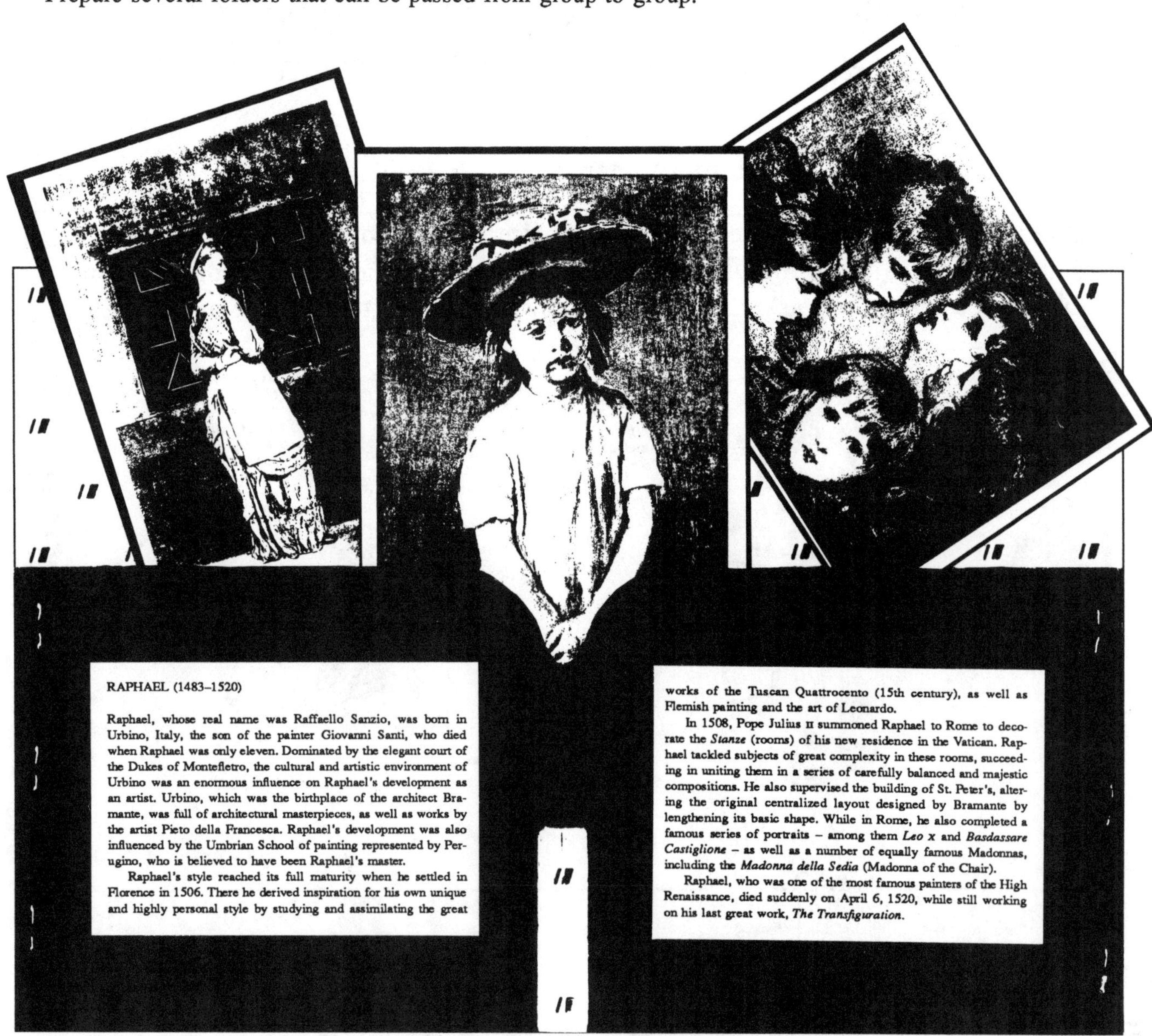

RAPHAEL (1483–1520)

Raphael, whose real name was Raffaello Sanzio, was born in Urbino, Italy, the son of the painter Giovanni Santi, who died when Raphael was only eleven. Dominated by the elegant court of the Dukes of Montefletro, the cultural and artistic environment of Urbino was an enormous influence on Raphael's development as an artist. Urbino, which was the birthplace of the architect Bramante, was full of architectural masterpieces, as well as works by the artist Pieto della Francesca. Raphael's development was also influenced by the Umbrian School of painting represented by Perugino, who is believed to have been Raphael's master.

Raphael's style reached its full maturity when he settled in Florence in 1506. There he derived inspiration for his own unique and highly personal style by studying and assimilating the great works of the Tuscan Quattrocento (15th century), as well as Flemish painting and the art of Leonardo.

In 1508, Pope Julius II summoned Raphael to Rome to decorate the *Stanze* (rooms) of his new residence in the Vatican. Raphael tackled subjects of great complexity in these rooms, succeeding in uniting them in a series of carefully balanced and majestic compositions. He also supervised the building of St. Peter's, altering the original centralized layout designed by Bramante by lengthening its basic shape. While in Rome, he also completed a famous series of portraits – among them *Leo x* and *Basdassare Castiglione* – as well as a number of equally famous Madonnas, including the *Madonna della Sedia* (Madonna of the Chair).

Raphael, who was one of the most famous painters of the High Renaissance, died suddenly on April 6, 1520, while still working on his last great work, *The Transfiguration*.

CHAPTER 9

INTEGRATING ART THROUGHOUT THE CURRICULUM

Art plays a very important role in the overall curriculum of the Principle Approach school. As a handmaid of the Gospel and a tool for nurturing aesthetic tastes and sensibilities, art should be integrated into the whole curriculum. The following are several suggestions that elementary classroom teachers could incorporate in their lessons:

1. Student illustrations and coloring for notebook work
2. Using masterpieces for inspiring the writing of compositions
3. Using masterpieces to highlight an historical event or teach the individuality of a nation
4. Sketching on a Field Study Tour
5. Using masterpieces to appoint the classroom or for use on a bulletin board

EXAMPLE OF ART IN THE LITERATURE PROGRAM

To culminate the study of the classic *Hans Brinker, or The Silver Skates* by Mary Mapes Dodge in the third grade literature curriculum, a Special Day Celebration called **"Dutch Day"** makes the culture and individuality of Holland come alive for the students. Dressing up in simple Dutch costumes, the students participate in a morning of all things Dutch! They enjoy a Dutch breakfast, a visitor from Holland, the music and dance of The Netherlands, and walking in their *klompen*. The Art Department participates with a program on Dutch artists. In the classroom, the students are directed to observe the style, subject matter, and the use of the elements of design by two Dutch artists. They compare and contrast self-portraits and a sampling of other works by these artists. Then the Art Director "takes them to the Rijksmuseum" – a wall outside the classroom filled with masterpieces of Rembrandt and Van Gogh. Each student becomes an "art detective" and identifies which artist created each masterpiece. An "Art Detective" badge is awarded to the student who identifies the most masterpieces correctly.

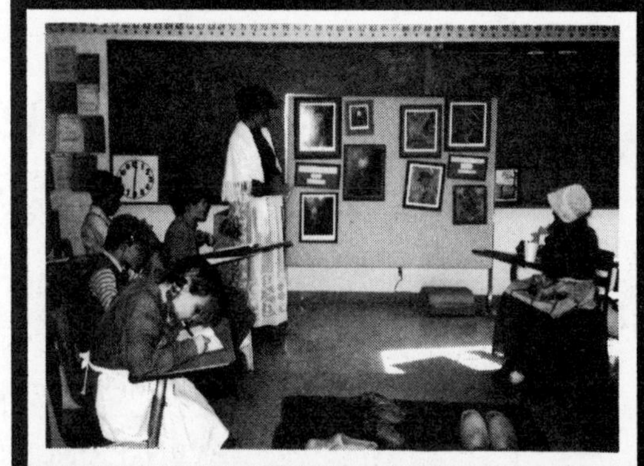

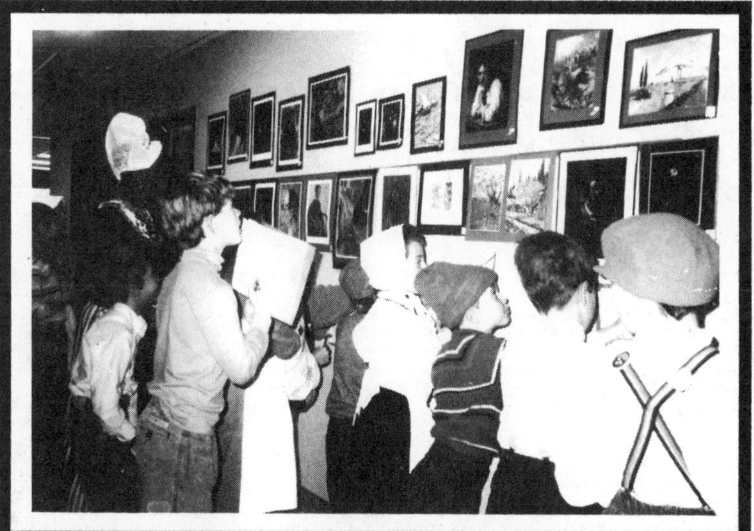

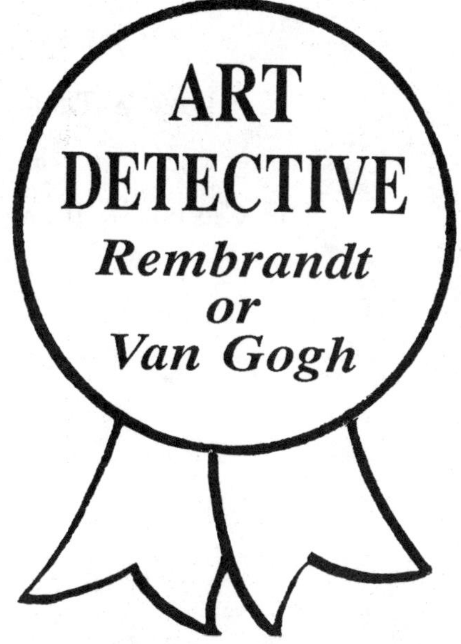

APPENDICES

APPENDIX I

ART GLOSSARY

APPENDIX II

ART APPRECIATION STUDY HELPS FROM
The Book of Life

APPENDIX III

READY REFERENCE:

SUMMARIZED AND PRESENTED BY ELIZABETH YOUMANS

The Philosophy of the Principle Approach

Seven Principles of the Principle Approach

The Providential View of History

The Chain of Christianity

Continents on the Chain of Christianity

Major Links Taught Each Year

Using a Time Line in Teaching Providential History

How to Think Governmentally

The Christian Idea of God, Man, and Government Summarized

4 R-ing Curriculum

APPENDIX I

ART GLOSSARY*

Artist – One skilled in an art or trade; one who is master or professor of a manual art; a good workman in any trade. A skillful man, not a novice. In academical sense, a proficient in the faculty of arts; a philosopher. One skilled in the fine arts; as a painter, sculptor, architect, etc.**

Artisan – An artist; one skilled in any art, mystery or trade; a handicraftsman; a mechanic; a tradesman.**

Abstract – Having little or no reference to the appearance of the natural objects; pertaining to the non-representational art styles of the twentieth century.

Academy – A place of study. Giorgio Vasari founded the first academy of arts in Florence in 1563.

Altarpiece – A panel, painted or sculptured above and behind an altar.

Architecture – The science and art of building for human use, including design, construction, and decorative treatment.

Background – In pictorial art, that part of the composition which appears to be behind forms represented as close to the viewer; the most distant of the three zones conceived in linear perspective to exist in deep space, beyond the foreground and middle ground.

Baroque – A style of artistic expression prevalent especially in the 17th century that is marked generally by extravagant forms and elaborate and sometimes grotesque ornamentation.

Basilica – In the Roman period, the word refers to the function of the building – a large meeting hall – rather than to its form, which may vary according to its use; as an official public building.

Cartoon – A preliminary sketch or drawing made to be transferred to a wall, a panel, or canvas as a guide in painting a finished work.

Catacombs – Underground tunnels in which the Early Christians in Rome and other communities buried their dead. Some catacombs also contained chapels and meeting rooms. The painted decorations found in the catacombs are the earliest known forms of Christian art.

Chiaroscuro – In painting or drawing, the treatment and use of light and dark, especially the gradations of light that produce the effect of modeling.

Classical – Used generally to refer to the art of the Greeks and Romans.

Color – The choice and treatment of the hues in a painting.

Composition – The arrangement of form, color, line, etc. in any given work of art.

Contour – In the pictorial arts, an outline that forms the boundary of one shape and defines it in relation to other shapes and is expressively handled so as to suggest fullness and recession of forms and varieties in texture, such as those in body structure and soft tissues. Contrasts with simple outline, which is no more than the boundary of a form defining silhouette.

Contrast – Closely related to emphasis, this term refers to a way of combining art elements to stress the differences between those elements.

Design – The organization, plan, or composition of a work of art. An effective design is one in which the elements and principles have been combined to achieve an overall sense of unity.

Drawing – A sketch, design, or representation by lines. Drawings are usually made on paper with pen, pencil, charcoal, pastel, chalk, etc.

Engraving – A design incised in reverse on a copper plate; this is coated with printer's ink, which remains in the incised lines when the plate is wiped off. Damp paper is placed on the plate, and both are put into a press; the paper soaks up the ink and produces a print of the original.

Etching – Like engraving, etching is an incising process. However, the design is drawn in reverse with a needle on a plate thinly coated with wax or resin. The plate is placed in a bath of nitric acid; the etched lines are produced on the plate by the coating. The coating is then removed, and the prints are made as in engravings.

Foreshortening – A method of representing objects as if seen at an angle and receding or projecting into space; not in a frontal or profile view.

Form – The external shape or appearance of a representation, considered apart from its color or material.

Fresco – A technique of wall painting known since antiquity; the pigment is mixed with water and applied to a freshly plastered area of a wall. The result is a particularly permanent form of painted decoration.

Genre – In the pictorial arts and sculpture, the casual representation.

Gradation – A way of combining art elements by using a series of gradual (step-by-step) changes in those elements.

Harmony – A way of combining elements to accent their similarities and bind the picture parts into a whole.

Horizon Line – A real or implied line across the picture plane parallel with its top and bottom edges, which like the horizon in nature, tends to fix the viewer's eye level, and toward which in linear perspective all receding parallel lines seem to converge.

* Definitions, unless otherwise noted, are taken from *History of Art for Young People* by H. W. Janson. Harry N. Abrams, Inc., NY, NY (1987).

** Definition from *American Dictionary of the English Language* by Noah Webster. F.A.C.E., San Francisco, CA (Facsimile 1828 Edition).

Hue – The property of color that distinguishes one color from another, as red, green, violet, etc.

Illumination – A term used generally for manuscript paintings. Illuminated manuscripts may contain separate ornamental pages, marginal illustrations, ornament within the text, entire miniature paintings, or any combination of these.

Image – A representation of an object, an individual, or event. An image may also be an evocation of a state of being in representational or nonrepresentational art.

Impressionism – A style of painting that started in France during the 1860s. Impressionist artists tried to paint candid glimpses of their subjects and emphasized the momentary effects of sunlight.

Landscape – In the pictorial arts, the representation of scenery in nature.

Limner – One that colors or paints on paper or parchment; one who decorates books with initial pictures. A portrait painter.

Line – A mark left in its path by a moving point, or anything, such as an edge, a boundary, or a horizon, that suggests such a mark; a succession of notes or ideas, as in a melodic line or a line of thought. The linear might be considered one-dimensional, as opposed to the spatial, which is either two- or three-dimensional.

Linear Perspective – A mathematical system for representing three-dimensional objects and space on a two-dimensional surface. All objects are represented as seen from a single viewpoint.

Medium – The material with which an artist works, such as marble, terra-cotta, oil paint, watercolor, etc.

Miniature – A painting or drawing in an illuminated manuscript; also a very small portrait, sometimes painted on ivory.

Mobile – A type of sculpture made of movable parts that can be set in motion by the movement of air currents.

Modeling – In painting or drawing, the means by which the three-dimensionality of a form is suggested on a two-dimensional surface, usually through variations of color and the play of lights and darks.

Mosaic – A design formed by embedding small pieces of colored stone or glass in cement. In antiquity, large mosaics were used chiefly on floors; from the Early Christian period on, mosaic decoration was increasingly used on walls and vaulted surfaces.

Painting – The art of forming figures or resembling objects in colors on canvas or other material, or the art of representing to the eye by means of figures and colors, any object of sight and sometimes the emotions of the mind. A picture; a likeness or resemblance in colors. Colors laid on.

Pastel – Powdered pigments mixed with gum and molded into sticks for drawing; also a picture or sketch made with this type of crayon.

Pietà – In painting or sculpture, a representation of the Virgin Mary mourning the dead Christ whom she holds.

Portrait – A picture or representation of a person, and especially of a face, drawn from life. In portraits, the grace, and we may add, the likeness, consist more in the general air than in the exact similitude of every feature.

Portraiture – A portrait; painted resemblance.**

Realism – A mid-nineteenth century style of art in which artists discarded the formulas of Neoclassicism and the theatrical drama of Romanticism to paint familiar scenes and events as they actually looked.

Relief – Forms in sculpture that project from the background, to which they remain attached. Relief may be carved or modeled shallowly to produce low relief, or deeply to produce high relief; in very high relief, portions may be entirely detached from the background. "A relief is when the figures are only partly freed from their background." – *Michelangelo*

Renaissance – A revival or rebirth of cultural awareness and learning that took place during the fourteenth and fifteenth centuries, particularly in Italy.

Representational – As opposed to abstract, means a portrayal of an object in recognizable form.

Rhythm – The regular repetition of a particular form; also, the suggestion of motion by recurrent forms.

Sculpture – The creation of a three-dimensional form, usually in a solid material. Traditionally, two basic techniques have been used: carving in a hard material, and modeling in a soft material such as clay, wax, etc. "I mean by sculpture that which is done by taking away. That which is done by adding is like painting." – *Michelangelo*

Sketch – A rough drawing representing the main features of a composition; often used as a preliminary study.

Stained Glass – The technique of filling architectural openings with glass colored by fused metallic oxides; pieces of this glass are held in a design by strips of lead.

Still Life – A painting or drawing of an arrangement of inanimate objects.

Symbol – A form, image, or subject representing a meaning other than the one with which it is usually associated.

Tempera – A painting process in which pigment is mixed with an emulsion of egg yolk and water or egg and oil. Tempera, the basic technique of medieval and Early Renaissance painters, dries quickly, permitting almost immediate application of the next layer of paint.

Watercolor – Pigments mixed with water instead of oil or other mediums, or a picture painted with watercolor, often on paper.

Woodcut – A printing process in which a design or lettering is carved in relief on a wooden block; the areas intended not to print off are hollowed out.

APPENDIX II

*Art Appreciation Study Helps From The Book of Life**

HOW TO STUDY A PICTURE

To enjoy and understand a painting of any period, certain principles must be understood. First of all, the picture must be considered with interest and attention. We must *want* to know about it. Many people do not make any effort to understand the best pictures. They merely glance at a picture, say they are "not interested in art," or that they "cannot understand what anyone sees in those old pictures," and turn away without making any attempt to understand or appreciate. But the effort is very much worthwhile. These old pictures are some of the most precious things which the world has to offer; it is our great loss and our children's loss if we do not appreciate them.

The important points in considering a picture are these:

1. The Center of Interest. Every good picture has a center of interest. It may be the face of the Madonna, it may be a hut in the landscape, but you will always find it, and it is the key to the artist's purpose in painting the picture. Take, for example, *The Transfiguration* by Raphael (see p. 92), which now hangs in the Vatican at Rome, one of the most splendid of the world's pictures. The center of interest is the figure of the transfigured Jesus. The arm of the demoniac boy, the uplifted arms of the disciples lead the eye to that figure rising in glory above the mount. Raphael is telling here that wonderful story of the transfiguration so that the most unlearned peasant could understand it. There are many pictures like the very beautiful *Madonna and Child* by Murillo, now in the Pitti Palace at Forence, in which the center of interest is unmistakable; the mother and the child comprise the whole picture. The painter aimed to show the tender and divine beauty of both, without any distraction or wandering of the attention.

2. The Composition. This is the artist's term for the grouping and arrangement of the figures with relation to the center of interest. The figures are the actors in the story which the artist places before our eyes. In *The Transfiguration,* Raphael combines two events in the life of Jesus in a masterly way. At the top of the picture is the figure of Jesus, the center of interest. The disciples are on the ground, sleeping or just awaking. The august figures of Moses and Elias appear on either side of the transfigured Jesus. It will be noticed that the figures are symmetrically arranged, – there is a figure on each side of Jesus. The small figures on the left do not really belong in the picture. Raphael would never have put them in himself. They were ordered by the donor of the picture. To the left are two adoring figures, St. Lawrence and St. Julian. It will be remembered that when Jesus came down from the mount, he was met at once by the old problem of sin and suffering. He found and healed the demoniac boy. In this composition, some of the people are pointing to the boy, the problem of suffering, but he and three of the disciples are pointing to Jesus, the Lord of healing. The composition is thus aranged in a most masterly way to teach the great story of the glory and the humanity of Jesus, the heavenly and the earthly aspects of his life. The demoniac boy is really a secondary center of interest, and the figures are arranged with reference both to the boy and to the supreme interest, the figure of Jesus. It must be remembered also that color adds to the significance of the composition. The balancing of the composition may be accomplished by a bright spot of color on one side.

3. Detail. Every picture has more or less of detail. In the *Madonna and Child* of Murillo, it almost vanishes; other pictures are crowded with detail. To study this is one of the greatest joys of the appreciation of painting. The child will delight in such study. It is like a game of "observation." Sometimes much of the charm of the picture is revealed in these minor features. Some of the Italian painters were very fond of detail, and the sort of detail which delights children. For example, take the *Nativity* by Girolamo dai Libri (see p. 94) in the Civic Museum at Verona. Here is a wealth of detail. It will be noticed at once that the Italian painters made no attempt

---

* *The Book of Life*, Vol. 8: *Bible Educator Indexes,* arranged and edited by Hall and Wood (1923). Used by permission of The Zondervan Corporation, Grand Rapids, Michigan.

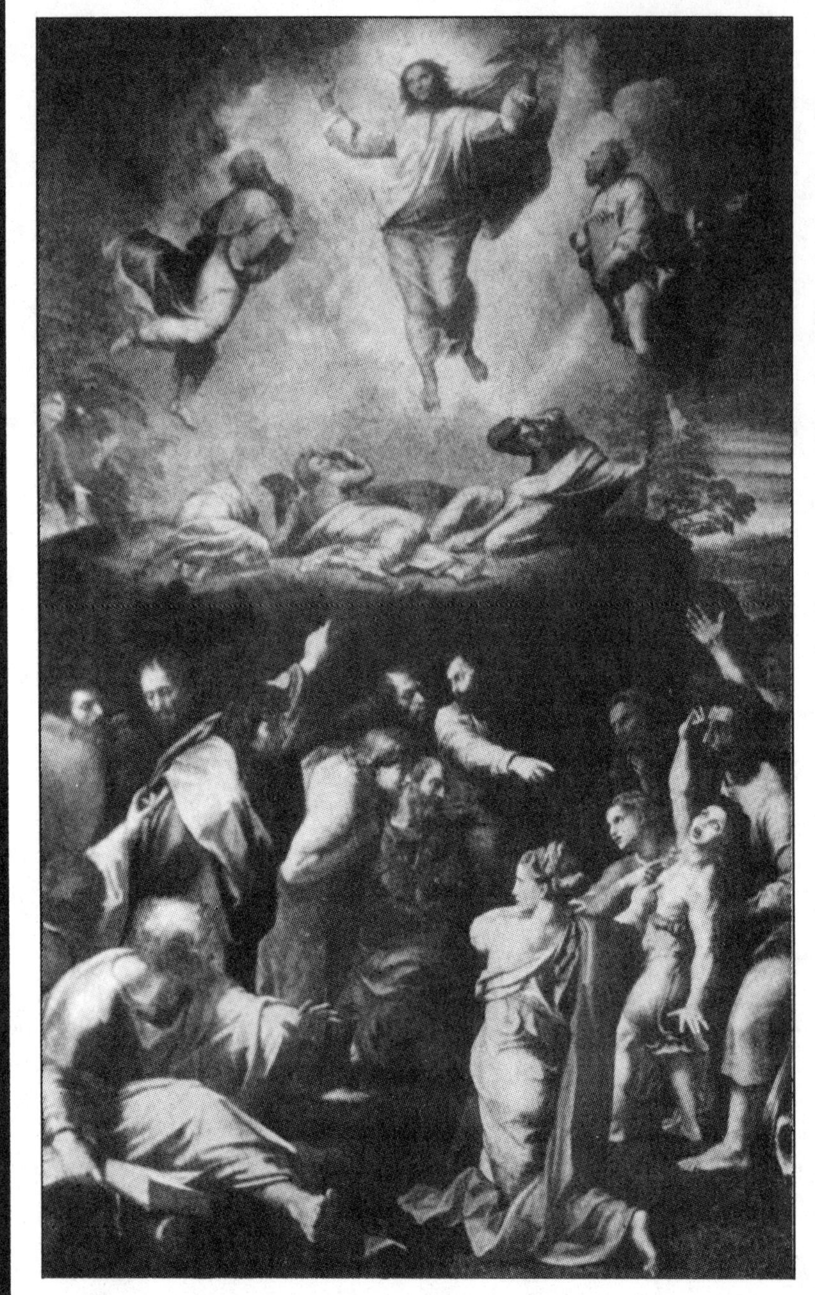

The Transfiguration

by Raphael Sanzio

(1483–1520)

Vatican Gallery, Rome, Italy

This famous painting shows a double scene, the Transfiguration above and the incident of the demoniac boy below.

Above we have a representation of that scene on Mount Hermon where Jesus went to pray, taking with him Peter, James, and John. "And as he prayed, the fashion of his countenance was altered, and his raiment was white and glistening. And behold, there talked with him two men, which were Moses and Elias." At His feet are the three prostrate figures of the dazzled disciples. It is a vision of heavenly peace and serenity. At the left are two kneeling figures representing relatives of the donor, as was the Renaissance fashion.

Below is the scene of noisy crowds and earthly lamentation that met Jesus and His disciples when they came down from the mountain. At the left are nine of the disciples. Facing them is the crowd accompanying a father who calls upon the disciples, in the absence of Jesus, to heal his son. The prayers and demands of the crowd are met with the consternation and helplessness of the disciples. Some point upward, away from the tumult and confusion, to the vision overhead, suggesting that through the Saviour the boy will be cured.

Thus the artist, by placing together these two contrasting scenes of heavenly aspiration and earthly suffering, helps us to understand more clearly and vividly the meaning of these Bible events.

This picture, the last work of the great Raphael, was designed by him, but only the upper part was painted in 1520, when he was stricken with fever, and in thirteen days was dead. This and other unfinished works were left to pupils to complete.

to reproduce the scenery of Palestine. They had never seen it; they had never seen the costumes of its people; so they calmly used as models the people they saw about them, and the scenery with which they were familiar. They introduced figures also of saints who were not living at the time of the pictures; sometimes the donors of the pictures to the church were included as a compliment. We must always remember this and make due allowance. After all, what did it matter to them or to us, if only the picture carried its meaning, told the story?

In this charming picture by Libri, the center of interest is, of course, the child lying on the folds of a garment on a rocky platform. Around the child are grouped the figures of Joseph and Mary and two saints. We know that the saints are Jerome, because the lion which was always the symbol of Jerome is seen in the corner of the picture, and St. John the Baptist, who carries the slender cross with the pennant bearing the words in Latin, "Ecce Dei Agnus," "Behold the Lamb of God," always the symbol of St. John. Mary, dressed as a peasant woman, is looking at the child, and Joseph, an elderly man in a flowing robe, looks down with rather an anxious expression. All the figures have halos. The stable is just a cleft in a great rock, with a rustic canopy built over it. The child will be interested in the ox and the ass, solemnly eating their dinner from woven baskets of a kind peculiar to northern Italy. Then there are two rabbits which have just come out of their home beneath the rock. What place have rabbits in a religious picture? They were put there, perhaps, because the artist knew that children would be interested in them and because he himself had a gentle, child-like heart. The lion seems to be regarding the rabbits with rather a fierce expression. Call the child's attention then to the other details of the picture. There are two figures; perhaps they are farmers or hunters passing by. One has a large knife in a sheath slung at his girdle and carries a staff; the other has some sort of an implement on his shoulder. Down in the valley where the lake or inlet of the sea is crossed by a bridge runs a white road with tiny figures of men in it. There is an old stone farmhouse also. Look closely and you will see a well with a sweep like that once used on New England farms. Then there are still more minor details, – the trees growing out of the cliff, the pebbles, the flowering weeds. All these make up the picture. It is a pleasure to see them all, to think of the artist as he lovingly painted, not only the little Child Jesus, but the little black and white rabbits and the weeds growing out of the rock.

4. Colors and Symbols. In painting, and especially in the painting of the old Italian masters, color had an especial significance. White is for light, purity, innocence. Jesus is clothed in white after the resurrection and Mary, in the picture of the annunciation. Red represents divine love, royalty; white and red together, innocence and love. In the opposite sense red signifies war, blood, hatred, punishment. Blue stands for constancy, truth; Jesus and Mary wear a red tunic and a blue mantle, representing heavenly love and truth. St. John wears the same colors, except that his tunic is blue and his mantle, red. In some cases the colors are red and green. Yellow is the color of the goodness of God, of love, of marriage, of faith. Joseph wears yellow. Peter wears a yellow mantle and a blue tunic. In the opposite sense yellow stands for inconstancy, jealousy, deceit. Judas Iscariot is usually clothed in yellow. Gold suggests brightness, royalty. Green stands for hope of immortality, victory. Violet symbolized love, truth, passion, suffering. These colors are by no means universally used, but this list will be a guide to the meaning of the older pictures.

Emblems also have an important place in the meaning of pictures. The halo or nimbus is painted as a circlet of gold or a radiance extending in a circular form from the head of a holy person. Sometimes, especially in earlier pictures, the halo was pictured as a solid gold disk, sometimes as a golden band around or behind the head. The lamb is the symbol of Christ, the "Lamb of God"; sometimes it is given to John the Baptist, sometimes to St. Agnes. The lion is a symbol of Christ, the lion of the tribe of Judah, used especially in very early Christian art. It is often the companion of Jerome, because of the story that he once pulled a thorn out of a lion's paw, and the lion ever afterward followed and protected him. The peacock is an emblem of immortality; the dove, of the Holy Ghost; the sword, of martyrdom. The arrows are given to St. Sebastian, St. Ursula, and St. Christina, who were martyred by arrows. The wheel stands for St. Catherine. The palm is the emblem of victory. The lily stands for purity; it is often seen in pictures of the annunciation.

In early Christian art the symbols of the evangelists were these: for St. Matthew, a cherub; for St. Mark, a lion; for St. Luke, an ox; for St. John, an eagle. In later art the other disciples are sometimes distinguished by an emblem illustrating in some cases the manner of their death: St. Andrew, by the transverse "St. Andrew's cross";

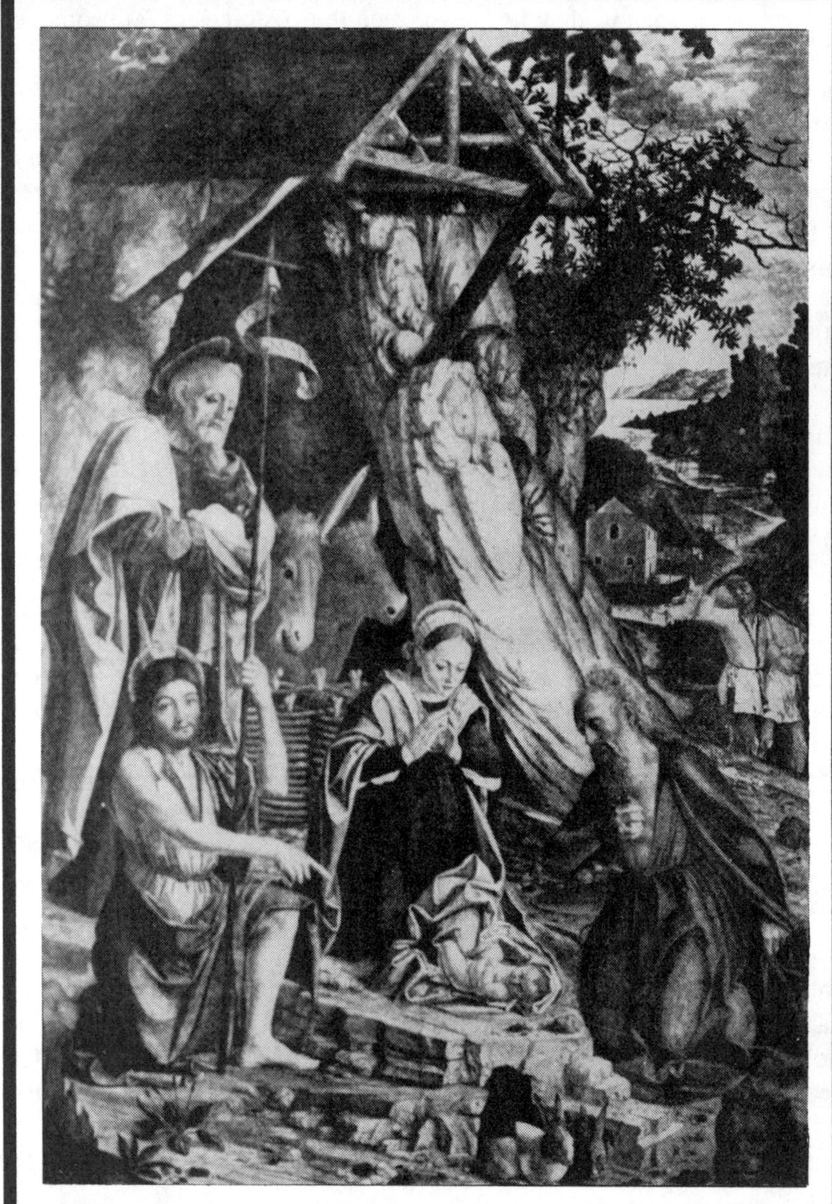

The Nativity

by Girolamo dai Libri

(1474–1556)

Civic Museum, Verona, Italy

This delightful picture called **The Nativity,** *shows Mary, Joseph, John the Baptist, and St. Jerome adoring the Christ Child. How can one tell which figures represent the Baptist and St. Jerome?*

The scene is a rocky, mountainous place where a few flowers and trees have taken root. In the distance, buildings and the shore of a lake are pictured. Near by, two peasants are passing, one shading his eyes and looking at the holy group. Behind the gentle Mary we see a stable in the opening of which an ox and ass are standing. Two rabbits, which seem to have attracted the Babe's attention, and the head of St. Jerome's lion are visible in the right foreground. Do you feel the reposeful devotion expressed by the figures and by the tranquil landscape?

This picture is of the kind known in Italian art as a "sacra conversazione" or communion of sacred personages. It is important to note that the people in devotional pictures of this kind are brought together without relation to historical facts. Thus, John the Baptist, who was actually but six months older than Jesus, appears here as a grown man beside the infant Jesus, and St. Jerome, who lived some four hundred years after Jesus, is shown worshipping the Holy Child. We must not think that the artist did not know the Bible and Church history, but rather must we acquaint ourselves with the true object and feeling of such representations. For here, the primary purpose is to create a spirit of devotion in the beholder by presenting sacred beings whose lives were outstanding examples of faith in Christ.

The painter, Girolamo dai Libri, was born in Verona, Italy. He was educated for a miniaturist and was consequently known as "dai Libri" from the choral books which he illuminated. His fondness of detail and his feeling for the poetic beauty of landscape show clearly in his work. Girolamo was one of the most talented artists in the local school of Verona, but only a minor artist in Italian painting.

St. Peter, by the keys, sometimes by a fish; St. James, by the pilgrim's staff; St. John, by the eagle; St. James the Less, by the club; St. Thomas, by a builder's rule; St. Bartholemew, by a large knife; St. Matthew, by a purse; St. Simon, by a saw or a small cross; Judas, by the money bag; St. Paul, by a sword.

The early leaders and martyrs of the church are usually represented with their own especial symbols. St. Jerome is often seen in pictures. A spare, half-naked, emaciated man with a high forehead, and a long beard, he sometimes has a book as a translator of the Scriptures, and his lion is usually with him. St. Agnes is represented with a lamb; St. Anna is often shown in pictures of Mary, the mother of Jesus; St. Barbara, with a tower, sometimes a palm and a sword; St. Cecilia, the patroness of music, often with a crown of red and white roses. St. Elizabeth, mother of John the Baptist, is often shown in groups of the Holy Family. As a man, St. John the Baptist is sometimes clothed in skins. His emblem is usually a cross and a long slender pole, sometimes with a pennant bearing the words, "Ecce Agnus Dei," "Behold the Lamb of God." St. Sebastian is a young man bound and pierced by arrows.

5. The Story. Not all pictures tell a definite story but many do and each picture has a purpose. The child should be taught to observe the story or meaning of the picture. This will not always be easy and help must be given by the parent.

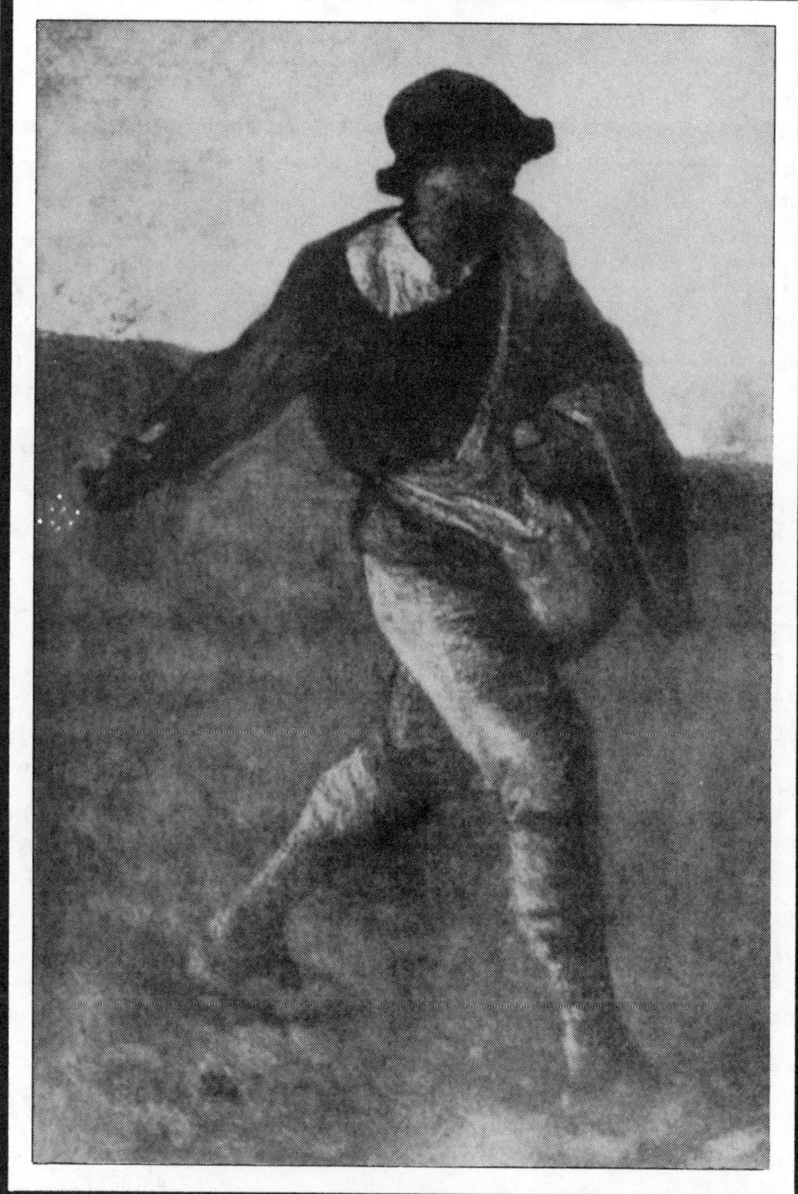

The Sower

by Jean François Millet (1814–1875)

While this famous picture represents a sower in the fields of France it might well have been painted to illustrate the parable, "Behold a sower went forth to sow."

Besides the pictures whose subjects are taken directly from the Bible narrative, there are many which may teach great moral lessons, though they do not illustrate directly Biblical material. The child should be taught to recognize in such pictures the spiritual meaning. Two pictures have been chosen to illustrate this type, – two of the great French artist, Millet: *The Sower,* and *The Angelus.*

Geographical pictures, photographs of localities in the Holy Land, bring very closely to those who cannot travel, the exact aspect of these places which were familiar to the heroes of the Old Testament, to our Lord, and to the apostles. Geographical pictures are valuable also in showing the dress and occupations of the natives of Palestine, which have changed very little.

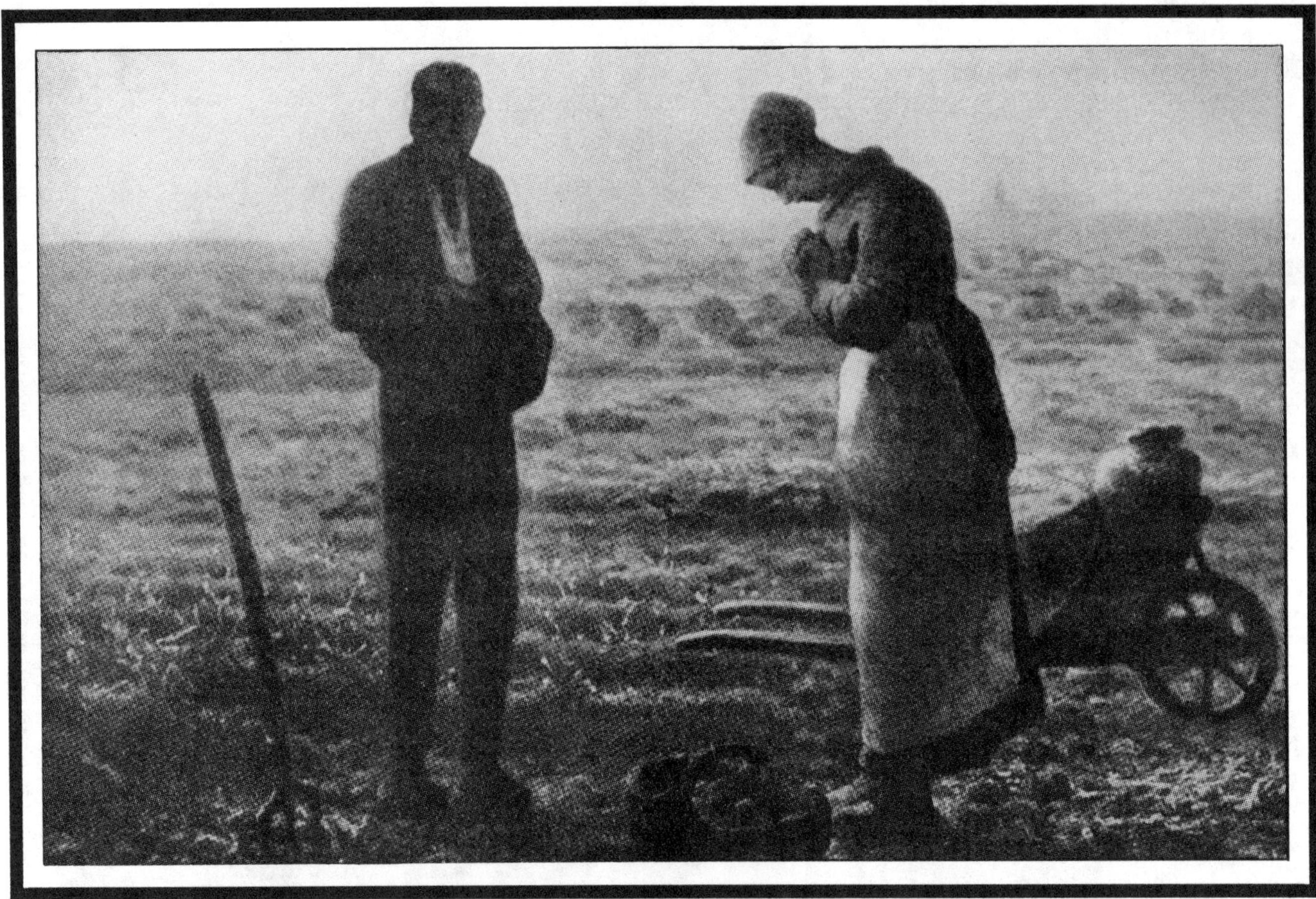

The Angelus

by Jean François Millet
(1814–1875)

In this very famous picture the French peasants working in the fields hear the bells in the far-off church sound The Angelus, the evening call for prayer. They stop work, the man removes his cap, they both bow in an attitude of prayer.

This picture teaches a great lesson of reverence. Even though we are not in church, it is possible to have the attitude of prayer, to remember that God is our father, and to thank him for his goodness.

THE BIBLE AND RELIGIOUS ART

THE WIDE USE OF PICTURES IN EDUCATION

"We ought to form the habit of looking at a beautiful picture every day." – GOETHE

The use of pictures in education is steadily increasing. In the early days the walls of school rooms were bare and unattractive; today there are few schools so poor that they cannot possess at least one copy of some great painting, perhaps in colors, or a good photograph of a magnificant building, or a reproduction of a great historical scene. The textbooks of the public schools are now for the most part attractively illustrated with good pictures.

The use of pictures as an aid to religious education is also becoming general. Fortunately in this field the greatest pictures of the world are upon religious subjects. Religious pictures make an especially strong appeal to young children. A mother wrote recently to a religious journal saying, "A picture of a little girl kneeling at her mother's knee hangs in my children's nursery. The baby girl has studied it so closely that she is not content to kneel anywhere for prayer but at her mother's knee. My other daughter, whose age is ten, likes the picture of Christ in Gethsemane, which hangs in her room, and she always kneels in that attitude."

A little American girl, ten years old, was taken by her parents to see the great picture by Holman Hunt, *The Light of the World,* which hangs in a chapel of Keble College, Oxford, England. After they had left the chapel, her parents missed the little girl, and going back, found that she had returned to the picture and was gazing at it with rapt attention. The same child, when three years old, was seen one day looking with the greatest earnestness at a picture of the head of the suffering Christ, which hung upon the wall of her father's study. After a while she said to herself, "Poor man, dear man!"

Many instances are recorded by library workers of children who come to the library and demand to see some of the great religious pictures. A recent writer tells of a ragged boy from the slums, who came with his little brother to the Art Institute at Chicago, and asked to see "the picture that's so great hanging on the wall." He had been brought by his kindergarten teacher the previous week to see a fine copy of *The Sistine Madonna*. He had returned with his brother to see the picture. They gazed at the picture for a long time and returned again and again to see it.

NO CHILD SHOULD GROW UP WITHOUT OWNING A GREAT PICTURE

Every child should have a religious picture of the very best nature hanging upon the walls of his own room. The constant pervasive influence of a great picture upon the mind of a child cannot be estimated. Never was the need greater than at the present time, when the mind of the child is flooded with sensations received through the eye, – glaring advertising signs; the grotesque pictures, poor in drawing, hideous in color, which almost every child sees every week in the "Sunday supplement"; the pictures, sometimes good, but often poor and demoralizing, at the "movies." To counteract this flood of impressions, we have these great pictures of the past, teaching the divinest truths, glorious in their beauty, executed by master artists. What parent can be so indifferent to the welfare of the child as not to desire this influence for him?

PICTURES CANNOT BE APPRECIATED WITHOUT STUDY

The appreciation of pictures is, like everything else, a matter of close observation and study. While a young child may be attracted and influenced by a great masterpiece, the power to understand and enjoy religious art is gained only by careful attention. The excellence of many paintings of minor rank is very great, the help which they may give to an understanding of the Bible incalculable; but this is often all lost, simply because people do not know what to see in a picture or how to study it. Many business men go to Europe and wander aimlessly through the great galleries, seeing nothing, enjoying nothing, appreciating nothing, simply for lack of a little intelligent application. The study of religious pictures may become a very great source of pleasure to both parent and child, by even a very simple knowledge of the fundamental principles of art.

THE EARLIEST CHRISTIAN ART

The earliest Christian paintings are very rude. Many of the converts to Christianity were people of poverty and small education. They drew at first only the symbols of the new faith. These were the symbols most often used: "the anchor, expressive of hope; the dove, symbolical of the Christian soul released from its earthly tabernacle; the sheep, symbolical of the soul still wandering amid the pastures and deserts of earthly life; the phœnix, 'the palm bird,' emblematical of eternity and the resurrection; the fish, typical of our Saviour – from the word, ἰχθύς, formed by the initial letters of the titles of our Lord – Ἰησοῦς Χριστὸς Θεοῦ Υἱὸς Σωτήρ – 'Jesus Christ, the Son of God, the Saviour'; the ship, representing the Church militant, sometimes seen carried on the back of the fish, bread, represented with fish, sometimes carried in a basket on its back, sometimes with it on a table, in allusion to the multiplication of the loaves and fishes – in ancient times a meal was not thought complete without fish, whenever it could be had, – 'bread and fish' went together like 'bread and butter' in our time; a female figure praying; a vine, in allusion to the Church; an olive branch, as a sign of peace; a palm branch, as a sign of victory and martyrdom."

These symbols were rudely scratched, where they may still be seen on the walls of the passages of the catacombs at Rome, those subterranean retreats where the Christians worshiped to escape persecution, and where thousands are buried. They are also upon the walls of the chapels in the catacombs. Recently there have been discovered in a catacomb just opened two portraits believed to be very early, perhaps contemporaneous, portraits of Peter and Paul. They are very striking pictures, of better workmanship than is usual at this period.

THE GLORIOUS MOSAICS

Later, when the age of martyrdom was over and Christianity began to build its own churches, often upon the ruins of pagan temples, a new form of art came into being. The people were still ignorant and unlettered. How better could Bible stories be taught to the people than by picturing them upon the walls of the places of worship? These early pictures were of mosaic. They are called "Byzantine" because they originated in Byzantium, the old Constantinople. There are marvelously beautiful examples of this art still surviving at Ravenna in Italy, the old capital of the later Roman Empire, at the Palatine Chapel of the Royal Palace at Palerno in Sicily and at the great church at Monreale, a suburb of Palermo. This mosaic work is made of thousands of little cubes of glass, in glowing colors, blue, green, red, gold, creamy white, in more than twenty different shades. The artist used these cubes just as the artist in oils uses his colors. Laying his cubes in a bed of cement upon the walls of the church, he depicted saints and angels, Jesus enthroned in glory, the whole history of the Old and New Testaments. In one of the churches at Ravenna, there is a splendid procession of saints, men on one side, women on the other, their robes brilliant with color, shining with actual jewels and mother of pearl. You can almost see them march and hear the trumpets of victory blow – "For all the saints who from their labors rest, Alleluia! Alleluia!" The colors of the great oil paintings have faded, but these colors are as fresh and glowing as on the day in which they were laid. No photographs can, of course, do justice to these pictures of everlasting charm. The drawing seems crude and the figures seem awkward, but they are really glorious in their beauty, and they taught the first great lessons of Christianity to the people of that age. The mosaics represent Jesus and Mary, the saints, and apostles as very glorious in gorgeous robes glittering with jewels.

HOW KNOWLEDGE WAS SAVED TO EUROPE AFTER THE BARBARIAN DELUGE

After this period Europe was overrun by the barbarians of the North, and almost everything which was precious and beautiful was destroyed.

Then came the forming of the great monastic establishments, and Christian art was saved by the monks, who themselves practised, and taught the people, not only the practical arts – agriculture, metal-working, building; – but also the fine arts and crafts. However much monastic life may have degenerated later, the world owes to the monks of this period all its possessions of knowledge, saved from the utter wreck of the barbarian invasion. "Pictures are the books of the ignorant," said Augustine. It was necessary to teach the Bible to people who had no books, who could not have read them if they had had them. So the Bible stories began to appear again upon the walls of the churches in pictures and sculpture, crude at first but gradually growing more beautiful. The Bibles of this period were lettered on parchment and adorned with exquisitely beautiful initials and miniature pictures of Biblical scenes and characters.

THE BIBLE IN STONE

Then came the great building age all over Europe, lasting for nearly four hundred years, when the wonderful Gothic cathedrals were built, – such glorious buildings as those of Amiens, Chartres, Rheims, in France; Lincoln and Durham in England; Burgos in Spain. It was a time of great religious fervor. Everywhere over Europe churches were built, not only the great cathedrals but churches in every town and village. They were built not by ecclesiastics but by the people themselves, "a free will offering unto the Lord." When the mighty cathedral of Chartres was built, even the women harnessed themselves to the carts upon which the stones were drawn. The building itself and its adornments, the most glorious windows in the world, the sculptures which tell the Bible history in stone – were all produced in the little town of Chartres by the people themselves. These great buildings were built and the Bible was illustrated so completely in the carvings of the great western portals that Ruskin called that of Amiens, "The Bible of Amiens." Every important incident of Bible history is portrayed. In the chapter-house of the cathedral at Salisbury, England, there is a frieze in which the whole Bible history is shown. While these sculptures are crude, still they are very vigorous and expressive, and there was no more effective way of teaching the Bible to the people of that time.

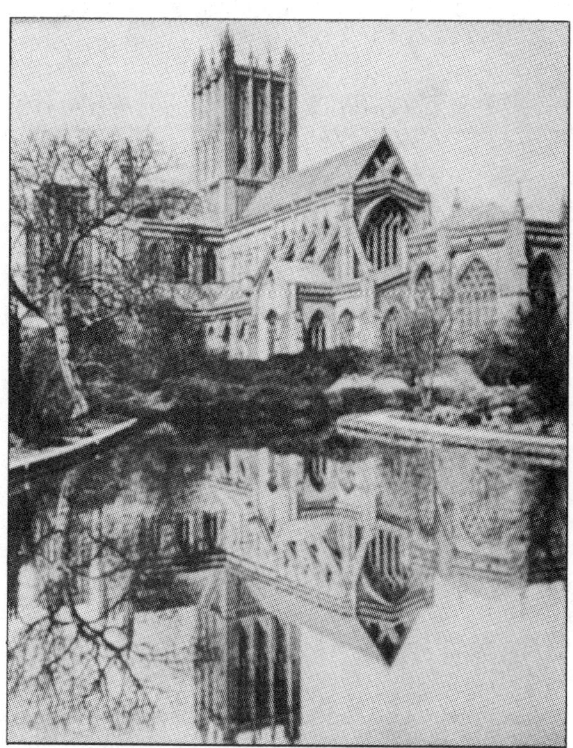

WELLS CATHEDRAL

THE WEST FRONT IS COVERED WITH SCULPTURE DEPICTING SCENES FROM THE BIBLE

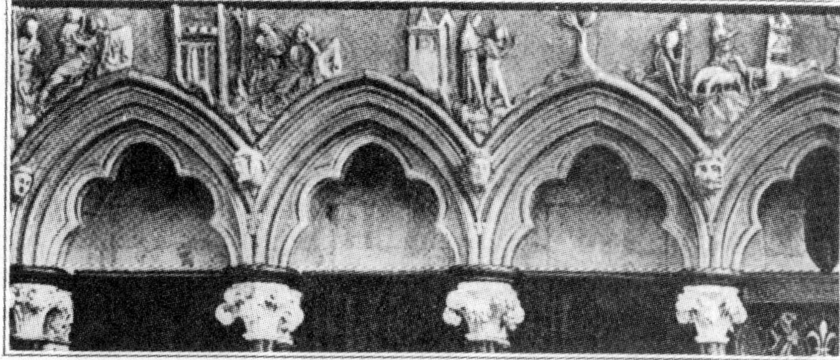

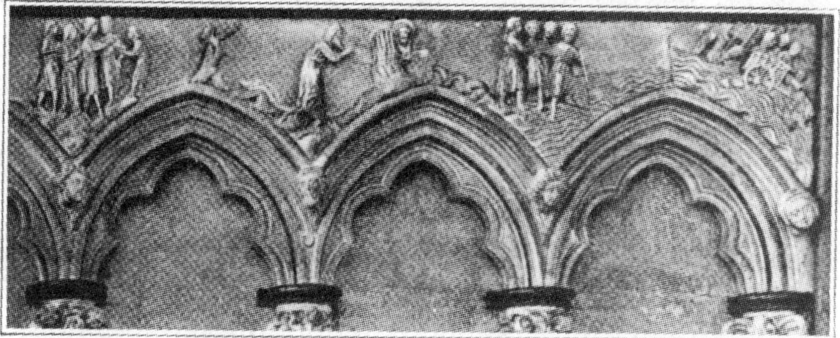

SCULPTURE IN CHAPTER HOUSE AT SALISBURY CATHEDRAL

UPPER, LEFT TO RIGHT: ISAAC BLESSING JACOB, THE BLESSING OF ESAU, REBEKAH SENDING JACOB TO PADAN ARAM, AND THE MEETING OF JACOB AND RACHEL

LOWER, LEFT TO RIGHT: JOSEPH ASSURING HIS BRETHREN OF HIS PROTECTION, MOSES AND THE BURNING BUSH, THE PASSAGE OF THE RED SEA, AND THE DESTRUCTION OF THE EGYPTIAN ARMY

EARLY ITALIAN PAINTING

In Italy there began to be felt the need of a finer way of teaching the Bible than by sculpture, and out of this desire came the development of pictorial art. The earliest period, which is called "The Gothic period," was from about 1250 to 1400. Among the earliest painters were Cimabue and Giotto. The paintings were upon the walls of churches in fresco, and the subjects were practically all Biblical. The influence of the mosaic art of the earlier days is seen, and yet there is one very important difference. The pictures of Cimabue and Giotto of the earliest school of Fra Angelico, whose pictures greatly resemble those of Giotto, are extremely simple. The gorgeous robes of Mary disappear; and she becomes a sweet and natural woman, in the plain dress of the peasant. The paintings seem flat. The figures are often poorly drawn, but there is a sincerity, a power about them which is appreciated when they are carefully studied.

THE PIONEERS OF MODERN ART

Then came the periods of the early Renaissance, 1400–1500, and later Renaissance, 1500–1600. To these periods belong the mighty masters: Raphael, Leonardo da Vinci, Correggio, Michael Angelo. At this time classic art was studied; careful attention was given to drawing, color, "chiaroscuro" (light and shadow). While painters gradually chose more secular subjects, even during the later periods religious subjects were most often used. It must be borne in mind that this great development of art, the greatest the world has ever seen, was called out by the Church and was devoted to the Church in its efforts to teach the Bible to the people. Many of these paintings are in galleries now, but originally they were painted for the walls and altars of churches.

CHRISTIAN ART THE HERITAGE OF ALL THE WORLD

It must be constantly borne in mind that the Church of this time was the sole Church of the people. It was not Protestant nor Catholic, for the division into Protestant and Catholic did not come until the 16th century, the time of the Reformation. All the beautiful buildings, all the paintings and sculpture, all the heroic lives of saint and martyr, the prayers of St. Augustine, the holiness of St. Francis, belong just as much to the Protestant Church as to the Catholic Church. The past is our heritage and our glory. Because two sons of the same house part and go in different directions, it does not follow that either forfeits the memories and the precious heritage of the old home. We may enjoy the great paintings of this period, feeling happily secure that they belong to us, not to any one Church, but to all the Christian world.

NOTES ON THE GREAT PAINTERS OF RELIGIOUS PICTURES

The personalities of the great artists are of much interest and value in the interpretation of their work. A few notes are accordingly given to aid in such interpretation. One of the editors has recently visited nearly all the great galleries and churches of Europe, where he has seen the majority of the pictures in this work. Some notes of this pilgrimage are also given.

1. Early Christian Martyrs. We have no record of the names of those who made the first crude drawings in the catacombs. A visit to such catacombs as that of St. Calixtus in Rome and the even more extensive underground galleries and chapels of Syracuse in Sicily is a very moving experience. Here are symbols in thousands. These are most touching memorials of faith and hope and affections.

2. The Mosaics. The editor has seen the mosaics of Palermo in the Palatine Chapel of the Royal Palace, and those in the cathedral at Monreale, a suburb of Palermo, and most interesting of all, those at Ravenna in the great churches of San Vitale, St. Apollinaris in Nuova, and St. Apollinaris in Classe. It is impossible to describe the fresh beauty of these wonderful pictures in mosaics. They told the whole story of the Bible in colors to people who could not read, but who could be educated and moved by these wonderful pictures. It is marvelous to see how these old artists working with little pieces of stone managed to give expression to the faces of these characters and to make the scenes vivid and realistic. The photographic examples of these mosaics may seem dull, but they show how the people of that far-off day studied and loved the Bible stories.

3. The Bible in Stone. A subject for endless study is the Bible in stone as it is found sculptured on the porches and walls of all the great Gothic cathedrals and churches. These figures are even less accurately drawn than those of the mosaics. Some may even seem hideous and grotesque. They doubtless did not seem so to the people who carved them and learned the Bible stories through them. All the stories of the Bible are thus portrayed, in stone or in bronze, on the great doors. While these figures are crude, they are full of life and character. The main thing is that they accomplished their purpose. They carried the knowledge of the Bible in a vivid and comprehensive way to people who could not read. Stone and bronze were not the only materials used. The Biblical scenes were carved in ivory, wood, and gold and embroidered in tapestry. In the city of Milan, in one of the churches, there is an altar of solid gold upon which are portrayed in panels scenes from the life of Jesus. This is the sole remaining example of the goldsmith's art of this period.

4. The Early Masters. CIMABUE (1240–1302) was the first great painter to abandon mosaic and use the new medium. He began to paint pictures of the life of Jesus which may still be seen on the walls of the churches of Florence. Then came a greater painter, his pupil, Giotto. Cimabue found Giotto one day, a shepherd boy with his sheep. The lad was drawing pictures of his sheep with a pointed stone on a smooth piece of slate. The sketches showed so much talent that Cimabue asked the shepherd boy to become his pupil.

GIOTTO DI BONDONE (1266–1336) became one of the greatest painters of any age. Giotto was a man of a sweet and child-like nature, gracious to all with whom he came in contact. A story is told which illustrates his skill and his sense of humor. A messenger came from a prince to ask for specimens of Giotto's drawings. The artist took a sheet of paper, dipped a pen in red and firmly fixing his arm against his side so as to make a compass of it, with a turn of his pen made a perfect circle.

Having done it, he turned smiling to the courtier and said, "Here is the drawing." But he, thinking he was being laughed at, asked, "Am I to have no other drawing than this?" "This is enough and too much," replied Giotto; "send it with the others and see if it will be understood." The messenger, seeing that he could get nothing else, departed ill-pleased, not doubting that he had been made a fool of. However, sending the other drawings to the prince with the names of those who had made them, he sent also Giotto's, relating how he had made the circle without moving his arm and without compasses, which when the prince and many of his courtiers understood, they saw that Giotto must surpass greatly all the other painters of his time. This thing being told, there arose from it a proverb which is still used about men of coarse clay, "you are rounder than the O of Giotto," which proverb is not only good because of the occasion from which it sprang, but also still more for its significance, which consists in its ambiguity, tondo, "round," meaning in Tuscany not only a perfect circle, but also slowness and heaviness of mind.

The religious paintings of Giotto are characterized by a supreme simplicity and dramatic power. They are child-like in their naturalness and in the power to tell a story clearly and convincingly. Compared with the old mosaics, they are extremely simple. There is none of the regal color and splendor of the mosaic. Joseph is a carpenter and Mary, sweet and tender, is a woman of Nazareth. It is true that there are crudities in drawing. Giotto had not mastered the art of painting accurately figures or landscapes, but he was one of the very early pioneers of his art. Learn to forget any such imperfections and look for the story told by the hand of a master. There are pictures which are better drawn, more elaborate, glowing more richly in color, but none more sincere, more devout, more truly spiritual in their nature. When the editor visited Padua, it so happened that an exhibition of modern paintings was being held in the ancient guild hall. These paintings seemed monotonous, dreary, uninspired. Some were simply commonplace, some were grotesque in their attempts to be original and daring. After seeing these, we went to the little "Chapel of the Arena," the walls of which are covered with the frescoes of the great master. It was a holy place. We sat spellbound, not heeding the passage of time, before these wonderful pictures, faded, imperfect in many respects, but possessing an immortal significance and a fadeless charm. The Chapel of the Arena is one of the most precious shrines of art in all the world. Several of these pictures are given in *The Book of Life*. Study them with reverence and remember that a man who possessed a simple and child-like heart, who "walked with God," poured out his soul to tell to people, who had no other means of knowing, the great stories of the Bible and especially to illustrate the life of the Master.

Another of the great early masters was **Fra Angelico** (Giovanni Guido, 1387–1455), who was for thirty years a monk in the monastery of San Marco in Florence, the monastery which also sheltered the great reformer and martyr, Savonarola. He painted his pictures on the walls of the cells of the monastery, where they may still be seen. There is also a wonderful collection of the paintings of the master in rooms of the monastery recently opened. It is one of the most inspiring places in the world, this old monastery, now owned by the State. Here the painter worked not for money, not for fame, but for the "love of the working" in the true spirit of sincerity and faith. His work in many respects resembles that of Giotto, as it naturally would, for both were men of sincerity, simplicity, and spirituality. It is said that Fra Angelico began all his paintings with prayer, and that he would alter nothing he had ever begun, so firmly did he believe in the guidance of the Spirit. He might have been rich, but did not care about it, saying that true riches are nothing else but being content with little. He might have governed many and would not, saying that it was less troublesome to obey and one was less likely to err in obeying. He was never seen in anger.

The same things may be said of the work of this great artist and devout man that have been said of the work of Giotto, and it is a most instructive exercise to compare the pictures of these two early painters of religious pictures.

Raphael Sanzio (1483–1520). Raphael was one of the greatest – some consider him the very greatest – of the world's artists. He was born on Good Friday, 1483. His father, Giovanni Santi, was an artist, but of no distinction. Nevertheless, he was a good teacher, and Raphael received his early education from him. His father took the boy, who early began to show great talent, to Perugia, and placed him under the tutelage of Perugino, one of the best teachers of his time. The boy showed great ability and soon was able to imitate his master so closely that it was impossible to tell his work from that of Perugino.

From Perugia he went to Florence and then to Rome, where he painted the masterly frescoes in the Vatican. *The Sistine Madonna* is the crown of all his work, one of the very greatest pictures in the world. The great number of his pictures shows how untiring was his industry, and the quality reveals his supreme genius. He was a man of the very highest moral and intellectual character, seeking the noblest and the best.

Vasari, most famous of biographers of artists, says of Raphael, "In addition to the benefits which this great master conferred on art, being as he was its best friend, we have the further obligation to him of having taught us by his life in what manner we should comport ourselves towards great men, as well as towards those of lower degree, and even towards the lowest; nay there was among his many extraordinary gifts one of such value and importance, that I can never sufficiently admire it and always think thereof with astonishment. This was the power accorded to him by Heaven, of bringing all who approached his presence into harmony . . . all, I do not say of the inferior grades only, but even those who lay claim to be great personages became as of one mind, once they began to labour in the society of Raphael, continuing in such unity and concord, that all harsh feelings and evil dispositions became subdued and disappeared at the sight of him . . . . Whenever any other painter, whether known to Raphael or not, requested any design or assistance, of whatever kind, at his hands, he would invariably leave his work to do him service. He was never seen to go to Court but surrounded and accompanied, as he left his house, by some fifty painters, who attended him thus to give evidence of the honour in which they held him."

Leonardo da Vinci (1452–1519). This great painter was born at the little town of Vinci near Florence. He was a genius not only in painting but in many other lines. He was a great architect, sculptor, engineer, and inventor, and, in a lesser degree, he was an expert in the fields of mathematical astronomy and botany. He had some skill as a poet and musician.

His greatest picture, perhaps the best known and most famous picture in the world, rivaling in this respect *The Sistine Madonna*, is *The Last Supper*, painted for the refectory of the monastery of Santa Maria delle

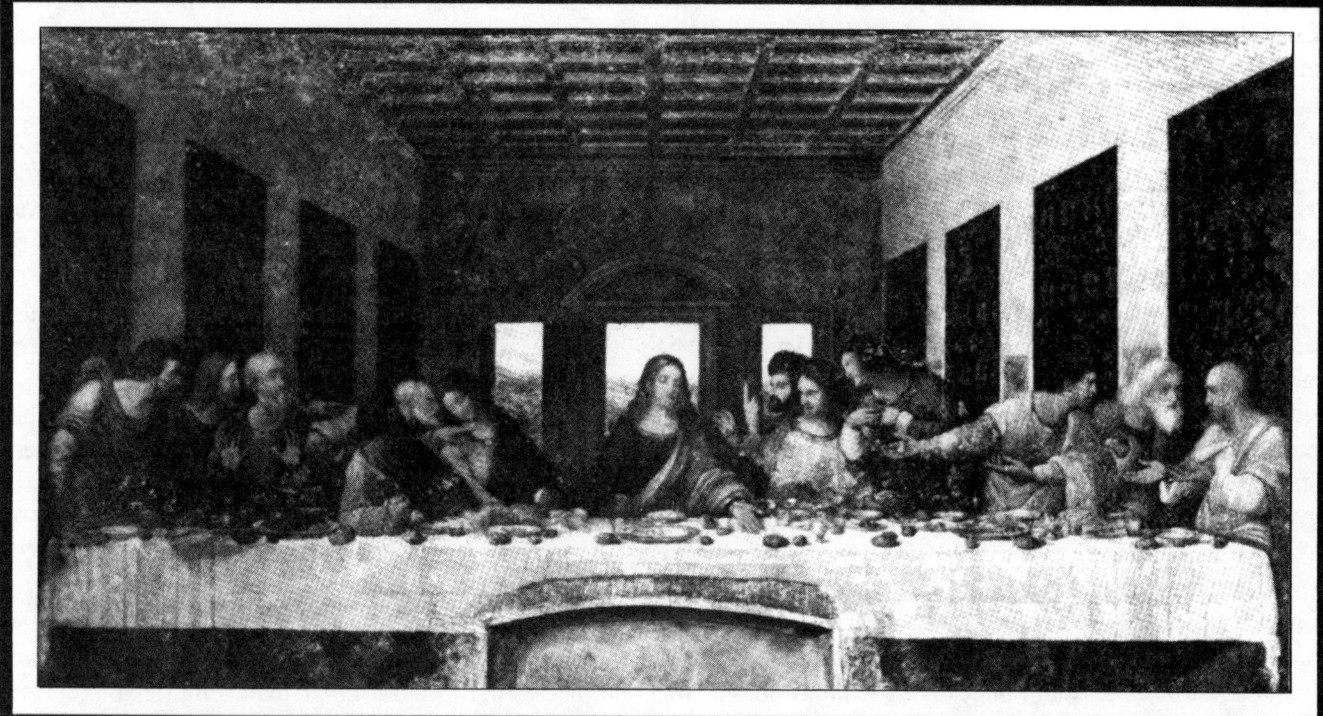

The Last Supper

by Leonardo da Vinci

(1452–1519)

*Next to Raphael's **Sistine Madonna,** da Vinci's **The Last Supper** is the most popular picture in Italian art. Leonardo worked on it for at least three years. It decorates the end wall of the former refectory of the Monastery of Santa Maria delle Grazie in Milan, Italy. It is so simple and impressive that it stamps itself on all memories and remains the greatest expression of the subject in painting. It suggests awe and tenderness, and religious emotion is stirred to tragic depths. Jesus has just said, "One among you shall betray me," and this unexpected announcement of treachery has thrown the twelve apostles into confusion.*

We see Jesus sitting motionless in the midst of the tumult which his announcement has caused. On his left, Thomas is pointing and seeming to ask, "One of us?" and James throws his arms out widely "as if he suddenly saw an abyss opening before him." Jesus alone remains calm, his eyes fixed downward, his hands stretched out listlessly with the gesture of one who has said all he has to say. His is the terrible silence which leaves no hope and seems only to repeat the utterance, "Yea, it is so, one there is among you who will betray me."

The mural, finished in 1498 possesses power which time cannot dim. It shows that eternal values are not measured in terms of material perfection, of newness, or of commercial value. This picture as it stands today is priceless. Even if it could be removed, the Italian nation would not part with it for any price. It is one of the supreme productions of that artistic people, a possession which is shared with the world.

Grazie in Milan. We were almost afraid to visit the picture for fear of disappointment. No picture has received harder treatment. The room in which it was painted has been inundated by water. It has been used in time of war as a stable and storage house. The picture has been frequently restored, but there was no disappointment when we came out of the sunshine of the streets of Milan into this cool, quiet room, paneled in dark oak, containing no furniture, nothing but the picture at the end. We sat down as others did on the benches at the side of the room and gazed with reverence upon that marvelous picture which conveys, as perhaps no other picture in the world conveys, the very spirit of the Master and that company of the apostles gathered for the Last Supper. The power of the picture, abused and defaced as it has been, shows better than anything else that the most precious things of the world are not material but spiritual.

Michelangelo Buonarroti (1475–1564). It is generally considered that the four greatest painters of the world were Raphael, Leonardo da Vinci, Titian, and Michelangelo. In his boyhood Michelangelo was bound for three years to Ghirlandajo, and attracted the notice of the great patron of art, Lorenzo de Medici, who gave him a home in his own palace. Although he was at first exclusively a sculptor and distrusted his powers as a painter, his wonderful mural decorations in the Vatican, in the Sistine Chapel, have raised Michelangelo to the very highest rank as a painter. In personal character he was distinguished for his tremendous capacity for toil. His innate strength is impressed upon all that he ever accomplished. He has been called a Titan among men.

Andrea Verrocchio (1435–1488). Verrocchio was another universal genius like da Vinci. He was a goldsmith, a master in perspective, a sculptor, a wood carver, a painter, a musician, and for those early days a student of science.

Sandro Botticelli (Alessandro Filipepi, 1447–1510). Botticelli's lovely pictures of the Madonna show a characteristic sadness and delicacy of expression. He was one of the first to paint other than religious pictures.

Titian (Tiziano Vecellio, 1477–1576). Titian is reckoned among the very greatest of the world's painters. He was a Venetian and his pictures partake of the gorgeous and sensuous beauty of that rich city of the sea. His pictures as a rule are not marked by deep spirituality like those of Raphael.

Among other great Italian painters represented in the pictures in *The Book of Life* are Pinturrichio, Crivelli, the Bellini Brothers, Francia, Correggio, Borgognone, Gozzoli, Melozzo da Forli.

An artist who must be reckoned among the greatest is **Bartolomé Estéban Murillo** (1618–1682), born at Seville, Spain. He painted very many religious pictures and especially those beautiful Madonnas with the Infant Jesus which are so much loved, more popular perhaps than those of any painter except Raphael.

Peter Paul Rubens (1577–1640) is the greatest of the Flemish school of painting. His *Descent from the Cross* in the Cathedral at Antwerp, Belgium, must be counted among the masterpieces of all time. Had he continued his early style, he would have been among the very greatest of painters. His later style is, however, heavy, gross, and sensuous.

Anthony van Dyck (1599–1641), first among the actual pupils of Rubens, is especially famous for his portraits. Religious subjects, however, were treated in his earlier years.

Rembrandt van Ryn (1607–1669) is the foremost painter of the Dutch school. The characteristic feature of his technique is his treatment of light and shade. A profound student of humanity, he reveals his interest both in his secular and religious pictures. His "Christ" is a universal Christ, present among the multitudes of Amsterdam as really as among the crowds of Capernaum.

The English Pre-Raphaelites were a group of painters who went back to the style of the early painters before Raphael for their inspiration. Some of the religious pictures of this group, which includes Hunt, Rossetti, Millais, Brown, Burne-Jones, Watts, and others, possess a deep spirituality.

Albert Dürer (1471–1528) was born in Nüremberg, Bavaria, and is the most celebrated painter of Germany. He studied in Venice and formed an intimacy with Giovanni Bellini. Raphael was his friend and admirer. He was not only an artist but he was an author of some note. Besides his paintings, he made many wood cuts and he is also said to be the inventor of etchings and of wood cuts in two colors. He was a warm friend of Martin Luther and some of his pictures were painted with the express purpose of persuading people to a personal study of the Bible.

BIBLE STORIES TOLD BY CRAFTSMEN OF THE EARLY CENTURIES

The following pictures, which are used by the courtesy of the Metropolitan Museum of Art, New York, show how universally the Bible was taught by means of the crafts. These stories were depicted not only in stone and mosaic upon the exterior and interior of the great churches, but they were illustrated also in many different materials – ivory, wood, silver, stained glass. The vast majority of the people of these centuries were unable to read and this constant portrayal of the Bible even upon familiar objects of household use made the incidents of the Bible almost universally known.

This work may seem crude and even inartistic to us, but it must be remembered that it is the work of very early periods and it must be studied from a devotional rather than from an artistic standpoint. The craftsman in his shop doing the best he could with the material at hand and his own limited knowledge was a real preacher of the Bible to the people. While this work may seem primitive, compare it with some of the illustrative work of the present time, which is not only crude and bad from an artistic standpoint, and not only teaches no great moral lesson as the craftsmen of the Middle Ages attempted to do, but leaves an effect which is often vicious and harmful.

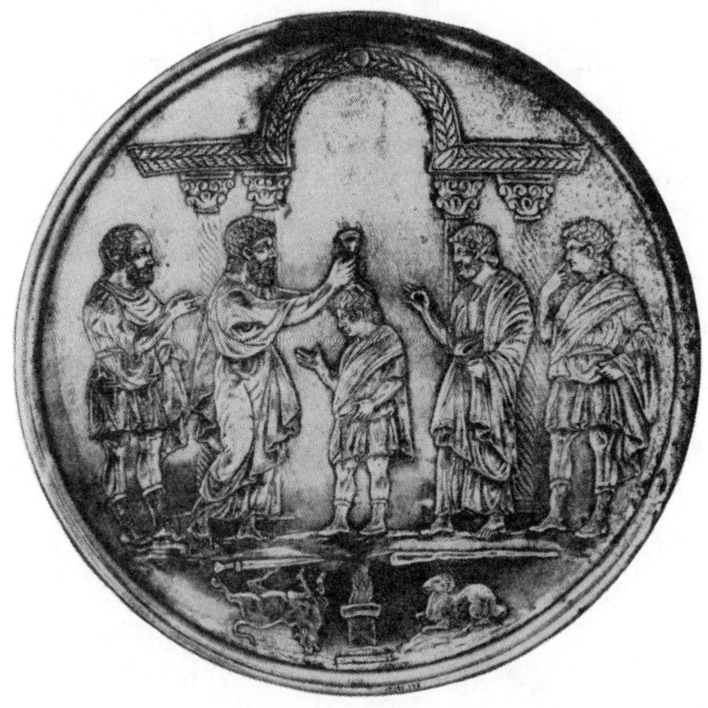

DAVID ANOINTED BY SAMUEL – A BIBLE STORY TOLD IN SILVER
THIS PICTURE IS OF BYZANTINE MOSAIC ON SILVER. THE ARTICLE IS A SILVER DISH.

APPENDIX III

READY REFERENCE

SUMMARIZED AND PRESENTED BY ELIZABETH YOUMANS

THE PHILOSOPHY OF THE PRINCIPLE APPROACH

"The Principle Approach is America's historic Christian method of Biblical scholarship which makes God's Truths the foundation of every subject in the school curriculum."[1] It incorporates seven minimal Biblical principles, identified by Miss Slater, co-founder of the Foundation for American Christian Education, that explain the relationship between Christian character and America's history and government. In Noah Webster's 1828 Dictionary, the word ***principle*** is defined as: "the cause, source, or origin; the first cause; that from which a thing proceeds; ground; foundation; that which supports... a series of actions or of reasoning." Principles are **seeds**, the **internal causes** for external conditions.

THE SEVEN PRINCIPLES (Described on the next page):

1. God's Principle of Individuality
2. The Christian Principle of Self-Government
3. America's Heritage of Christian Character
4. "Conscience is the Most Sacred Property"
5. The Christian Form of Our Government
6. How the Seed of Local Self-Government is Planted
7. The Christian Principle of American Political Union

The Principle Approach is the Biblical method of scholarship that birthed America's Christian Republic and her noble Christian character. Christian scholarship, like salvation, is individual and internal and begins by restoring the **4 R's – Researching, Reasoning, Relating, and Recording** – to their identification in the various curriculum subjects. "Truth becomes the private possession of the individual by application of the 4 R's. Each one educates himself in the unchanging laws of God's Word, the primary source of all knowledge and wisdom.... By means of Christian scholarship every sphere of human activity is brought under the subjection and authority of Biblical principles."[2]

1. The Principle Approach is **expansive** not evolutionary. It gives the **whole** from the beginning rather than building as in evolution. The rudiments and tools for every subject are presented to every student each year and are expanded throughout the grade levels. Against the backdrop of the whole, the separate elements unfold.

2. The Principle Approach is **reflective learning** as opposed to rote learning. It produces **mastery** of the subject.

3. God's Word and His principles are used to illumine and bring form to each subject. Scripture is the standard for discerning truth from error.

4. The curriculum is predicated on the Christian idea of man and government. Christian liberty provides a different foundation, development, and use of a subject than the bondage of the pagan view.

5. The Principle Approach encourages the development and use of Christian character, liberating the God-given potential in every student. It produces an enterprising spirit bearing the fruit of **productivity**.

---

[1] Rosalie J. Slater, *Teaching and Learning America's Christian History: The Principle Approach.* F.A.C.E.: San Francisco (1965), p. 83.

[2] Katherine Dang, *A Guide to American Christian Education: The Principle Approach* by James B. Rose. A.C.H.I., Palo Cedro, CA (1987), p. 15.

SEVEN PRINCIPLES OF THE PRINCIPLE APPROACH

1. **God's Principle of Individuality:** Everything in God's universe reveals His infinity and diversity. Each person is a unique creation of God, designed to express the nature of Christ individually in society. The quality of man's government is primarily determined in his heart.

2. **The Christian Principle of Self-Government:** God ruling internally from the heart of the individual. In order to have true liberty man must be governed internally by the Spirit of God rather than by external forces. Government is first individual then extends to the home, church, and community.

3. **America's Heritage of Self-Government:** The image of Christ engraved upon the individual within, bringing dominion and change to his external environment. The model of American Christian character is the Pilgrim character with these qualities:

   Faith and Steadfastness
   Brotherly Love
   Christian Care
   Diligence and Industry
   Liberty of Conscience

4. **"Conscience Is the Most Sacred of All Property:"** God requires faithful stewardship of all His gifts, especially the internal property of our conscience, thoughts, and convictions. This is a tool for self-government as each child learns the revelation of consent. Each individual governs his life through the voluntary consent to do right or wrong and is protected by laws established by the consent of the governed.

5. **The Christian Form of Our Government:** The divine flow of spiritual power and force through self-governing individuals whose God-given rights are protected by laws established by their elected representatives. Proper government requires a balance of internal power and its external form as seen in the separation of powers and its dual form with checks and balances.

6. **How the Seed of Local Self-Government Is Planted:** Christian self-government begins with salvation and education in God's Law and Love and flows to governing oneself, one's home, church, and community.

7. **The Christian Principle of American Political Union:** Internal agreement or unity, which is invisible, produces an external union, which is visible in the spheres of government, economics, and home and community life. Before two or more individuals can act effectively together, they must first be united in spirit in their purposes and convictions.

THE PROVIDENTIAL VIEW OF HISTORY

PROVIDENCE: THE HAND OF GOD IN HISTORY

"The hand of our God is upon all them for good that seek him; but his power and his wrath is against all them that forsake him."

[EZRA 8:22]

"In *theology,* the care and superintendence which God exercises over his creatures. He that acknowledges a creation and denies a *providence,* involves himself in a palpable contradiction; for the same power which caused a thing to exist is necessary to continue its existence. Some persons admit a *general providence,* but deny a *particular providence,* not considering that a *general providence* consists of *particulars.* A belief in divine *providence,* is a source of great consolation to good men. By *divine providence* is often understood God himself."

– NOAH WEBSTER, *American Dictionary* (1828)

The Providence of God in history is a Biblical doctrine. Divine Providence, understood as God Himself, filled the literature of England and America for over 500 years until the 20th century. Abundant evidence can be found in the original historical documents. The American Christian philosophy of education and government is predicated upon the teaching of the Providential view of history. As American Christians we know something of the saving grace of Christ, but very little about how God brought forth this nation. This ignorance of the Hand of God in America has diluted our love for our nation and our uniquely Christian institutions. If we do not know of God's directing Hand in America's past, how can we be certain of it today or in the future? The consequence of this uncertainty is the lack of knowledge of our own call and purpose in God's plan for us as individuals and the nation at large. Raised in a secular educational environment, America and Christianity have become separated in our thinking. As identified by her in an address to the Pilgrim Seminar in Plymouth, Verna M. Hall profiled modern Christians in two categories: One group is "known for attempting to make Christianity more human, and more like secular institutions in attempting to solve our national problems. Indeed it is difficult to tell where this type of Christianity leaves off and good humanism begins. The other group has become so concerned with endeavoring to defend the faith itself, that they have withdrawn almost completely from the affairs of man in his daily walk.... Forgetting or forsaking the Hand of God in history, forgetting or forsaking the Word of God as our American political textbook, our economic textbook, our social, cultural, educational textbook; this alone has produced the results we have in our nation today."[1] **Providence** is the ***key*** to understanding history as it reveals God's Hand moving in the affairs of individuals and of nations to fulfill His purposes here on earth. It presents the **whole view** from eternity's perspective. It plants **hope** and **purpose** in the hearts and minds of individuals, challenging them to assume their God-ordained purposes in directing human events.

TEACHING HISTORY PROVIDENTIALLY ANSWERS:

Who? **God**
What? **Events and Individuals**
Where? **Geography – the Stage for Man's Activities**
Why? **The Gospel**

---

[1] *A Guide to American Christian Education for the Home and School: The Principle Approach* by James B. Rose. A.C.H.I., Palo Cedro, CA (1987), p. 28.

THE CHAIN OF CHRISTIANITY

The **Chain of Christianity** is defined as God's use of individual men and of nations to move the Gospel westward and the effect of internal liberty in the civil sphere. The concept of the Chain of Christianity has several themes:

1. How are men governed?
2. How did God use individual character to forward Christ, His Story?

Since Adam's disobedience and fall, man has been trying to establish a government to hold in check his wickedness and inhumanity. While God's principles were related to the civil sphere, the concept of ***individual liberty*** came into existence and increased the desire to restrain the power of government over those it governed. It took 1620 years from the time Jesus Christ appeared for Christian liberty to be seen as God-given, not government granted. The Pilgrims understood that government is first ***internal*** as each individual accepts the liberty which only Christ can give. It is ***external*** in the civil sphere and, if Christian in nature, will reflect a greater freedom from the restriction of government in the life of the individual. The concept of government on the Chain of Christianity reveals **more liberty for the individual** as the **Gospel** continues moving **westward**. Liberty culminated in the civil sphere in America with the formation of the world's first Christian Constitutional Republic. This is one of two major themes that should be taught to the students every year, beginning in kindergarten.

The second theme that should be included when teaching the Chain of Christianity is how God has used **individual character** to forward His plan and purposes on the earth. After the appearance of Jesus Christ, the focal point of all history, character becomes related to individual salvation. The Old Covenant required obedience to God's Law which was written on stone tablets. However, in the New Covenant, God's indwelling Spirit writes His Law on the tablets of human hearts and minds, providing greater internal liberty.

A **time line** is an excellent tool for illustrating the major links on the Chain of Christianity. One should be developed for each classroom and hung over the chalkboard for easy reference and use in all subjects. See an example of a time line on pp. 24–25, and a discussion of time lines with examples on pp. 112–118, in this *Guide*.

CONTINENTS ON THE CHAIN OF CHRISTIANITY

In God's Providence, Christianity took a westward move, originating in Asia, developing in Europe, and establishing in America the most complete expression of the Christian civilization.

> "...the entire globe is a grand organism, every feature of which is the outgrowth of a definite plan of the all-wise Creator for the education of the human family, and the manifestation of His own glory."
>
> — Arnold Guyot, *Physical Geography* (1873)

1. **Asia**, the largest, most central continent, has the greatest contrasts in physical regions, separated by the greatest barriers.
   a. It is the continent of origins.
   b. Races, civilization, religion, and language all began there.
   c. Its climate and barriers isolated its diversity of races from one another.
   d. Its close connection to other continents facilitated the dispersion of races throughout the globe.
2. **Europe**, smaller, with more moderate forms of relief, less extreme contrasts of climate, a more fertile soil, an abundance of minerals, has a coast line greater than any other continent.
   a. It has a diversity of structure greater than Asia, contributing to the development of distinct nationalities.
   b. Its nations have proximity to one another and greater communication between them, with common access to the sea.
   c. It is the continent of development.
   d. The Indo-European race finds expansion and development not in Iran, its original seat, but in Europe.
   e. The arts and learning of antiquity attained their highest development in Europe.
   f. Christianity became the foundation of modern civilization in Europe.
3. **America** is characterized by unity and simplicity.
   a. Its climate is moderate.
   b. Its physical structure provided for the blending of a population into one.
   c. Its rich plains are turned toward Europe; its rivers provide passage.
   d. Its physical features were designed to receive a ready-made civilization and to furnish it with a scene most worthy of their activity.
4. In God's Providence America's harvest is the development of the individual.
   a. All the past contributed to the excellence of her foundation.
   b. Asia, the ancient Greek and Roman civilizations, and Modern Europe all provided America with all their lessons, discoveries, and disciplines of thousands of years.
   c. America ennobles man with a sense of his own dignity through the practice of a system of self-government under law.
   d. America furnishes to each individual such aid as a state can give to make the most of himself and to reach the fullest expression of his value.

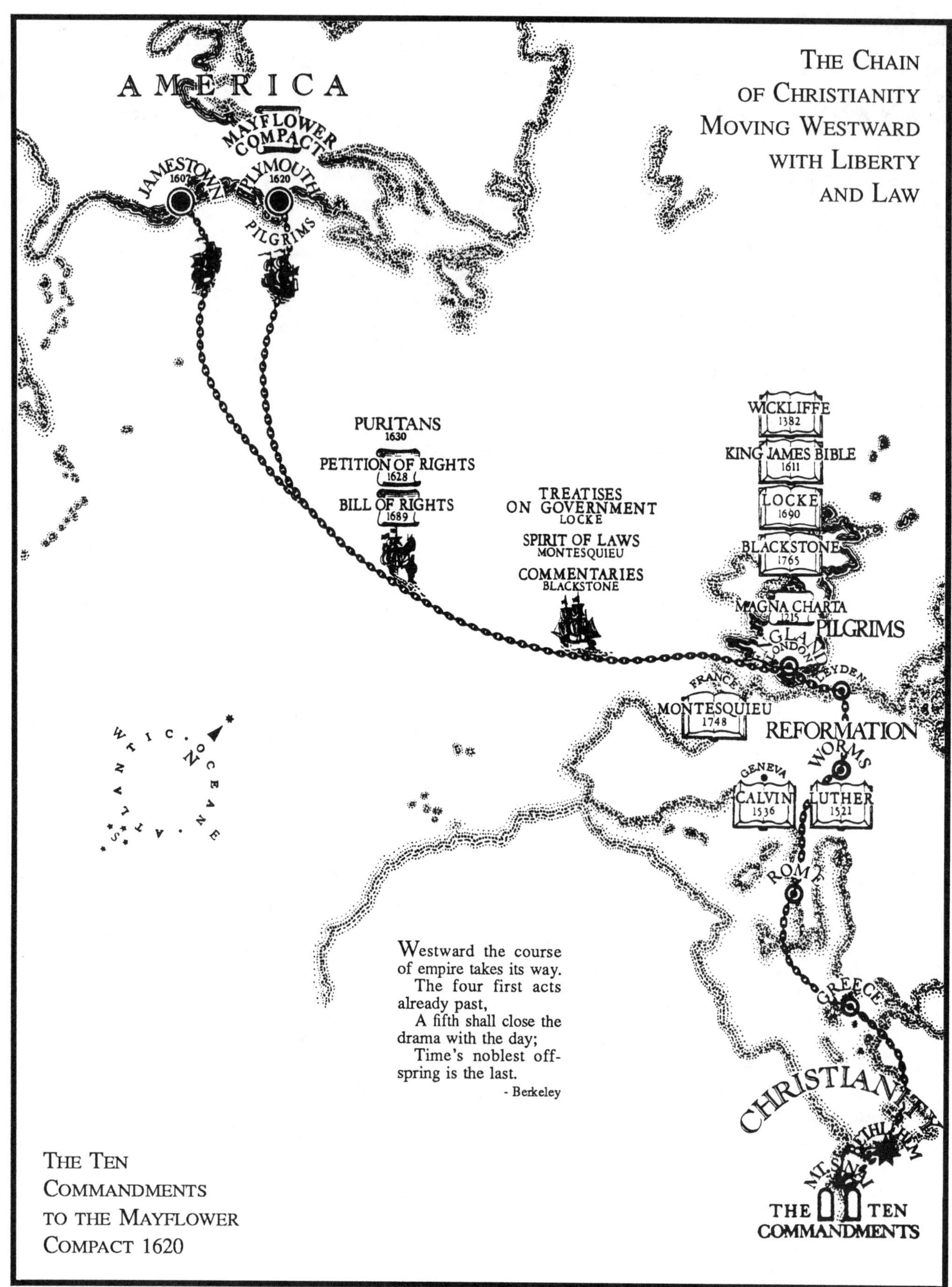
THE CHAIN
OF CHRISTIANITY
MOVING WESTWARD
WITH LIBERTY
AND LAW
AMERICA
MAYFLOWER COMPACT
JAMESTOWN 1607
PLYMOUTH 1620
PILGRIMS
PURITANS 1630
PETITION OF RIGHTS 1628
BILL OF RIGHTS 1689
TREATISES ON GOVERNMENT LOCKE
SPIRIT OF LAWS MONTESQUIEU
COMMENTARIES BLACKSTONE
WICKLIFFE 1382
KING JAMES BIBLE 1611
LOCKE 1690
BLACKSTONE 1765
MAGNA CHARTA 1215
PILGRIMS
LONDON
LEYDEN
FRANCE
MONTESQUIEU 1748
REFORMATION
WORMS
GENEVA
CALVIN 1536
LUTHER 1521
ROME
GREECE
CHRISTIANITY
MT. SINAI
THE TEN COMMANDMENTS
Westward the course
of empire takes its way.
The four first acts
already past,
A fifth shall close the
drama with the day;
Time's noblest off-
spring is the last.
- Berkeley
THE TEN
COMMANDMENTS
TO THE MAYFLOWER
COMPACT 1620

MAJOR LINKS TAUGHT EACH YEAR IN THE HISTORY CURRICULUM*

The elementary school years provide an opportunity for the classroom teacher to establish a solid foundation upon which students can continue to build and refine a Biblical philosophy of history and government. Teaching children the major links every year, beginning in kindergarten, expanding the curriculum year by year, line upon line, precept upon precept, and progressing through the elementary grade levels, gives the students the opportunity to develop mastery of the Providential view of history. This method firmly establishes the Biblical principles upon which the students can interpret the cause and effect of all historic and current events throughout their lives.

Ten key links on the Chain of Christianity are presented chronologically each year in the elementary history curriculum. Each year one of the links is highlighted and taught in depth, while other material is included. The seedbed (the primary, recurring Biblical principles and ideas) of each link is presented in the kindergarten program and expanded throughout the elementary grades.

The First Link: **CREATION** – God's Principle of Individuality is emphasized and expanded throughout the years to include: God as Creator, His character, Christian individuality, geographic individuals, man is God's property, origin and dispensation of the races, establishment of civil government, and the Christian versus the pagan idea of man and government.

The Second Link: **MOSES AND THE LAW** – The Providential preservation and preparation of Moses for God's purpose as the first historian and first lawgiver are emphasized including: the Ten Commandments, the basis of civil law and dual form of government, the Principle of Representation and the relationship of the Old Testament Law to the New Testament; the distinctives of moral law, ritual law, and civil law.

The Third Link: **CHRIST, THE FOCAL POINT OF HISTORY** – Christ's birth and purpose for coming to the earth and His effect upon history are studied including: Christ fulfilled the law; the character of Christ; Jesus – the basis for Christian self-government; Greece and Rome prepared the soil for Christianity; two systems of law – external and internal.

The Fourth Link: **PAUL AND THE WESTWARD MOVE OF THE GOSPEL** – Paul, heeding the Macedonian cry for help, proved to be one of the most important links for America's Christian history. The establishment of the Gospel in Europe, the purpose of civil government as declared in Paul's writings, and the establishment of the New Testament Church – "a little republic" – are all studied in the life of Paul.

---

* See also the work of Ruth J. Smith on teaching the Links in "Teaching America's Christian History in the Elementary School," in *A Guide to American Christian Education for the Home and School: The Principle Approach* by James B. Rose. A.C.H.I., Palo Cedro, CA (1987), pp. 201–227.

The Fifth Link: **THE BIBLE IN ENGLISH** – In order to understand the history of civil liberty, the history of the Bible in English must be studied. The history of liberty for the individual is directly proportionate to the Bible in the hands of the individual. Supporting this link is the study of how the Bible in the hands of the individual brought reformation internally and then in the civil sphere. Wycliffe – the "Morning Star of the Reformation," Tyndale, Coverdale, the *Geneva Bible,* the *King James Bible,* the *Magna Charta* which protected individual rights of the Englishmen, and the *Bible* and the *Constitution* are included.

The Sixth Link: **COLUMBUS, CHRIST-BEARER TO THE NEW WORLD** – The preparation of Christopher Columbus, who knew God had a distinct call upon his life, is studied. Providential preparation is seen in Marco Polo's journals, Prince Henry the Navigator, and the invention of navigational instruments as the Era of Westward Exploration began. One of the themes studied is the preservation of the mainland of North America until God had a people prepared to establish the fullest expression of a Christian civilization.

The Seventh Link: **PILGRIM, SEED OF OUR CHRISTIAN REPUBLIC** – In the Pilgrim dynamic was the seed for our Christian republic. Providentially prepared, the Pilgrims possessed the Christian character, self-government, economics, education, and unity needed to produce a Christian Republic. America's heritage of Christian character, the Providence of God through the Reformation, Holland, God's preservation through Squanto, Thanksgiving, voluntary consent – the key to self-government, the writing of the *Mayflower Compact,* Jamestown and Plymouth colonies contrasted, and communism versus free enterprise are taught.

The Eighth Link: **PATRIOT, FIRST CHRISTIAN REPUBLIC** – As Christianity moved westward with its fullest expression in civil government, the contributions and Christian character of many individuals are studied including George Washington – Father of our Country, Sam Adams and his Committees of Correspondence, Patrick Henry, John Adams, and Benjamin Franklin. Other areas emphasized are: Boston Patriots and the Boston Tea Party, *Declaration of Independence,* the writings of the Patriots, the Revolutionary War, and the formation of our Christian Constitutional Republic.

The Ninth Link: **PIONEER, WESTWARD EXPANSION, AND EROSION** – The Bible, the Biblical principles of self- and civil government, and Noah Webster's "blue-backed" Speller went westward with the Pioneer. Various pioneers and pathfinders are studied as the nation expanded. The Era of Enterprise and Invention is highlighted leading up to the Civil War with the erosion of unity. The character and contributions of such Christian men as Noah Webster, Matthew Maury, Abraham Lincoln, and Robert E. Lee are identified.

The Tenth Link: **MY PLACE IN GOD'S PROVIDENCE** – The role of the American Christian in the 1990s is to aid in restoring and reclaiming the heritage of Christian character and civil liberty in America. God has a unique and special purpose and place on the Chain of Christianity for each one of us as well as for each individual nation. Each student is inspired and encouraged to assume his responsibility for the stewardship of his internal and external property, his scholarship and productivity, and to follow Christ in his daily walk, thereby fulfilling God's purpose for his life as a young American Christian.

USING A **TIME LINE** IN TEACHING PROVIDENTIAL HISTORY

The use of a **time line** and its role in teaching any subject, especially history, are vital. All subjects have a history and a God-given purpose and should be initially introduced to students by imparting that knowledge. In history there is a natural order, that of chronological sequence. If you mentally examine your own history memory bank, you will find that your understanding of chronology was added piecemeal as your knowledge of history increased, forming associations with prominent events and historic characters. Memorizing a list of dates and events serves no purpose in historic literacy, for it does not provide the discernment needed to distinguish between the important and the inconsequential. It is of far more value to know the order of the relative significance **providentially** and to be able to **reason from *cause* (God) to *effect*.** This is where the role of **time mapping** or the use of a **time line** is so worthy.

We are not born with an innate or developed sense of chronology. Time is a developing concept in the young elementary-aged child, one that must be learned. Young children initially require concrete or visual impressions for learning (pictures, maps, globes, handling objects). The abstract capability of reading, with its symbols, must be learned and developed. In order to introduce the concepts of sequence and time, the time line serves as a concrete method. Children first learn the idea of sequence as a preliminary step for the understanding of chronology and dates later on.

There are many ways to divide time. All of history can be divided into millennia, or centuries, or epochs and the critical events and characters mapped that way. But there would be many events that would be inconsequential in the study of the Providential hand of God in history. As the Chain of Liberty moved westward from Creation to the present, ten major events, characters, or links on the Chain of Christianity have been selected. (See pp. 116 & 118.) The birth, death, and resurrection of Jesus Christ is the focal point of ***all*** history and should be highlighted in some way on each time line. These links become "**pockets**" into which children deposit their growing knowledge of history. For example, when the establishment of Jamestown, the first permanent English colony in America, is studied, the children are taught that its founding lies within the same time frame as **The Pilgrims**, a major link in America's Christian history. Therefore, the children quickly learn the significance of events in ***God's*** timetable and then grow in their sense of time and chronology in relation to Christ, His Story.

THE STRUCTURE OF PROVIDENTIAL HISTORY IN THE ELEMENTARY CURRICULUM

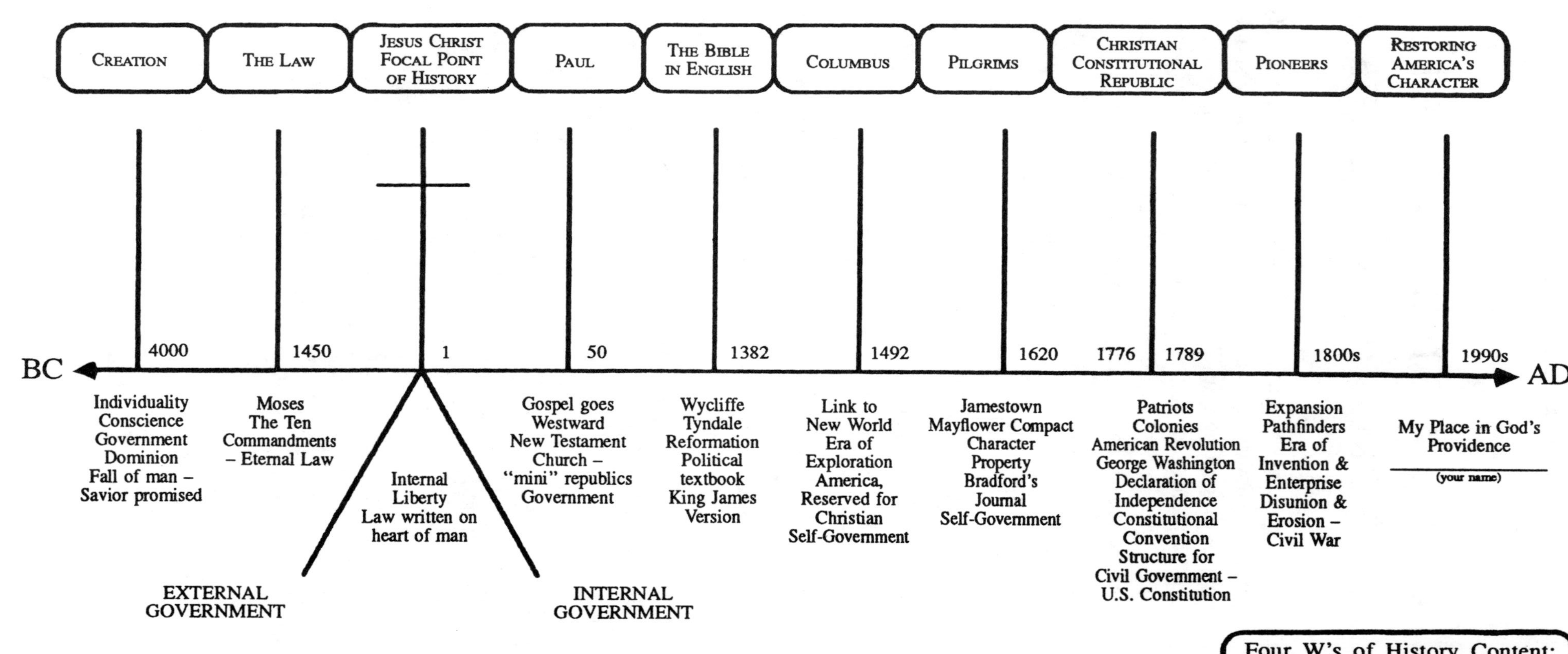

At StoneBridge Schools every teacher makes a time line that is placed over the chalkboard in front of the classroom. Each one reflects the creativity of its designer, but all have the same ten links or "memory pockets" represented. In this way, characters and events that are taught in each grade can be added to highlight the curriculum.

Following are several examples of successful StoneBridge time lines. In kindergarten one teacher used pictures, the same ones she had the students place in their history notebook when they were studied. These pictures represented the event or character of the ten links. She then joined them together with a paper chain. She collected from parents a picture of each of her students and placed them under the tenth link, so that when the children arrived the first day of school, they realized there was something important about the chain on the wall and it had something to do with them!

One sixth grade teacher designed her time line and placed it on the wall prior to the first day of school. Then in the first few weeks she had the art teacher work with the children to create the figures and representations of events using construction paper in three-dimensional designs. This was a very successful way of deepening the students' understanding of the value of the time line and their sense of time and chronology.

One first grade teacher had her six-year-olds create a personal time line with the help of their parents. Several time lines that were brought in extended nearly the length of the classroom wall! These young children and their parents were drawn into the concepts of the Providential hand of God, sequencing, and time.

Quite often in individual lessons, teachers have asked children to represent characters on the time line. A human time line is formed in front of the class and then the character or event being taught that day is represented by a student and placed in the "line."

Time lines can be designed vertically or horizontally, and one should always be placed in each student's notebook accompanying the subject overview. When introducing new material, it is very beneficial to have the students quickly draw a time line in their notes with the ten key links and place the character or event being studied on the time line in a different color. Then through the years of elementary education, students master the chronology of the Chain of Liberty and are able to place all other historic information within those "memory pockets," discerning whether they contributed or not to the westward move of the Gospel. God's plan for internal and external liberty is visually and permanently recorded in their brain!

PROVIDENTIAL TIME LINE OF LIBERTY IN ENGLISH HERITAGE

B.C.

Event	Date	Significance
Creation		Individuality – Conscience – Government
Moses	1450	The External Law
Jesus Christ	Focal Point of History	Internal Liberty & The Gospel
Paul	50	New Testament Church
Joseph of Arimethea	1st Century	Introduced Christianity in Britain
Patrick (Celtic Pastor)	432	Rule of Law & Local Self-Government
Alfred the Great	850	Tree of Liberty – Local Self-Government Laws based on Scripture
Magna Charta	1215	Power of King is Limited
Wycliffe	1382	Bible in English – Textbook of Liberty
Cabot	1497	Claims North America for England
Tyndale	1525	English Reformation
Geneva Translation	1560	Political Textbook & Bible of Pilgrims
Mayflower Compact	1620	Seed of Christian Republic Planted
Declaration of Independence	1776	Sovereign Rights of the Individual
U.S. Constitution	1789	Christian Document of Civil Liberty
Restoring America's Character	1990s	My Place in God's Providence

A.D.

HOW TO THINK GOVERNMENTALLY *

"THINK GOVERN MENTALLY"

Thinking governmentally means that the flow of force or power has been identified internally and externally in any given situation. Thinking governmentally asks who or what controls, directs, regulates, or restrains. Traditional American Christian education has always put an emphasis upon thinking governmentally. Government by God, or Christian self-government, occurs through the individual's ***voluntary consent***. The goals of Christian education are to fit the child with the character of Christian self-government and to reclaim the character of the republic: the character of Christian self-government. A philosophy of education is based upon a philosophy of government. One's view of the principles of teaching and learning is determined by one's idea of who or what is exercising control and ultimately becomes the authority. Every form of government is the result of a philosophy of education.

God ordained three governmental institutions: in the **home**, the **church**, and in **civil government**. The Christian idea of man and government is that God ordained civil government for man's good to **protect** man's God-given life, liberty, and property. The Christian view of government is first ***internal*** – causative, and then ***external*** – with civil government the effect, as each individual acknowledges the sovereignty of God in his life.

EVERY FORM OF GOVERNMENT HAS ITS PHILOSOPHY OF EDUCATION

INTERNAL (Causative)			➡	**EXTERNAL (Effect)**		
PHILOSOPHY OF GOVERNMENT (the source of authority or power)	➡***determines***➡	PHILOSOPHY OF EDUCATION (the wisdom in teaching and learning)	➡***produces***➡	FORM & QUALITY OF EDUCATION (the practice and product of education)	➡***shapes***➡	FORM & QUALITY OF GOVERNMENT (the form and functions of government)

Our Philosophy of Government *IS* Our Philosophy of Education
either by intent or unintentionally!

The concept of thinking governmentally (internal to external, cause to effect) is inculcated with the students beginning in the kindergarten program, not only in reasoning in the academic subjects but in character building as well. It is a wonderful tool for use in positive disciplining of children.

---

* From the teachings of Verna Hall and Rosalie Slater, as discussed and charted in *A Guide for American Christian Education* by James B. Rose, A.C.H.I., pp. 20–25.

THE CHRISTIAN IDEA OF GOD, MAN, AND GOVERNMENT SUMMARIZED

"It is in the man of piety and inward principle that we may expect to find the **uncorrupted patriot**, the **useful citizen**, and the **invincible soldier**. God grant that in America **true religion** and **civil liberty** may be inseparable."
– John Witherspoon, 1776

CHRISTIAN IDEA OF MAN	PAGAN IDEA OF MAN
1. All things are created by God.	1. All things came into being by chance.
2. Man is fallen and needs a Savior.	2. Man is simple, primitive, becoming better.
3. Progress for man is to alter his internal character to affect his environment.	3. Progress for man is to alter his environment to produce a better people.
INTERNAL TO EXTERNAL	EXTERNAL TO INTERNAL
4. Man's heart is cause of events.	4. Man's environment is the cause.
5. The goal: a new creation of individuality.	5. The goal: to change society.
6. Success is to overcome, have dominion.	6. Success is to adapt and adjust to society.
7. The effect: individual is free, independent, self-governing.	7. The effect: individual is in bondage to his environment.
8. The purpose of history: to glorify God – **Christ, His Story!**	8. The purpose of history: to glorify man.

4 R-ING CURRICULUM

Your personal research and written record should be organized in such a way that it will enable you to teach any age group of learners.

Compile your research in a three-ring binder with dividers that reflect the **whole** subject. This will enable you to recover your research quickly, to add to your research, or to teach the subject at any time.

RESEARCH SUGGESTED ORGANIZATION FOR COMPILING RESEARCH:

- Definition (1828 Dictionary)
- Vocabulary of subject
- Biblical foundation
- Christian history of the subject
- Key individuals
- Key events
- Key institutions
- Literature of the subject
- Geographical setting
- Art, music, and drama of the subject
- Leading ideas from your research
- Bibliography
- Inspiration for use with students
- Student activities to enliven and enrich
- Contributions to the spread of the Gospel and liberty for the individual

BIOGRAPHICAL RESEARCH ORGANIZATION:

Conscience and character (***internal***) are always ***causative.***

- Historical setting
- Geographical setting
- Physical description
- Family history
- Education
- Childhood anecdotes
- Christian influences
- Personality, affections, tastes
- Character qualities
- Contributions to the Gospel and liberty
- Account of life works
- Complete a time line

BASIC TOOLS AND PRINCIPLE APPROACH READINGS:

- *The Christian History of the Constitution of the United States of America: Christian Self-Government,* compiled by Verna M. Hall. Foundation for American Christian Education (F.A.C.E.), San Francisco, CA (1960).
- *Teaching and Learning America's Christian History: The Principle Approach* by Rosalie J. Slater. F.A.C.E., San Francisco, CA (1967), pp. 90–110.
- *A Guide to American Christian Education for Home and School: The Principle Approach* by James B. Rose. American Christian History Institute (A.C.H.I.): Palo Cedro, CA (1987), pp. 113–158.
- *American Dictionary of the English Language* (Facsimile 1828 Ed.) by Noah Webster. F.A.C.E., San Francisco, CA.
- *The Bible* – the *source* and *seedbed* of every field of study.
- *Commentary on the Whole Bible* by Matthew Henry.
- *The Exhaustive Concordance of the Bible* by James Strong.

OTHER BASIC RESEARCH TOOLS:

- *The Book of Life* (eight volumes, arranged and edited by Hall and Wood). John Rudin and Company, Inc., Chicago (1923–1952 editions).
- Original sources and documentation
- Autobiographical materials
- 19th and early 20th century books
- Contemporary Christian authors
- *World Book Encyclopedia* for basic information; a time line is often available for many subjects

REASON LEADING IDEAS:

- The Biblical principles of the subject and God's purpose for it must always be deduced from God's Word using the 1828 vocabulary of the subject.
- Contributions the subject has made to the spread of the Gospel and liberty for the individual should always be identified.
- Many others present themselves as the subject is researched.

RELATE IDEAS FOR DEVELOPING CURRICULUM FOR YOUR GRADE LEVEL

RECORD YOUR WRITTEN WORK

THE TEACHER'S ROLE IN AMERICAN CHRISTIAN EDUCATION

1. Exemplify Christian self-government
2. Demonstrate the tools of scholarship
3. Instill the ability to think governmentally
4. Inspire a lifelong love of learning, wisdom, and knowledge
5. Relate to each child individually, calling forth and thereby liberating his individuality

Mar. 21, 1989

Mrs. Giancoli,

I would like to take this time to thank-you for your preparation of your inspiring classes in Art! You have been the best art teacher I've had in 8 years of school. Expect a surprise towards the end of school (June)! May God bless and enrich your life! See ya Mrs. "G."

- From the second Bernini, Giotto and Michelangelo,

Adam Fell "89"

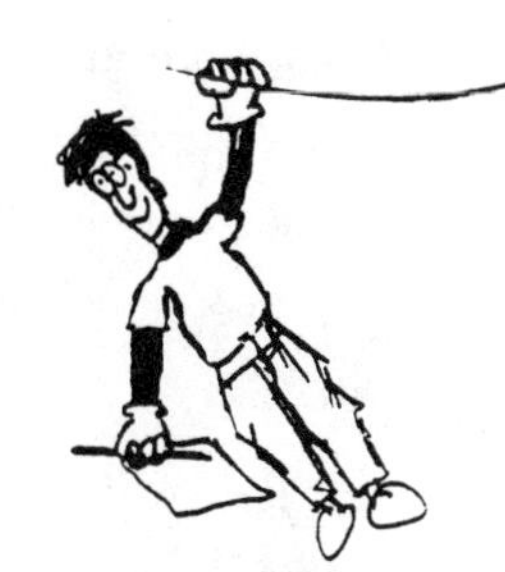

Starting With Me

God made me special –
Like no one else you see.
God made me a witness
To His diversity.

I Am God's Property

God made me for His purpose
He fashioned me to be
An image for His glory,
Almighty Father He.

– Rosalie J. Slater

CREDITS FOR ART

Cover Graphics – Mrs. Sylvia Terpstra

Page xii Jeni Giancoli, 8th Grade

Page xiv Inspired by 15th C. European woodcut

Page 1 Courtney Buck, 8th Grade

Page 7 Becky Williams, 4th Grade

Page 9 Inspired by 17th C. European woodcut

Page 11 Daniel Keller, 5th Grade (left)
Timothy Parker, 6th Grade (right)

Page 15 Tara Peppos, 5th Grade (right, top)
Devin Whalen, K-5 (right, middle)
Natalie Thompson, K-5 (right, lower)

Page 19 Heather McCauley, 10th Grade

Page 21 Dee Dee Riggan, 4th Grade

Page 22 Timothy Andrus, 4th Grade

Page 27 Ami Giancoli, 5th Grade

Page 33 Ami Giancoli, 1st Grade

Page 35 Thomas Merrell, 5th Grade (right, lower)

Page 36 Benji Wilkerson, K-5 (right, top)

Page 37 Erica Ward, K-5 (left)
Maddie Leiter, K-5 (middle)
Sarah Spruill, K-5 (right)

Page 41 Robby Ingram, 8th Grade (top)
Sarah McCartney, K-5 (portfolio)
Ryan Leadem, K-5 (flowers)
Brandon Griffin, K-4 (portrait)

Page 50 Erin Cheeseman, 8th Grade (left)
7th & 8th Graders (right)

Page 51 Alex Podesta, 7th Grade (left)
Daniel Keller, K-5 (right)
Mark Blevins, 6th Grade (lower)

Page 57 Zachary Beale, K-4

Page 58 Michael Daulton, 10th Grade

Page 59 Ryan Leadem, K-5

Page 60 Faith Shaw, 1st Grade

Page 61 Mickey Eaddy, 2nd Grade

Page 62 Mike Funk, 3rd Grade

Page 63 Israel Cartier, 4th Grade

Page 64 Joey Ferrell, 5th Grade

Page 65 Peter Davis, 6th Grade

Page 66 Courtney Buck, 7th Grade

Page 72 Laura Hocter, K-5 (left, top)
Joy Parker, 8th Grade (left, middle)
Andrea Smith, 4th Grade (left, lower)
Marie Bryan, 3rd Grade (right, top)
Alex Pendleton, 3rd Grade (right, lower)

Page 73 Michael Merrell, 4th Grade (left, top)
David Early, 5th Grade (left, middle)
Meagan Griggs, 5th Grade (left, lower)
Alex Podesta, 8th Grade (right, top)
Jenny Cuthrell, K-5 (right, lower)

Page 76 Joshua Kennedy, 4th Grade

Page 83 Mrs. Sylvia Terpstra

Page 123 Adam Fell, 8th Grade

Page 124 Joey Ferrell, 4th Grade

. . . where art lives!

Notes

Notes